IN TANDEM

RECOVERING ME, RECOVERING US

What experts are saying about

In Tandem
Recovering Me, Recovering Us

"Dr. Bird has provided a fantastic tool for not only understanding the basis of addictive behaviors, but a roadmap for recovery. The 'workbook' format is both user-friendly and practical, and helps those traveling the road to recovery 'find' their true identities. The emphasis on individual recovery for those struggling with addiction and for loved ones experiencing betrayal trauma teaches both to understand that couples can connect again when each focuses on sweeping his or her own side of the street. Life can be meaningful and enjoyable again as recovery is internalized and lived, and this book is a powerful tool in helping those willing to undergo the journey arrive at this worthwhile destination."

- Donald L. Hilton Jr, MD, FAANS
Adjunct Associate Professor of Neurosurgery
University of Texas Health Science Center at San Antonio
Author of *He Restoreth My Soul*

In Tandem takes "an important step in laying the foundation for individual healing in a way that respects the uniqueness of both the addict's and partner's recovery, while simultaneously honoring the coupleship recovery."

- Janice Caudill, PhD, CSAT
Founding board member of APSATS

"*In Tandem* is thoughtfully organized with wonderful suggestions for soothing and coping skills at the end. I wish Dr. Bird's list of relational coping suggestions were taught in high schools everywhere."

- Kelly McDaniel LPC, NCC
Author of *Ready to Heal: Breaking free of addictive relationships*

"People's behavior in addiction wrecks relationships and it takes hard work to reconnect in a healthy way with those you love. *In Tandem* offers a framework that makes sense, goes slow enough that skills and new habits can really be learned in the process making repair possible. By focusing on the importance of involving both the addict and partner (or friend, family member, work mate, or sibling) in creating and sustaining a new road to recovery, Dr. Bird gives everyone a way to mend and rebuild safe relationships. Easy to read! Easy to use! Effective at every turn! I highly recommend this winner for anyone wanting to recover."

- M. Deborah Corley, PhD
Co-founder and owner of Santé Center for Healing,
and co-author of *Disclosing Secrets, Surviving Disclosure, and Making Advances*

"*In Tandem* by Dr. Mark Bird is a practical guide to awareness and healing for any couple struggling with intimacy and relationship issues. Based on the metaphor of a bicycle built for two, it presents a balanced 'how to' guide with practical tools for 'riding together.' Dr. Bird avoids typical pitfalls of emphasis on one partner more than the other and writes easy to understand prose that any layperson can understand and apply. I have worked in the field of sex addiction and intimacy disorder for 12 years and wholeheartedly endorse and recommend this book."

- Sherry Young, PhD, CSAT

IN TANDEM
RECOVERING ME, RECOVERING US

MARK H BIRD, PHD

Stemar Press

ISBN: 978-0-9994138-0-7

Cover Photography and Design by J. May Photo. jmayphoto.com
Book Design by Stevie Bird. steviebirddesign.com
Special thanks to Velo Republic for the cover bike. velorepublicbikes.com

Printed and bound in the United States of America.
Published by Stemar Press, Denton, Texas. StemarPress.com

To my mom — Dianne Carolyn Hilton Bird

Even though you are gone,
your love still inspires me.

Acknowledgments

There are so many people I need to thank for the work that was put into this book, both directly and indirectly. I am so grateful for the village that surrounds and supports me.

To God

I am tentative to write my feelings toward God, as they are very personal and may offend those who have a different experience of God than I do; however, I include some of those feelings here because I believe I would be deeply ungrateful if I did not acknowledge the role God has played in my life. There are so many ways that people view God—God as they know Him. The God I know is loving. I am His son, and He cares for me. In the book of Genesis in the Old Testament, it refers to God as a jealous God. The word in Hebrew is Qannah, which means "possessing sensitive and deep feelings." I'm so grateful for a God who feels deeply for His children, including me. While I know not all have experienced that feeling from God, I am grateful to know Him in that way.

I also acknowledge that the paths I have taken and the experiences I have had have been strongly influenced by God. If I had done according to my plans, I would have ended up in a very different place (in so many different ways). I am grateful to God for the guidance He has given me, directly and indirectly. I believe at their root, all the things I have learned individually and professionally have come as a result of following that guidance. I am grateful for a God who is patient in my growth and lets me have the space and time to learn, even when it is painful (to me and to Him, I believe). Lastly, I'm grateful for the gift of His Son, Jesus Christ, to help provide deliverance from problems I cannot resolve on my own. I love Them because They are perfect in Their love towards me.

To my wife, Stevie

I'm certain that in your decision to marry me you never imagined all the ups and downs that this world would bring us. I have tried hard to be a good husband and a good dad, but I know there are times I've fallen miserably short. I'm grateful for your patience, for your willingness to stand up to me even though it is hard, and for your long hours taking care of kids while I wrote this book, among other job responsibilities. I love you, for that and so many other reasons. Thanks for being mine for eternity.

In addition to being my wife, you've also been my technology person. Thanks for the time editing, formatting, and preparing the book. Thanks for your research to make sure that we were doing it well, and thanks for being patient as I tried to explain the various things that I was trying to accomplish. You are so talented! Thanks for putting those talents to work on this book.

To my Mom and Dad

I'm so grateful for the role my parents played in making me who I am. I'm so grateful to you, Mom, for the wonderful, affirming love that you showed me and all that you knew. To this day, all that I know about connection is influenced by having felt that love from you when I was young. You taught me that being a feeler was a valid and meaningful approach to life.

I know Dad was a hard worker, but as I have reflected I realize that I learned most of my ideas on hard work from you. You were always up before everyone else (as I generally am, too, with my family), preparing lunches, breakfast, or just doing other things. I remember the sound of the typewriter in the early morning, and I am grateful to have interviewed you as part of a class in college to understand at a deeper level what that work meant to you. You taught me what work was, and of the real work that being a mother was.

I remember when Grandma Hilton passed away while I was in college. I was staying at their old home with you, and Kevin and I were sleeping in the living room. As I woke, I heard you talking with Kevin on the couch in that room. You were telling him that you were proud of him, that he was the best at his combination of talents. I immediately remembered what you would say to me: "Mark, you are the best piano playing, trumpet playing, basketball playing, volleyball playing, soccer playing, singing, etc., etc., that I know." You taught me that I was worthy of love because I had a unique combination of talents that was only mine and because I was your son. I always knew that I was loved by you, even when I made mistakes. Even though you passed away several years ago, I feel your love regularly and am grateful to know that I will feel it again in its fullness after this life.

Dad, having a kid with ADD (although I was never officially diagnosed) must have been rough. I remember the many calls to school and the many teacher/principal meetings, from elementary through high school. I remember specifically two occasions that forever changed my life in a very subtle but powerful way. The first was in middle school, and they were going to give me more detentions. You said, "That won't bother Mark one bit. He'll go there and get his homework done, and it won't make a difference to him." Instead, you suggested you could come to school and attend a day with me if I misbehaved again. While I didn't like that idea at all (which was a motivation not to misbehave that worked), I remember thinking, "My dad knows me." What a powerful feeling to be known. Because of this experience (and other similar ones) and Mom's example as well, I have learned to live my life to know and be known—connection.

The second was with my ninth grade teacher. You had a meeting with her and wouldn't let me come to it, which was unusual. When you came home, you said the meeting went well and that you'd found some resolutions. You also told me that the reason you didn't want me there was because you knew that she was treating me poorly and that you were going to go to battle for me, if necessary. That memory—realizing that someone would go to battle for me—has stuck with me all my life. It has forever influenced how I understood love.

You also taught me to be a thinker: to use my head to find words and solutions. I learned early on that there were solutions for almost everything if you put your mind to it. I learned to fight for what I felt was right. Combined with Mom's feeling style, I learned to value my feelings and attach them to thinking to find solutions that really work. Your combined parenting created much of the way that I have learned to manage my feelings and connect them to my thoughts.

I remember when I was 16 years old, I came to you and asked you to explain eternity. I still believed you had all the answers, so when you said you didn't I was surprised. I said, "Come on, Dad, you can tell me. I can handle it." You insisted you didn't have that answer, and you taught me that some things in life might not be fully understood at first. You modeled for me that knowledge and answers could be found, but it was also important to know that those things usually come line upon line rather than all at once. I learned to be more patient but still very active in learning as much as I could about things that mattered to me.

Until I had people comment on my teaching, I never realized that you modeled an amazing approach to teaching and learning. I'm grateful to have seen that example to help me connect with others as we learn together.

Most importantly, I'm grateful to you, Dad, for modeling what it means to be loyal to your wife and family. I'm grateful for your patience with all eight of us kids. I remember a client in one of my groups who had disconnected from our conversation. When I checked in with her, she said: "When you said earlier that your Dad didn't beat you, it just threw me for a loop. I just assumed that all fathers beat their children." I had never fully understood how much pain there was in the world due to family-of-origin abuse. I regularly remember that statement and am even more grateful for the love and support you and Mom gave me.

Finally, I remember finding the song "It works" by Alabama. It talks about a man and a woman who still responded to each other in some ways that were different than "modern" times. While it wasn't your marriage exactly, it reminded me immediately of the unique ways that you and Mom showed love in your marriage. While I knew I wouldn't do exactly what you guys did, I know that Mom "lived her life for" Dad, and Dad "would gladly die for her." And as the song said, "It works." While your marriage wasn't perfect, you taught me that imperfection can be beautiful. Thank you both again for helping me to become who I am.

To Dr. Mark Butler

I'm pretty sure I'd not be where I am without you, Mark. Even though you've been a more distant part of my life in the past 10 years, your influence has been a huge part of what has allowed me to accomplish this book. Thanks for your friendship, your mentoring, your encouragement, the times you helped me grow through tough personal experiences, for your word-smithing and professional guidance, and for loving me as I have loved you. I'm so grateful for your friendship.

To Laney Knowlton

When I invited you to help edit the book, I never knew how much I needed that help. Your insights about the partner's perspective, your technical skills, and your passion about the work we were doing have all been so meaningful to me and to this book. I especially appreciate the time I called you and you gave me the courage to write about the partner's experience in ways that seemed, at times, so different from other things I had seen written. While I felt strongly about what I was writing, your willingness to sit with me that day and encourage me to continue courageously really meant a lot to me.

Thank you also for helping push the process along, for co-authoring the first chapter, and for being patient with my foibles and struggles all along the way. I know I have given you a serious test of your patience, and you have passed it in so many ways. Thanks for allowing me to share your perspectives on codependency and boundaries. Most importantly, I appreciate the many hours talking, working, sorting, and resolving. I appreciate your friendship and am glad to be your colleague.

Teachers, Researchers and Reviewers

Finally, I'm grateful to all those who helped in my learning over the years, participated in my research (both participants and those who helped me complete the research), and also to those who took time to review this book, both in the initial stages and in the final stages. There are so many hands that helped create what this final project has become. For all of you, I am profoundly grateful.

CONTENTS

Appendix 203

IN TANDEM

RECOVERING ME, RECOVERING US

Introduction

THE TANDEM BICYCLE: A METAPHOR

A couple sets out on a bicycle built for two, on an epic journey to explore wonderful vistas and experience the beauty the world has to offer. They are deeply in love and hope that the decision to be linked together as they travel will deepen their relationship and make the journey much more joyful and much less lonely; riding alone can be so lonely. Neither knows exactly where they are going, and neither are experts. Both have crashed before on their own, having little formal training; however, both have ridden a bicycle before with some success. Neither has ridden a bicycle built for two for such a long journey. They assume the road ahead will be similar to terrain they have managed with some success before in their individual cycling; they have studied and heard stories about others' journeys down this road. In the beginning, they enjoy the ride and the beauty and newness of the journey. It feels amazing to be connected in this way.

Because it is a long journey, they must pace themselves, alternating who pedals more. Sometimes she takes the front seat, where she controls the direction they are headed. When she's in the lead, he can relax some as she manages the upcoming terrain. However, in the back seat he cannot always see what is going on. He must trust that she will drive safely. When he is in the front seat, she relaxes and trusts him. They have a few small problems along the way. Both make mistakes, but they are able to continue forward. The journey seems manageable, though at times both feel the tediousness of the ride. They are occasionally lost; however, because they are not quite sure where their final destination is, they just keep pedaling until they seem to be back on track.

Weather and terrain change over time, sometimes making the journey more difficult or more pleasant. When they are exhausted or worn out, the journey doesn't seem as enjoyable, and of course they have their disagreements. With time and trouble, they do not talk and laugh as much as they once did, and they communicate even less about managing the journey (and when they do, it usually just ends up in a fight). Each at times is resentful, feeling like they are doing a lot more work than the other; however, they continue to move forward with hope that things will get better.

Then one day he gets careless while in the driver's seat. He turns down a road that seems good at first, even vaguely familiar. He realizes after a while that if she knew where they were she would not be happy. Although she senses some small changes as they go down the new road, she cannot see enough to know what is happening. So she trusts him as the driver. The long journey has made both a little numb and disconnected so the rougher terrain is not as noticeable as it might have been early in the journey. She notices some particularly tough climbs and a few slippery areas and attempts to talk to him about them. He is terrified she will be upset, so he plays off her concerns and even makes fun of her for having them. He tells her, and begins to believe, that she is a nag for constantly bringing it up. When things get particularly rough, he blames her for distracting him, for complaining too much, or for anything else he can: anything to take the focus off of his failures and try to distract her from the real issues. He must hide the truth about the path they are on while he works hard to try to get back on track on his own. Although she asks to drive at times, he insists that things are fine and that he likes to drive, because he is terrified to let her see where they are until he has made things right.

Soon exhaustion sets in and he cannot hide things as well. While he doesn't like the overall terrain, the rush of certain parts of it keep him going. It keeps him distracted, at least, from the terrible parts of the ride. He has all but given up on trying to find a way back. He crashes more, but makes excuses. She expresses her concerns and pain, but he finds ways to convince her that things are fine. Although things still don't feel fine to her, she continues to let him drive. He has become terrified of what will happen if she finds out. He works so hard to hide the path they are on that he cannot keep his focus on the road ahead, which leads to even more problems. Then one day it happens: a huge crash. As they get up from the crash, she sees clearly for the first time where they really are. The pieces of the journey over the last few months and years start to fall into place, and suddenly she can make sense of so many parts of the recent events: the truth about the path she'd been on with him for way too long. She never would have knowingly approved of this path, and she knows he knew that. Why would he do this to her? She is wounded and devastated.

She reviews how she had felt, thought and behaved in the past. She remembers how she had sensed things were off in the past and tried to talk to him several times about it. She keeps wondering how she did not see it sooner. As she reviews the events leading up to the big crash, she sees more clearly why they had crashed before. She reviews the events of the past over and over again with a new lens. Each time, the pain seems to deepen as it becomes more real.

What can she do now? She reviews her options. She could just stop the journey with him, but they had come so far together. She doesn't really want to journey alone. What had happened to all their hopes and dreams? Could they ever have the life they had intended to have together? She remembers how good things had been once, although it seems so far away now.

She knows that even if she parts ways with him she will still be in this really ugly, painful place. Does she want to journey through this land alone? She could go on with him, but how can she trust him? She wishes this nightmare would go away. She wonders why he had lied for so long. She sees the road back but wonders if he will be willing to travel it with her.

He is ashamed that she has found out about his mistakes and is terrified that she will see him as a failure. He is scared of abandonment and rejection, and wonders if she will ever trust or love him again if she knows the whole truth. He also wonders if everyone else will see his mistakes now and leave him completely alone. He watches her carefully, trying desperately to reassure her that things will be okay. But deep down he wonders if they will be, if he will be.

You and Me: Individual Recovery

Thus begins the road to recovery: two people, exhausted, wounded from the crash(es), fearful, and distrustful. Both are uncertain exactly how they got there. Both are spent from the journey. Both are wondering how they can survive after the big crash. Both wonder if getting on the road again will bring them what they want and if they can make it together. In this moment, they cannot make it on their own. They need triage. They need support to move forward, and they need a road map.

This story is more and more frequently occurring for either gender. In many cases, it is *she* rather than *he* who made the initial decisions to act out, to hide, and to deceive, and it is *he* rather than *she* who must deal with the trauma and betrayal.

Regardless of your particular story, recovering requires a lot individually from both the partner and the addict. It requires learning how to nurse and care for your own wounds. It requires being with yourself in the present, allowing yourself to feel, and learning how to manage your pain. It demands honesty with yourself. It requires learning from the past and practicing new things for the future. It requires humility to listen to and rely on others, acknowledging that doing it on your own did not, does not, and will not ever work. That is the "you" and "me" of individual work in recovery.

When I was a young and inexperienced cyclist, I crashed my bike several times. Initially, I didn't know how to use the brakes, so I rode around my block three times before my dad finally caught hold of my bike and slowed me down. I was fortunate to have parents who cared and knew how to help me manage things that I could not manage on my own.

With support, I eventually gained the skills I needed to cycle successfully most of the time and started trying out more difficult skills. I decided to jump curbs and was generally successful. Occasionally, I would time a jump poorly and crash. Each time I crashed I made adjustments to do better the next jump. I could not really get mad at anyone else because I was the only one on the bike. I cried when it hurt, learned from my mistakes, and kept on trying to make it an enjoyable experience.

Even as my skills improved, occasionally I got distracted while riding my bike. Once I was saying goodbye to my friend as I rode away from his house and crashed into a parked truck. A year later I was distracted by a boy and girl kissing and crashed into the same truck again. My face went right into the grill. After the second crash, I learned this lesson about riding a bike: stay aware of *all* of your surroundings, look forward and keep your eyes on the road!

As a proficient rider my ability to ride had improved, but the potential for a crash increased as I rode faster and paid less attention to my surroundings. In one incident, I was racing my friend around the block. I rode out of the alley and ran right into the side of a moving car. I flew over the hood, did a full flip in the air, and somehow landed on my feet. I think I freaked the driver out! I was worried about the damage I might have done to her car, not realizing how much danger I had been in. I was very lucky. My lack of awareness about potential risks, and a bit of carelessness, could have led to serious injury. I determined then that I would be more careful; I could have fun within limits.

Becoming a proficient cyclist did not mean that I would not crash. Crashes are part of the journey. Learning from the crashes made me a safer, happier and more successful cyclist.

The same is true in recovery. There will be crashes as part of recovery, because you are human and learning. The important thing is to keep the quantity and severity of the crashes to a minimum. There are several factors that can help ensure that crashes are minimized and less painful:

1. Stay watchful and attentive to your surroundings, especially potential dangers.

2. Learn or improve skills to manage yourself and the stressors in your environment more safely and successfully.

3. Develop an ability to recover from mistakes and even significant crashes.

4. Seek support from people who know and love you and people who know something about recovery and healthy living.

5. Practice patience as you and your partner work to learn and grow.

6. Exercise caution to experience life at a pace that is exciting yet safe (i.e. it might be fun to go flying down the alley, but there are significant risks, like getting hit by a car).

We: Couple Recovery

Couple recovery is a lot like tandem bicycling. Tandem bicycling can be really fun when both people are skilled and do their part, but the stakes are higher. You have less control than in individual biking. If the ride gets out of control and the bike goes down, there is damage to more than one rider, as well as damage to the trust between the riders (the relationship). After a crash or two it can become scary, especially for the person on the back. Because the driver makes decisions about what needs to be improved to prevent further injury or crashes, the person on the back seat often feels scared and out of control. They have handlebars, but they do not offer any real ability to guide the process.

Addict

If you are an addict, you represent the person in the front seat, and you have usually crashed several times. Recovery from crashes is not easy for you. You might struggle with feeling inadequate and frequently grapple to recover from spirals into shame. You might feel scared you will not manage it well and others will see your struggle and judge you. More specifically, you might be scared, even terrified, that if you crash again you will no longer be loved by your partner and that s/he will leave you, as others in your life may have done. You may feel fearful and out of control regarding your partner's willingness to stay in the relationship or your partner's trauma-based behaviors.

As you begin recovery, it is critical that you do more than just get up and start riding again. There are several important steps:

1. Take responsibility by acknowledging your part. Do not blame.

2. Autopsy: figure out what you did that got you into those situations and determine how not to let it happen again. This process often requires help from others to have a complete understanding.

3. Show empathy for the fear and other feelings your partner might now have.

4. Work to understand what your partner needs right now to help him/her recover from the effects of the crash.

This type of accountability, your ability to do your own work and learn to share the journey toward healing with your partner, can help establish trust again over time.

Partner

If you are a partner of an addict, you may feel scared and out of control. Despite feeling powerless, you can begin to find power over portions of the recovery process: your portions. Empowerment does not mean that you will not feel the pain of the bike crashing; that is painful no matter what.

I had an experience of tandem cycling on my two-seater Yamaha 150cc motor bike. I let a friend drive while I was on the back. She was inexperienced, and the ride quickly felt out of control. I tried hard to balance out the bike without overreacting. I talked to her as it became scarier. I asked her to brake and explained what that meant. Eventually she was able to slow down just enough that I could jump off and grab the back of the bike, stabilize it, and stop it completely. If she had not been able to slow down, I would have gone down with the bike no matter what I tried to do. Either way, I experienced intense fear and distrust about getting back on the bike again with her as the driver unless she learned some new skills first.

The tandem bicycle experience for partners is very similar: they feel out of control and scared to get back on the bike with the addict. Because most partners have crashed many times, the first step you must take is to find healthy people in your life that can help nourish you and heal your wounds: friends, family, a therapist, a group, a sponsor, and so forth.

Additionally, there are several steps from my tandem experience that model some of the ways that partners can create safety and empower themselves within the relationship in healthy ways:

1. Balancing the bike without overreacting: learning to manage your own emotions and trauma triggers successfully is a huge part of learning to see and claim your power.

2. Learning to identify dangerous situations: this includes understanding your own and the addict's warning signs and triggers.

3. Learning to connect with your partner around triggering situations in ways that increase the chance of having your needs met.

4. Developing healthy boundaries to buffer and protect you from the addict's mistakes.

    a. Boundary 1: Jumping off the bike. This is not always possible, but learning to disconnect in a healthy way if the addict is going down the same path can protect partners from being re-traumatized.

b. Boundary 2: Not jumping right back on the bike. In the story I shared, my friend's inexperience made riding with her dangerous. In order for it to be safe for me to get back on the bike with her again, I needed to know she had taken the necessary steps to individually improve her skills. It is healthy for partners to take time to fully commit to the relationship again until the addict has done his/her part to learn new skills that can build trust.

To the degree that you can learn the skills you need to care for yourself and protect yourself from going down with the bike (preventing further wounds), you will begin to feel better and more confident in your individual journey. You will feel empowered and safer as you develop these skills.

The Relationship

Ultimately, staying safer and healing your own wounds can prepare you for healing the relationship, with support. Self-trust gives you the foundation to begin to take steps to build trust within the relationship. Gradually, you will trust your spouse more as s/he displays trustworthiness in managing recovery more successfully. Relational safety will grow as you do your own work and communicate with each other, truly working *in tandem*. Some of the significant relationship pieces include the following:

1. Being honest: communicating successfully and courageously about your thoughts, feelings, and behaviors.

2. Learning to communicate safely by:
   a. Using time-outs.
   b. Using structure in communication patterns that creates a safer environment for sharing (I call this catching and pitching).
   c. Managing reactivity while talking about warning signs.

3. Developing empathy, the ability to understand and deeply connect with your partner's pain.

As you develop these and other relationship skills you will gradually be able to communicate safely and vulnerably, creating a trusting, empathetic and connected relationship.

Road Map for This Book

The purpose of this book is to help individuals and couples recover from sex addiction, heal individual wounds, recover from destroyed trust, and build healthy connection (with others and within the relationship). The ideas and skills I cover in this book are ones I use in my everyday counseling practice. I have seen many people succeed as they have applied these concepts and tools.

For many, this process can feel overwhelming. There are so many things to learn, and so many new steps to take, that it can often feel like too much. Long-term success comes one step at a time. I love the words of Ralph Waldo Emerson: "That which we persist in doing becomes easier for us to do—not that the nature of the thing is changed, but that our power to do is increased." As you use these tools, you will find that things that initially feel impossible to do will become second nature. As my clients have applied themselves one step at a time, they have found that those small steps have created new hope individually and relationally, as well as increased strength and self-confidence. These steps gradually accumulate into long-term recovery.

For those not in a primary relationship, certain tools, such as relational check-ins or couple planning, will not be directly applicable; however, this program applies directly to all relationships. Additionally, principles like honesty, empathy, trust building and communication are concepts that are absolutely critical to long-term recovery and connection.

I have often heard people say that starting recovery is like drinking out of a fire hose. Therapy lingo and recovery terminology can be difficult to understand initially. I have attempted to write this book in such a way that concepts are described in simple, plain language and that the flow of information is less overwhelming. The questions and assignments are organized so that they build upon each other. Reading through quickly and skipping the step-by-step personal work and assignments will ultimately lead to feeling overwhelmed. The fastest way to recover is to go slowly, one step at a time.

The goal of this book is to provide tools for early recovery that will help manage the chaos, provide stability, and create basic tools to care for yourself individually and begin building connection. The first chapter in this book focuses on the importance of connection, how connection impacts addiction and addiction impacts connection, and the power of labels. I review the way those addictions can appear and what the label of addiction really means. I review connective disorders and specifically look at sex addiction as a label.

Chapter Two covers the role of emotions and emotional management in recovery, using the metaphor of the thermometer to help outline the basic skills needed individually. Chapter Three reviews the trauma and addictive cycles, helping both partner and addict to understand how those patterns play out individually and within the relationship. Chapter Four provides individual tools for both addict and partner, organized as The Recovery Hill (recovery from trauma and from the addiction for both partner and addict). Chapter Five then combines all the skills you have learned into a relational context, applying them to early recovery tools for couples.

Middle and late recovery topics are not covered in this book, although I hope to write another volume that addresses middle and late recovery. Individual tools of middle and late recovery include the following:

1. Understanding shame and anger, including how they can destroy connection when not managed well.

2. Managing primary emotions more successfully.

3. Amends and impact letters: this is listed here because a successful amends and/or impact letter leads to greater personal insight and growth.

Middle and late recovery tools for increasing connection with others include the following:

1. Learning to build greater connection in all your relationships.
   a. Understanding connection as a process that occurs gradually over time.
   b. Managing social situations in ways that build greater connection.

2. Catching and Pitching: tools for safe communication within caring relationships.

3. Developing two types of empathy.
   a. Empathy related to the trauma of the addiction, including:
      i.   Disclosure and/or Amends letter (addict)
      ii. Impact letter (partner)
      iii. Responding in a safe way when triggers occur
   b. Empathy related to pain experienced in the past and present, including pain from the relationship and family-of-origin.

4. Healthy sexuality.

In summary, when you have completed this book you will have built a set of tools that will have brought you from the chaos of discovery/disclosure of the addiction into a more stable, less reactive place, personally and relationally. You will have the basic tools to care for yourself, acknowledging and managing your feelings and needs more successfully. You will also learn how to connect your new recovery skills within your primary relationship, and you will then have a solid foundation to be able to explore and implement the tools related to middle and late recovery.

While this book provides a strong foundation of tools for individual and couple recovery, I strongly recommend that you utilize this book in conjunction with individual therapy, couple therapy, group therapy, and 12-step programs whenever possible. Doing so will help you implement these tools with greater success.

Chapter 1

BEGINNING THE JOURNEY

Chapter Co-authored with
Laney Knowlton

Getting Started

Wherever you find yourself on the journey, facing your future can create a variety of feelings. If you've just experienced the crash, you may feel fear in different forms: uncertainty about the future and what steps can be taken, fear that things will not change or cannot be fixed, fear of losing the relationship and perhaps many others. You may feel shame: fearful that you will never feel worthy of love. You may feel angry, wounded or betrayed. You may feel immense grief as you consider all the losses in your life as a result of the crash.

On the other hand, some of you may feel relief due to coming out of hiding. For addicts that means getting honest about the addiction, and for partners that means not feeling alone in shouldering the impact of the addiction, having found some safe people with whom you can share your pain and find support. You may feel interested—or even desperate—to learn about why you do what you do and how to change those patterns. You may be excited to find something that can help you overcome your struggles and find greater success and happiness in your life. You may find hope in the fact that others have been down this road and know the way to a full recovery.

Throughout this book you will see exercises, called Reflections, that are intended to help you more completely process and apply the information and skills you are learning. Writing down your thoughts and feelings can be very vulnerable. In order to keep your answers safe and confidential, I urge you to find somewhere to keep this book and/or your journals where you know that they will not be accessed by others without your permission. If you and your spouse are both working through this book simultaneously (which is my hope), I suggest you write your answers in a journal and/or buy a second copy of the book so you can each keep your work private. Please do not allow your work to be read by your partner or read his/her work unless you have a specific reason to do so that is approved by your therapist.

There is a significant difference between keeping secrets and keeping something private. It is critical that you have the safety and confidentiality to be fully honest without needing to filter your answers or worry about your spouse's reaction to them. Part of healing is learning to choose wisely how and when to share with others, setting appropriate boundaries. Ultimately, as you sort through your thoughts and feelings, the goal is to be completely honest in a way that brings connection and healing. While the difference between privacy and secret-keeping may be difficult to understand now, please trust the recommendation to keep your work and your spouse's work private until it is the right time to share.

Reflections – Exercise A

1. What are your feelings as you start this book?

    _____

    _____

2. What are your biggest fears about it?

    _____

    _____

3. What are your hopes for this process?

    _____

    _____

4. What steps do you need to take to keep your work safe (i.e. buying a small safe or lock box, typing up your answers on a computer and using passwords to protect the files, finding a private blog website, etc.)?

_____

_____

Connection and Addiction

In the 1960's and 1970's, several studies were performed to help us better understand addiction. In the initial studies, the researchers put rats in small cages alone with just food and two water bottles. One bottle contained plain water and one contained water that had been laced with heroin or cocaine. The rats gradually became addicted, drinking the drug-laced water almost exclusively. Eventually, nearly all of them died. The conclusion the researchers made was that the chemical pull of addiction was strong enough to prevent the rats from stopping despite the obvious long-term consequences of starvation and imminent death.

Another group of researchers, led by Bruce Alexander, noticed that there were several variables in the initial experiments that might be important factors in why the rats became addicted: the rats were alone, the cage was very small, and there was nothing in the cage but bottled water. Alexander knew that rats were normally social creatures, and wondered if their isolation was perhaps another important factor in the problem of addiction. Wondering how they would react to the different bottles of water if their environment was changed, he built Rat Park, which included other rats to interact with, a large cage, toys and food. With the change in environment, most rats drank relatively small amounts of the drug-laced water (1/4 of the amount of the rats in the empty cage experiments), and not a single rat drank enough of the drug-laced water to result in death. In a second experiment, he even "hooked" the rats on drugs by putting them in the empty cages for roughly a month and a half, then moved them to Rat Park. Although the rats experienced withdrawal symptoms as part of their transition to Rat Park, they eventually stopped drinking the drug-laced water and went back to living a normal life.

In his research, Alexander identified several historical examples where an increase in addiction occurred. For example, when colonization occurred in the U.S. and Canada, the Native American population was forced from good farming land and/or their nomadic lifestyles into a very small area. Much like the rats in the small-cage experiments, the rates of addiction skyrocketed.

Recently, Alexander's studies have re-emerged as a more significant part of our conversation about addiction. In 2015, Johann Hari revisited these studies in his book *Chasing the Scream: The First and Last Days of the War on Drugs*. He identified another human equivalent to the rat experiments: The Vietnam War. With a high percentage of soldiers returning from the war addicted to heroin, there was a great fear that there would be major problems as they returned home. Remarkably, only a very small percentage needed treatment. While they experienced withdrawals and challenges, the return of connection and a better overall environment enabled them to stop using, just like the rats in Rat Park.

Alexander's conclusion about addiction based on his studies was this: drugs become irresistible when the chance for a healthy social existence (connection) is destroyed. At its core, addiction is about a lack of healthy connection, as well as the environment that the connection helps to create. In other words, *the opposite of addiction is not sobriety, it is connection* (Hari, 2015).

Connection does not merely mean physically being around other people or having acquaintances. It does not mean having relationships where you do all the work or the other person does all the work. True connection requires that you know and honor yourself. It means having relationships in your life where you are able to be your authentic self, keep healthy boundaries and have relationships at different levels of connection, including deep connections. In these connections, others also share their authentic selves with you. We will review connection in greater detail throughout this book.

In stating that the opposite of addiction is connection, I do not intend to discount the other realities of addiction. Addiction is also physical, physiological, and genetic. Addiction is fundamentally a brain disease. When you use an addictive behavior or substance it changes your brain in critical ways. That change then affects your ability to be connected, and the cycle continues downward.

What I am suggesting is that addiction is rooted in disconnection and the dis-ease (Washton and Boundy, 1990) that stems from lack of connection. While it is important to examine thoughts, behavior and physical aspects of addiction recovery, the underlying emotional and relational aspects must be treated for long-term recovery.

Reflections – Exercise B

1. What thoughts or emotions came up for you as you read this section?

_____

_____

_____

The Struggle for Connection

As I've read, studied, talked, and worked with my clients in therapy over the years, I have seen a lot of different ways that people talk about connection/disconnection and how it relates to addiction. As I have researched addiction, I have found that many therapists and authors use the term "intimacy disorder" to describe the addictive patterns that happen when people are disconnected. The word intimacy refers to the ability to form friendships, close personal relationships and connection with others. When your struggle to find or maintain connection leads to sexually acting out, it is considered disordered intimacy.

I have found that although partners of addicts may not have acted out sexually, they often struggle with the same problem of not being able to form healthy connections and close friendships with others; they struggle with disordered intimacy as well. Recognizing this in no way minimizes the need for the addict to take responsibility for his/her addictive behaviors, nor does it change the trauma that comes from those behaviors. However, it is important to realize that partners are struggling with connection too. That realization allows recovery work to include the necessary tools for partners to be able to heal that aspect of their lives, to whatever degree it is occurring. Without addressing those missing tools, complete healing from the pain that comes from being married to an addict is not possible. Partners are not considered secondary in this program. Partners' needs, pain and healing are an equally important part of the process of recovery.

The main problem with the label of "intimacy disorder" is that our culture generally uses the word intimacy to refer to sex. When my clients have heard the term intimacy disorder, they have often translated that to "sexual disorder." I even had one wife translate that to "you are not having enough sex with your partner, and that is the issue." Luckily her individual therapist was able to help her understand what it truly meant.

Another common term to describe the struggle to connect is "attachment disorder." This term was coined by John Bowlby (1969) as part of his *Attachment Theory*. Considerable research has been done to substantiate this theory. Basically, the research has shown that attachments (connections) we form as infants establish long-term ways of interacting with the world. In those formative years, the brain begins to send messages throughout the body using neurons, specialized cells for transmitting information. Based on the feedback from and connection to the outside world, these neurons begin to link together in certain ways. These links or connections of neurons are called neural pathways. If the message about connection to a baby is positive, neural pathways form that reinforce a sense of safety and connectedness. If the message about connection to a baby is not positive, neural pathways form that allow the baby to manage the distress and disconnection. Because these initial neural pathways are the first to form, they have a significant influence on how we tend to think about and react to others as we grow older.

Bowlby believed that the first year was very important, so much so that it almost determined the way you would connect with others throughout your life. However, research since then has shown that these neural pathways can be changed, with work and positive connection. I will discuss how that change can occur in future chapters.

In 2004, Philip Flores wrote *Addiction as an Attachment Disorder*, a groundbreaking book on how attachment/connection is related to addiction. He cites research about self-regulation, which is the ability to manage one's own feelings, and notes that it is biologically impossible to regulate our own emotions over an extended period of time outside of relationships. He then notes that "individuals who have difficulty establishing emotionally regulating attachments are more inclined to substitute drugs and alcohol for their deficiencies in intimacy." I would argue that there are many types of behaviors that are used for the same purpose: filling in for the gap created by disconnection.

Connection, Disconnection, and Connective Disorders

When you are unable to connect in a secure way, you find it difficult to create and/or maintain relationships with healthy, appropriate levels of connection. Some people are unable to share and be honest in their most caring relationships because it feels too risky to share with those you value the most. In other cases, the opposite occurs, and you are so desperate for the connection you want in your life that you share excessive and inappropriate levels of personal information before gaining the necessary trust for that level of disclosure (i.e. sharing a personal secret or deep emotions with someone you met only recently). Stuck in disconnection, you begin to search for something—anything—that will bring a sense of relief, comfort, and connectedness. The result is what I call connective disorders. While the term is similar in almost every way to attachment disorder, my clients have regularly reported that the term connective disorder is one they relate to better.

Bruce Alexander (2010) talked about our culture's impact on connection and the reasons why he believes so many people turn to addictions (and I would argue other connective disorders) for relief in today's world:

> The view of addiction from Rat Park is that today's flood of addiction is occurring because our hyperindividualistic, hypercompetitive, frantic, crisis-ridden society makes most people feel socially and culturally isolated. Chronic isolation causes people to look for relief. They find temporary relief in addiction to drugs or any of a thousand other habits and pursuits because addiction allows them to escape from their feelings, to deaden their senses, and to experience an addictive lifestyle as a substitute for a full life. (http://www.brucekalexander.com/articles-speeches/rat-park/148-addiction-the-view-from-rat-park)

Essentially, our current culture tends to create disconnection: training us to compete and isolate rather than connect. And for most of us, that also means that we get little training or tools to help us to create connection in our lives. This book represents one attempt to provide tools and training to help you gain and improve that connection in your life.

Symptoms of Connective Disorders

Without training and with so much disconnection, we turn to a variety of behaviors for relief: the symptoms of connective disorders. Because the ways we create relief from being disconnected are often difficult to discern, I have created a list of different symptoms that can occur with connective disorders. This list may not be completely inclusive, and many categories overlap. Many people relate to several of the categories. Some examples presented here may apply to you but may be more extreme than your situation. In those cases, hopefully you can connect to (or see in your spouse) less extreme versions of that symptom. Acknowledging the symptoms you relate to will help you begin to understand how connective disorders show up in your life and relationships. Noticing the symptoms you see in your spouse can help you understand him/her better. Over time, understanding the ways your and your spouse's connective disorders occur will bring a greater capacity to change and find real connection.

Before I move forward, let me clarify one thing. The goal in this section is not to place blame on either addict or partner. Understanding the symptoms of your connective disorder—the ways you disconnect, numb, or seek relief—allows you to begin to take your power back. Both addict and partner can only find power in realizing how you have struggled to connect and/or protect yourself in relationships.

Let me share an example. A couple comes to counseling because the husband had multiple affairs. The husband's acting out is his responsibility. He needs to take responsibility for his actions and work to repair the damage those actions have caused. That is an extremely important part of the process of healing. The wife is not responsible for the husband's affairs. If he was unhappy in the marriage, he could have taken many other healthy steps to address the disconnection.

His behaviors, however, signal the existence of a disconnection that affects the relationship. This disconnection is something we address with both partners so that as healing from the affairs occurs, both partners are able to connect in ways that are healthy and emotionally safe for *both* of them and in ways that meet *both* of their needs.

In many cases, the partner (or addict) may be displaying other symptoms of a connective disorder, such as codependency. Those symptoms need to be addressed as well. Again, this does not excuse or justify the addict's behaviors. Identifying and addressing all symptoms allows both partner and addict a chance to heal and find peace and connection. Thus, both addict and partner have a responsibility for their connective-disordered behaviors and for the ways in which they personally have affected the relationship. Both play a part in healing the relational disconnect.

If you are the partner of an addict, the most complete healing I can offer you includes applying the tools found in this book to yourself in addition to your spouse. You will not be ignored in this program. As stated earlier, your pain is not secondary to the addict's pain and your healing is not less important either. This is why I include you from the very beginning of the program and ask that you consider how the concepts apply to you as well as to your spouse.

With that clarification, let's review the different ways people try to cope ineffectively: the negative symptoms associated with connective disorders. While each definition is presented using only one gender's pronoun, all connective disorder symptoms can apply to both genders.

Compulsive Sex/Sex Addiction

Sex is like a drug. Any time the individual experiences overwhelming feelings, they bury them by acting out sexually. The fear of being alone terrifies them.

> "I had sex with him again. I know I wasn't supposed to, but I just felt so alone. I know he's bad for me. At least I made it three days this time!"

> "I love my wife, but the urges come and I can't seem to stop having sex with prostitutes. I know that she might leave me if I act out again, but I don't know how to stop."

Pornography Addiction

The individual spends an excessive amount of time watching or thinking about pornography. This may be a constant issue or may be something the individual binges on every few days, weeks or even months. Masturbation may or may not be involved.

> "I sat down for 30 minutes and realized hours later that it was 4 a.m. I had completely missed dinner and had to be at work in 3 hours."

Compulsive Masturbation

The individual masturbates excessively, even when no sexual urges are present. The behavior interferes with daily living activities and may lead to injury.

> "I couldn't make it through the 20-minute drive. I had to pull over and masturbate. I didn't even want to, but I couldn't stop myself."

Chronic Infidelity

The individual repeatedly has affairs, with or without telling their partner. These affairs may involve developing emotional relationships, or they may be one night stands, anonymous affairs or visits to prostitutes.

> "I seem to be utterly unable to be completely faithful."

Virtual Infidelity

The individual uses online message boards and chat rooms to develop and maintain relationships. These relationships may remain virtual or may become physical.

> "No one is being hurt. I'm not actually doing anything wrong. It's not a real affair because I've never touched her."

Chronic Inappropriate Flirtation

The individual's self-esteem is based off of other people being attracted to him. Suggestive conversations are a regular occurrence, despite the cost to the individual's primary relationships.

> "I just want to know I'm attractive. It's not like I do anything with them."

Compulsive Seduction

The individual is more interested in the initial conquest than in sex. The high comes from the other person's interest in them, not from physical activities with them. It is similar to chronic inappropriate flirtation, but takes the interactions a step further.

> "I'd call women listed on Craigslist and make them want to set up a meeting with me. I never showed up for any of the meetings. Just setting them up was my high."

Control Driven Sex

The individual has sex with those he or she is in a position of power over. Using power to convince others to have sex with her provides an ego boost and a feeling of control.

> "Of course they wanted to have sex with me. I can have any female in the company that I want. I am a VP."

Voyeurism

The individual is sexually aroused by watching others perform private acts, such as getting dressed or having sex, without their knowledge.

"The fact that they don't even know that I'm watching them turns me on as much as seeing what they are doing."

Subtle Exhibitionism

The individual deliberately wears tight or revealing clothing, or knowingly bumps into or rubs up against someone, attempting to elicit a sexual response. The high in this case comes from seeing the reactions in others.

"I know men look at me when I walk by. It gives me a high when I 'accidentally' brush up against someone and see their reaction."

Intrusive Sexual Behaviors

The individual subtly violates the personal boundaries of others. This can be achieved by brushing up against them or using strategic movements or positions. Unlike subtle exhibitionism, the violations are not obvious. Part of the high is that they go unnoticed by the victim, so the individual is taking something that was not offered.

"I walked past her and my arm brushed against her chest. No one was hurt; she didn't even notice."

Knight/Damsel-in-Distress Addicts

The individual perceives love as either rescuing someone or being rescued by someone. These relationships may be affairs, or the individual may use new partners to escape the struggles/pain of their current relationship.

"He sees what I'm going through. He won't let me keep hurting this way."

"She is trapped in a horrible relationship. She's not strong enough to get out on her own. I know I can save her."

Obsessive Fantasy

The individual imagines details of a relationship that may not even exist at all. This might include plans for the future or suppositions about another individual's thoughts towards them.

"I know he's meant to be with me. He really loves me, not her, and I can tell he knows that when he looks at me."

Sexual Avoidance (also called Sexual Anorexia)

The individual obsessively avoids all forms of intimacy or sexuality. This often involves significant fear or anxiety.

"It makes me sick to think about having sex or even having a boyfriend. I don't see how people could like sex."

Honeymoon Addicts

This type of individual is only interested in the initial stage of the relationship. The romance of the beginning of a relationship is intoxicating, but once it has worn off the individual is absolutely not interested in the idea of having to do the work of maintaining a relationship.

"I can't stand the thought of never having another first kiss."

Serial Monogamy

The individual maintains primarily monogamous relationships. However, when struggles arise or the initial "spark" has worn off, the individual quickly moves on to another relationship, often spending little or no time in between relationships. Relationships last longer and the individuals form more serious commitments than Honeymoon Addicts do.

"I just want to run. I know this is what I always do when things get bad, but I don't see any point in staying."

Excessive Fear of Being Single

The individual is so afraid of being alone that he goes to extremes to avoid being single. This may include staying in very unhealthy relationships, frantically searching for his next partner the moment insecurities arise in his current relationship, or maintaining multiple relationships at the same time so there is always a backup partner available.

"If she ever finds out who I really am, she'll leave, so I need to keep my backups ready just in case."

Idealistic Fantasy

The individual maintains an idealistic and impossible set of standards for relationships. Every new partner is her true soul-mate and the answer to all her prayers. When the partner fails to live up to the unrealistic expectations, the fairy tale comes crashing down and the relationship is over.

> "He's everything I've ever wanted, everything I've ever looked for. I know now why none of my other relationships worked out."

Romance Addicts

The individual looks for that one magic relationship in which she will be everything the other person has ever dreamed of, so she can hold on to it for the rest of her life. This relationship may be a very short-term relationship and may or may not be physical. Romance Addiction is similar to Idealistic Fantasy, except the relationship(s) end before the fairy tale comes crashing down and reality sets in, allowing for long-term fantasy. Often, the individual is in a committed relationship with someone else and has no desire to leave; she just needs that romance to deal with life's realities.

> "I don't want to leave my husband. I know my husband loves me, but my affair partner made me feel beautiful and wanted and like every part of me was perfect. Now I can go on for the rest of my life knowing that my affair partner remembers me that way."

Substance Addictions

The individual uses substances (alcohol, drugs, etc.) to escape from or cope with emotions or difficulties. In some cases, substances can be used to help create a sense of connection.

> "I just can't take it anymore. If I can get high for a little while, then I'll have the strength to keep going."

> "When I'm high, that's the only time I can be myself. I can let my hair down and everyone thinks I'm hilarious."

Eating Disorders

The individual becomes so preoccupied with food and weight that it consumes them. It gives them something they have control over in their life or provides them with an escape. They also tend to believe that if they can control their body, they will be able to gain acceptance and love.

Anorexia/Bulimia.

"If only I were thin enough, then I would be good enough and people would love me."

Overeating/Food Addictions.

"It's been a really hard day. I deserve this tub of ice cream. Plus, if I finish it off, then I won't be tempted to eat it anymore."

Work Addiction

The individual focuses almost all his energy and time on work. He may focus on making money, moving up in the company, or just the payoff of structure, effectiveness, and success. Unlike others who work hard, his work is relentless and obsessive, and comes at a cost to health, marriage, social life and other areas of his life.

"I don't understand why my wife is complaining. I have to work this hard to make money so my family can have the things they need. How else could we afford everything?"

"I have to work this vacation. My boss is going to be very upset. I'll eventually get to the beach, but I'll have to bring along my laptop."

Perfectionism

This type of individual relentlessly pursues unattainably high standards (as close to 100% as possible). The only measure of success is achievement. When perfectionists fail in any small way, they judge their self-worth to be low based on those mistakes. Unlike healthy striving for excellence, perfectionists experience negative consequences such as severe stress, self-shaming, and relationship problems (including demanding perfection of their partner).

"I can't believe I got a 98 on that test. I thought I had done better."

"What is wrong with me, I thought I had that work project in perfect order, and then I made that mistake. I'm not sure I can ever be successful at work."

"Why can't others get this right. I just need to do it myself. If only there were more time in the day!"

Codependency

The individual's thoughts, feelings, and beliefs are dependent on the thoughts, feelings, and beliefs of others. She constantly works to control or manipulate situations and individuals in an attempt to feel peace, connection, emotional safety or happiness. This can manifest in many ways, including the following:

- Protect someone else from consequences, often as a way of protecting themselves from feeling pain from watching their spouse experience those consequences and/ or suffering other consequences personally (e.g. other people finding out about the addiction and being shamed).
- Manipulate situations to try to change the behaviors of others, often as a way of avoiding the pain that comes when those behaviors occur.
- People please even when it is at significant personal expense (usually with a hope of some type of positive reciprocation).
- Live in the role of victim with the hope of being rescued, as that makes them feel cared about.

"He really doesn't know what he's doing. He doesn't mean it. He's already so upset over it. I don't want to show him that he's hurt me because that will just make it worse for him."

"If I just yell loudly enough, if I make her feel badly enough about it, she won't do it again."

"You don't understand. It's not my fault. It's just been so hard for me since . . . Why do things always happen to me?"

"If I can just keep the house clean enough, do the grocery shopping and give her a lot of time to herself, maybe she will not be so tired. Then she will be able to let me know I'm important to her, that she appreciates and loves me."

Rage

This individual reacts with strong, often sudden outbursts of uncontrolled anger (very different from healthy anger, which could guide him to healthy confrontations). He may stuff feelings, trying to accommodate others, then blow up in rage when things feel overwhelming. He may also use rage to manipulate or control others so that he can avoid feeling powerless, rejected, abandoned and/or unappreciated. He frequently blames others for causing the rage rather than taking responsibility himself.

> "If she would just stop ignoring me, I wouldn't have to keep blowing up like this."

> "He's just so inconsiderate. If he would just do things differently, I would feel loved and wouldn't have to rage like this."

> "Why can't others just work with me. I hate feeling like I'm the only one doing anything in this house. I wish I didn't have to yell to get people to respond."

Again, in most cases people will display multiple types of connective disorder symptoms in their lives. Sometimes they occur separately, at different times, and for different reasons. People will often use one for a while, then try to stop. When they are able to stop that behavior, they often begin a different behavior. This is referred to as cross-addiction. Other times, these behaviors are combined as a way of intensifying the high/payoff or as a way to ease the shame more effectively.

Reflections – Exercise C

1. Which descriptions do you most closely relate to? Why?

_____

_____

2. If you are in a committed relationship, which ways do you think your spouse might display connective-disordered behaviors? Why?

_____

_____

3. What feelings came up as you read through the descriptions?

_____

_____

4. I do not want to be perceived as _____; I want _____. (Ex: I do not want to be perceived as a victim; I want people to understand how I got here. Or: I do not want to be perceived as unfaithful, uncaring, and cruel; I want to be understood.)

_____

_____

These connective disorders are attempts to make up for the lack of connection in our life, to find relief from the pain of disconnection, and to meet various needs. Each of us longs for connection and love, but with connective disorders, we try to fill those needs in ways that are not healthy and only work short term. Each symptom of a connective disorder is a different way to try to meet our needs.

Whatever the symptoms of the connective disorder are, life without them seems impossible. If it is sex, then it seems impossible to live without sex (one of Carnes' [1983] four basic beliefs of a sex addict is "sex is my most important need"). If it is romance, then it seems impossible to live without romance. If it is codependency, then it seems impossible to get connection or feel loved or emotionally safe without manipulating or controlling the situation. At a much deeper level, what people are really longing for is to know that they are loved and wanted, worthy and enough. Human beings are made for connection. Our greatest joys come from relationships with others. If connection is missing in our lives, or we are unable to recognize it, we do whatever we need to do in order to feel it, even if it's only for a few minutes or hours.

Reflections – Exercise D

1. How do you define connection? In other words, life without _____ seems impossible, or my most important need is _____.

    _____

    _____

2. Do you believe connection is important? Why or why not?

    _____

    _____

3. What do you do to feel connection?

    _____

    _____

Labels

"What's in a name? That which we call a rose
By any other name would smell as sweet."
Romeo and Juliet (II, ii, 1-2), Shakespeare

As you may have noticed, many of the symptoms of connective disorders could be classified as addictions. Because the word addiction is a difficult diagnosis for people to understand and even more difficult to accept, I'll spend some time now focusing on that term specifically: what it does and does not mean. I worked in a residential treatment center that specialized in drug and alcohol addiction, sex addiction, eating disorders and a variety of other process addictions. Occasionally during group I would ask them to tell me the first thing(s) they thought of when I said the word 'addict.' They would typically respond with a list like this one:

Wino	Bum
Loser	Shameful
Poser	Junkie

Destitute	Out of Control
Reject	Manipulative
Broken	Weak
Strung out	Liar
User	Self-centered
Ruined	Worthless

Sex addicts would always add a few more to their list: pervert, sicko, depraved, deviant, slut, etc. My next question would always be followed by silence: "If that's what you think addict means, why in the world would you want to call yourself an addict?" Eventually they would admit that they called themselves an addict because they had been told to in treatment, because they didn't have a better name for it, or even worse, because they thought their words were actually a good representation of them.

Labels are tricky things. Without them we can't clearly understand the different aspects of what we struggle with or how to overcome them. They give us power to identify and treat appropriately. At the same time, labels can cause us to focus only on weaknesses and not strengths. In the end, finding ways to label our strengths and weaknesses/problems can be very helpful, but embracing a label can also lead to accepting additional shaming messages that are not helpful (or even downright destructive).

Let me use attention-deficit disorder (ADD) as an example of one diagnosis where the label can either help or harm. When parents first discover their child has ADD, they have different reactions: some feel so much shame, they deny that it exists. They may pretend it never came up and/or go to specialists to find a different label.

In other cases, they may see the child as deficient: they are just broken in that way. They do not do any real work to emotionally support the child or to help them learn to cope with the challenges of ADD. Instead, they medicate the child. Let me clarify that medication is absolutely an essential part of treatment for many ADD clients I have; however, this type of parent *only* uses medications and does not provide other necessary support to the child. In these cases, the child often internalizes the message that they are broken/incapable. In other cases, the child is left feeling like they are alone in the struggle to succeed.

Other parents accept the label for their child, but go into a shame spiral, feeling like a failure as a parent, wondering how others will judge them, and feeling hopeless; life will never be the same. Others use the ADD diagnosis as an excuse to disable the child further, suggesting that the child can't do homework, chores, or other tasks due to ADD: things that might be achievable with appropriate support.

Finally, there are parents who respond in a healthy way, acknowledging the struggles related to ADD but not taking them personally. They didn't cause it. They embrace the good and find better ways to provide the support the child needs to be able to succeed. They read books, talk with others, go to therapy if necessary, consider medications that might help, and work to find solutions that are a fit: solutions that offer support while not enabling, or disabling, their child.

Much like ADD, we do the same with the label of addiction.

We *deny* that it exists:

"I just have a drink occasionally."

"Everybody watches a little porn sometimes."

"What man isn't attracted to other women? It's not realistic to expect me to be satisfied with only one sexual partner for the rest of my life."

"He just likes to gamble a little."

"I'm just trying to reach my ideal weight, and I'll stop when I get there."

We *excuse* ourselves or those we love from responsibility:

"It's not my fault that _____ (I can't pay the mortgage, I'm so attracted to women, I say or do the things I say/do). I'm an addict."

"I'm just an addict. It is something I've struggled with my whole life. There's nothing I can change. I wish we could just get the balance right with my medications, then I might stay sober. I wish I weren't so broken."

We try to find someone or something to *blame* for the problem:

"If only he had a better job, he wouldn't feel so stressed and drink so much."

"If my wife would just have more sex with me, then I wouldn't have to act out sexually."

"If I had lots of money, no one would complain about my gambling."

We go into a *shame/despair* spiral:

"Now I'm going to lose everything!"

"I'm broken."

"What's going to happen if people find out? They'll think I'm a _____ [you can insert any of the negative things my group members said here]."

"It's my fault. If only I were enough, she wouldn't act out."

Identifying a connective disorder can empower and enable healing. With help, you can learn to manage addiction and/or to respond to the addictions of others in healthy ways. You can read books, go to meetings, and get and stay connected with others: *You cannot do it alone.* They work to find solutions that are a good fit for their lives. They see the label as a way to identify and begin to learn and grow. That perspective is what leads to long-term recovery. Being the spouse of an addict is a label as well, one that has potentially damaging and painful consequences if not understood in a healthy way. Interestingly, addicts and spouses of addicts often share similar traits, although at times for very different reasons.

Reflections – Exercise E

1. Before reading the next few paragraphs, take a minute to consider the positive aspects of addicts and partners of addicts. What might you include?

   _____

   _____

   _____

My experience in working with addicts and loved ones of addicts has brought a clearer definition to the label "addict" and "family member of addict" for me. When someone self-identifies as an addict or a loved one of an addict, I assume the following about that person:

Strong	Feels powerless/stuck
Tender hearted	Skilled in some ways but not in others
Wounded	Overwhelmed
Resourceful	Fearful/anxious
Shame-based	Hard working
Wants to be loved/connected	

One way to recognize the strengths of an active addict is to watch how they utilize those strengths as they act out addictively. For example, when addicts want to use, they are extremely resourceful in connecting with others, finding financial support and making things work when everything seems tough. They are amazingly resourceful. Recovery can capitalize on these strengths.

There are strengths specific to spouses of addicts as well. Partners manage to make their resources stretch when it seems impossible, have the strength to hold everything together when it appears that it will all fall apart, and have the love and belief to try again and again. It may appear weak to stay in a relationship with an addict; however, I have found the opposite to be true. One goal of this book is to help partners see, understand and access their strengths: to see the good in themselves.

I hope that your work in this book will help to increase your understanding of the strengths both addicts and partners possess, even though those gifts/talents are typically seen as negative when associated with the addiction.

Reflections – Exercise F

1. What labels do you give yourself? What labels do you think other people give you?

2. What are the commonalities/differences between the labels you give yourself and those you believe others give you? Why do you think those similarities and/or differences exist?

3. What are some of your strengths (positive labels)?

4. What are some of the labels you feel apply to your spouse? What labels do you think other people give your spouse?

_____

_____

5. What are the commonalities/differences between the way you view your spouse and the way you believe others view your spouse? Why do you think those similarities and/or differences exist?

_____

_____

6. What are some of your spouse's strengths (positive labels)?

_____

_____

Defining Addiction

I have used the term "addiction" and "addict" several times so far. Before I go any further, let's talk about what I mean by those terms. Addiction is defined as *an escalating pattern of out of control behavior over time (six months or longer) that continues despite negative consequences and significantly affects the individual's life* (summary based on the *Diagnostic and statistical manual of mental disorders*, 5th ed.; *DSM–5*; American Psychiatric Association [APA], 2013).

There are several important components in this definition. Addiction is not something that has happened once or twice, or even a few times. It is a reccurring pattern. Addiction escalates over time, meaning the person develops a tolerance for the substance and/or behavior and has to use more, use more often, or use more powerful material to get the same high. Due to the development of tolerance, the body goes through withdrawal if the behavior stops (although this is not experienced in all cases of addiction). In an addiction, negative consequences do not prevent the behavior from happening. The human mind and body are created to incorporate feedback. If someone touches a hot burner on a stove and gets burned, they instinctively pull back their hand

and learn from that situation that they will get burned if they touch a red burner again. Addicts continue their behaviors even when they know from experience that they will be hurt or will hurt the people they love.

Finally, addictions significantly impact the life of the addict. This impact can happen in several areas:

- Social/Relational: marital problems, decrease in friendships, etc.
- Financial: money spent on the behavior, negative effect on income, etc.
- Occupational: loss of job, poor work attendance or reviews, etc.
- Physical: health issues, loss of sleep, effect on nutrition, etc.
- Mental: increased depression, anxiety, etc.
- Emotional: increase in stress and feelings of loneliness, fear, powerlessness, etc.

Several years ago the American Society of Addiction Medicine (ASAM) made a clear statement that declared addiction as a brain disease and included the use of behaviors (like sex addiction) in their definition. This declaration made a significant impact on the acceptance of behavioral addictions. I include it here for you to review, with emphasis added as it relates specifically to behaviors.

> Addiction is a primary, chronic disease of brain reward, motivation, memory and related circuitry. Dysfunction in these circuits leads to characteristic biological, psychological, social and spiritual manifestations. This is reflected in an individual *pathologically pursuing reward and/or relief by substance use <u>and other behaviors</u>*. [Emphasis added]

> Addiction is characterized by inability to consistently abstain, impairment in behavioral control, craving, diminished recognition of significant problems with one's behaviors and interpersonal relationships, and a dysfunctional emotional response. Like other chronic diseases, addiction often involves cycles of relapse and remission. Without treatment or engagement in recovery activities, addiction is progressive and can result in disability or premature death. (ASAM, 2011)

Sexual addiction is a pattern of sexual behaviors, existing for a minimum of six months, which negatively affects life and continues despite consequences. Behaviors escalate over time and tolerance is developed. If the behaviors stop, the individual may or may not experience withdrawal. When withdrawal is experienced, the symptoms may look different and/or take longer to appear than with substance addictions.

There are several misconceptions as to what falls under the umbrella of sexual addictions. Some people associate sexual addiction with homosexuality, cross-dressing, fetishes, child pornography and child molestation. Although sex addiction can include any sexual behavior and is not limited to a set of sexual behaviors, these behaviors alone do not mean that a sexual addiction exists. Some (such as child pornography and child molestation) are always unhealthy, significantly damaging to yourself and/or others, and illegal. It is important to identify that sexual addictions do not necessarily, or even usually, lead to those behaviors; however, in some cases they can occur as an escalation in acting out. Other behaviors, such as homosexuality, cross-dressing or fetishes, may be part of an addiction, but do not indicate an addiction in and of themselves.

Enjoying sex does not make you a sex addict. Incorporating sex toys into your sex life does not mean you are an addict. Sexual addiction does not mean experimenting with different positions or behaviors with your partner, although those may be problematic if those behaviors put you or your partner at risk of being hurt physically or emotionally. Sex is a healthy part of a relationship and allows for greater connection when used appropriately.

I use the term addict because it represents a simple, concise and potentially non-shaming way to address a set of behaviors that have escalated and become problematic. By my definition, an "addict" is someone who is trapped in a pattern of behaviors that are preventing him/her from feeling peace, joy, and connection. *The opposite of addiction isn't sobriety, it is connection.* Addictions are symptoms of a connective disorder.

Although there are those who feel like the first time they tried their addictive behavior they were hooked, most people begin addictive behaviors merely out of curiosity and are not immediately addicted. As they continue to use, they move, sometimes quickly, sometimes slowly, toward the more addictive side of the spectrum. Some people can maintain use at a level that never becomes problematic (although even at small levels there can be problems: disconnect from others, hangovers, etc.). Others continue to move into greater and greater problems.

As problematic behaviors increase, individuals shift further down the continuum of addictive behaviors. The *DSM–5* has specifically identified and defined two places on the spectrum of addictive behaviors: abuse and dependence (APA, 2013). Abuse refers to problematic use that occurs less frequently (like binge drinking on the weekends), while dependence/addiction, as noted previously, is more severe and continual use. The dilemma created by these two labels is that they identify only two points on the line, as demonstrated in the following diagram.

Casual Use   Abuse   Dependence
                                                       (Addiction)

As addictive behaviors increase, people try desperately to deny their problems and avoid these labels that, for them, mean all the negative things my group members listed earlier. So instead of embracing the reality that there are problems that are increasing and need to be addressed, they do all they can to avoid the shame they would feel if they accepted one of these labels.

Many clients get hung up on whether or not their behaviors constitute an addiction. Addictive behavior is addictive behavior (and the outcomes are the outcomes—positive or negative) no matter where you are on the continuum. And regardless of whether or not it is an addiction, it is still a symptom of a connective disorder and is worthy of addressing. No matter what label you feel fits best, it is critical to recognize the impact of the addictive behavior and address it as soon as you can—because the long-term negative consequences will become more and more severe the longer you wait.

It is also important to understand that, just like drug addiction, sexual addiction changes your brain. Even though the drugs are not ingested or injected, addictive behaviors cause your body to produce significantly higher levels of substances such as adrenaline, dopamine, and endorphins. These substances occur naturally in your body, but not at the high levels the body produces when you participate in addictive behaviors. Additionally, your brain changes when you are addicted. For example, evidence has shown that the prefrontal cortex—the part of the brain that control impulses, is critical in decision making, and helps us stick to our own values—shrinks significantly due to addiction. Because of these changes, addictions are considered brain diseases (as we discussed earlier). If you don't address the problem as soon as possible, then over time, the changes in your brain can make it more and more difficult to address it at all. My hope is that you will begin to heal wherever you are on the continuum, the sooner the better. The changes these behaviors have made to your brain can be reversed through sobriety, recovery, and healthy living. There is so much hope and opportunity in recovery.

Partners

While I will discuss this later, it is also important to mention here that trauma has an effect on the brain as well. Because discovery of the sexual acting out is so traumatic for partners, it is also critical that you get help as soon as possible in the process. The sooner you can manage the crisis and trauma, the more likely the negative impact of the trauma will be reduced and remedied. I urge you to engage in the recovery process as quickly as you can.

Reflections – Exercise G

1. What thoughts or emotions came up for you as you read this section?

    _____

    _____

2. What questions do you have about this section?

    _____

    _____

Origins of Addiction

Now that we have defined addiction, let's discuss its origins. First, genetic studies have been able to show a link between genes and addiction (for a basic understanding, see http://learn.genetics.utah.edu/content/addiction/genes/). Science may understand more perfectly in time, but for now it establishes what we have believed for years: our genetic makeup influences our susceptibility to addiction. So if your parents or grandparents were addicts, you are more at risk than others. Also, as we reviewed earlier, addiction affects the brain and body, creating dependence on the drug/behavior of choice. Additionally, other genetic predispositions like depression, anxiety, ADD, OCD and impulse control disorders have been linked to addiction. In other words, the likelihood of becoming an addict increases if you also struggle with other psychological issues.

These genetic factors are also influenced by the environment and the level of stress and support provided to the individual. A major long-term study measured the effect of Adverse Childhood Experiences (ACE's) on long-term well-being. ACE's include things such as physical abuse, sexual abuse, emotional abuse, physical and/or emotional neglect, household substance abuse, mental illness in the household, parental divorce/separation, an incarcerated household member, and so forth. The more ACE's an individual experienced, the higher the likelihood that the individual would participate as an adult in high-risk health behaviors such as smoking, alcohol and drug abuse, and promiscuity.

Additionally, the more ACE's present, the more likely the individual would experience physical health issues such as severe obesity, heart disease, cancer, stroke, diabetes, and a shortened life span. Finally, the higher the ACE's the more likely the individual would experience mental health issues such as depression and suicidality.

Experience has also taught me that addicts, and those who are in a committed relationship with addicts, are extremely tender-hearted, sensitive people. I consider this a genetic factor because that sensitivity has been part of their lives since they were very young, not just as part of the addiction. As children, they are often very attuned to others' feelings and are compassionate and empathetic. They reach out to connect and help others readily.

For example, being tender-hearted can be a strength, but when combined with a hostile environment can cause problems (intense rejection, abandonment, etc.). I believe this sensitivity is a gift, but without the right support and guidance, such sensitivity can lead to intense pain and trauma.

Reflections – Exercise H

1. What did you connect to in this section?

_____

_____

2. How did this section influence your view of claiming the label "addict" or "partner of an addict?"

_____

_____

Trauma

Traumas can occur as a result of natural disasters, war, family-of-origin issues, the culture we grow up in, our social contexts (i.e. school, work, friendships), and religious shaming or abuse. There are two types of trauma: big T and little t. Big T traumas are things like war, rape, natural disasters, physical abuse (including witnessing the abuse of a loved one), sexual abuse, neglect, or abandonment. Typically, big T traumas are recognized by society as being traumatic. Little t traumas (also sometimes referred to as relational traumas) are not as obvious, so we commonly ignore or minimize them: moving frequently, death of a loved one, peer rejection, divorce, affairs, difficulty in school, emotional abuse and so forth. Little t traumas often look insignificant to the outside observer, or are even discounted by those who experience them because they "aren't a big deal." My experience is that little t traumas are like "death by a thousand cuts" and can add together to create big T types of trauma. In other words, little t traumas can be just as traumatic as big T traumas to the individuals that experience them, *especially if left unresolved.*

My clients rarely think they have experienced trauma. Those who do acknowledge it often discount the severity of the impact. One woman I worked with experienced sexual abuse at a young age and was raped in her teens. As she shared the struggles that resulted, she qualified it with, "But I know others who have had it way worse." Another young man witnessed domestic violence between his parents and ultimately experienced it directly from his father. He had struggled to move out of his parent's home and overcome severe depression. As he processed his father's abuse he said, "I feel like this is such small stuff. I should just get over it. I feel like I'm wasting your time." In both examples, these clients had experienced trauma and were only able to heal once they had identified and worked through the impact that trauma had in their lives.

It is important not to discount the potential role trauma can play in both the development of the addiction and the recovery process. Trauma can shape our ability to respond to challenges in life and in relationships. In recovery is it critical to learn new ways to respond, rather than trauma-based ways, so that you can honor yourself and form healthy relationships. The key to healing from trauma is to acknowledge it, not blame yourself for it and work through it so that it no longer has the same negative impact on your life.

Reflections – Exercise I

1. What did you read in this section that related to you?

    _____

    _____

    _____

2. What memories resurfaced for you as you read through this section?

_____

_____

_____

3. What are the big T and/or little t traumas that you can identify in your life? Reflect for a moment on the memories you may not have identified as traumatic, but that come up often for you and still provide some level of disturbance (things mom, dad, siblings, peers or others said or did). Include those things on your list.

_____

_____

_____

_____

If you're still struggling with the label of sex addiction, I have included a Connective Disorder Screening Questionnaire in the Appendix. I suggest you answer the questions honestly and reflect on the outcome as suggested at the end of the questionnaire. I have also found that discussing the results with a sponsor or therapist can be helpful.

Separating the Authentic You from Your Addict or Traumatized Self

The first step in changing your addictive patterns of behavior is learning to separate yourself from the addict. This is also the first step partners can take to create safety and set up the foundation to rebuild trust and connection. Being trapped in an addictive pattern divides a person into two people: their authentic self and their addict. Being married to an addict can also divide a person into two people: their authentic self and their traumatized self. While I will address this in later chapters, I present this idea briefly here as a small step to helping you begin to recover your authentic, true self.

When the addiction ("the addict") hijacks your brain, you do things that your authentic self would never do. Activating the traumatized portion of your brain also hijacks your behavior. In both cases, you say and do things you would never say or do when you are your authentic, true self. You hurt yourself and other people in your life. It prevents your authentic self from managing your life. This is why I use the term addict: because addiction refers to behaviors that are out of your control. Partners of addicts may not act out in the same ways, but when you are in your traumatized self, your reactions are out of your control as well. I am not excusing addictive behaviors or saying that a trauma response is the same as an addictive behavior; I am working to give both of you the power to take control back from either your addict or your traumatized self.

Recognizing that stepping into that behavior is out of your control (Step One of the 12 Steps; Alcoholics Anonymous, 2001) does not absolve you of responsibility for your actions. It identifies areas in which your addict or traumatized self has control and allows you to start differentiating between those behaviors and who you really are and want to be. Recognizing this in your spouse, whether partner or addict, allows you to begin to create safety for yourself. It is the first step in taking back control of your life. You cannot fight a war if you do not know who your opponent is. The opponent here is the addict or the traumatized self. We will do more work in identifying the specific thoughts and behaviors that belong to your addict or traumatized self in upcoming chapters.

As noted earlier, it is also important to recognize that, while the behaviors of your addict or traumatized self are not things your authentic self would do, their strengths and weaknesses are your strengths and weaknesses. For example, addicts are incredibly resourceful. I've had clients who didn't even have the money to put gas in their car but were able to figure out how to acquire drugs. The resourcefulness in that case is expressed as part of their addict, but it is available to the authentic self as well. The reason this is important to understand is that your authentic self is not made up of only good traits, and your addict or traumatized self is not comprised of only weaknesses. Addicts often see things in extremes, but the goal of recovery is to find balance, acceptance and connection, not perfection. In fact, often really deep connections are created through being able to share weaknesses and struggles with others who can empathize with you in a healthy way.

The addict or traumatized self shows up when life gets overwhelming, when needs are not getting met (often over longer periods of time), or to help manage past traumas that are too painful. While this side of us can help to avoid, mask, escape and even feel temporary pleasures, it cannot bring long-term connection, serenity, happiness, and peace. The addict or traumatized self also prevents the authentic self from (1) developing tools and skills to manage difficult situations and emotions and (2) building healthy long-term connection with others.

The goal of this book is to help you develop a stronger sense of self and an ability to manage the difficult aspects of your life. As you strengthen your authentic self and learn to meet your needs and develop connection, you will also learn the tools to help avoid the destructive effects of addictive behaviors or trauma responses.

Reflections – Exercise J

1. What emotions and thoughts came up for you as you read through the preceding section?

   _____

   _____

2. What are some of the differences between your authentic self and your addict or traumatized self?

   _____

   _____

3. If you are married, what are some of the differences between your spouse's addict or traumatized self and their authentic self?

   _____

   _____

Wrap-Up

As you finish this chapter, I want to congratulate you on taking this first step towards recovery, connection, and peace! In this chapter I have reviewed the relationship between addiction and connection, connective disorders, labels, addiction, and sex addiction specifically. I hope that you have been able to relate to several of the ideas and that you are connecting with how those pieces related to you. Having a basic personal understanding of these concepts will help you know how best to engage in the recovery process. In Chapter Two we will focus on the role of emotion as it relates to addiction and trauma, the tools for recognizing and managing emotion, and the specific tools related to time-outs and self-soothing. These tools provide an essential foundation for managing the reactivity of early recovery but will continue to be useful as you move into middle and late recovery.

Chapter 2

FEELINGS AND THE THERMOMETER

Learning to Manage Emotion

Feelings, nothing more than feelings...
- Morris Albert

Before I address some of the perspectives and tools related to addiction recovery, it is important to first understand some basics about feelings. First, we all have them. While they are a constant part of our lives, we generally tend to ignore them, not notice them, and/or overreact to them. One thing is certain, as a culture we generally do not manage them well. Addiction and trauma add additional layers of unmanageability. Addicts have been numbing their feelings for a long time, and partners are often in such emotional pain and turmoil that they do all they can to avoid or numb the pain as well.

Learning to care for ourselves (self-care) is directly linked to emotional awareness, so it is essential to resurrect emotion in a healthy way to facilitate healing in recovery. In fact, Bill Wilson (1958), one of the founders of AA, called emotions the next frontier; he suggested that emotional sobriety needed to come as a part of healthy, long-term recovery. Some of the basic principles of emotions are discussed in this chapter. Before I begin, though, take a minute to answer the following questions. Please give them some time and thought before you move on. Doing this will help you internalize what you will learn as you work through this chapter.

Reflections – Exercise A

1. Where do emotions come from?

    _____

    _____

2. What purpose do emotions serve?

    _____

    _____

3. Why do people avoid them?

    _____

    _____

Origins of Emotions

Now that you have had a chance to reflect on emotions, let's consider them together. Let's begin with where emotions come from:

The Head—Neuroscience studies have clearly established that the signals which trigger emotion occur initially in the brain and are, in fact, a result of complex calculations based on external stimuli. Some research suggests that we can feel more quickly than we can consciously think. Additionally, feelings provide assessments of situations that are equally as accurate as conscious thoughts. Feelings are important, valid data (although how we *react* to them may not be healthy).

The Heart—This is the colloquial answer we often give, and the reality is not too far off. We often experience emotions in our bodies, although they originate in the brain, as a physical reaction which we attribute to our heart.

Relationships—Our interaction with other people, or lack thereof, elicits an emotional response from our brain.

Higher Power—I have found that when I am connected to my Higher Power, I often receive communication through my feelings. Many of my clients have reported the same experience.

What Purpose Do Emotions Serve?

Having discussed the sources of emotion, let's review some of the reasons we have emotions:

Protection—Have you ever been walking down a dark street and had the feeling it wasn't safe? Feelings like fear, surprise and anxiety can alert us to *potential* and real dangers.

Connection—Feelings like love, loneliness, insecurity, rejection, and abandonment all alert us to the need for, *potential* for and loss of connection.

Identity—Our likes, dislikes, passions, interests and focus in life are determined by the way we feel as we encounter life. These feelings help shape who we are and who we will become. They influence to a high degree where we choose to spend our time and energy.

Guidance—I call emotions our GPS, Global Positioning System, because they provide useful data to guide us in our lives. The first time my Dad got into a rental car that had GPS, he was driving alone and suddenly heard another voice in the car (the GPS). Obviously, this surprised and even scared him a little. Because he was uncomfortable with it, he eventually found a way to turn it off, despite its usefulness.

I think that's often what we do with feelings. We don't understand them. They don't make immediate sense. No one has ever explained them to us, and we certainly don't have a manual. Figuring out the unknown can be scary initially. In our discomfort, we find a way to numb and avoid them, despite the expert guidance they could give us if we could only discover a way to harness and manage their power.

Why Do We Avoid Them?

The number one reason we want to turn off emotions is because they are often painful. Who can't remember a time they felt rejected, abandoned, unloved or lonely? Why would we want to be attached to something that made us feel so much pain? Almost instinctively, we find ways to numb, avoid, cover up, discount and run from feelings in an attempt to avoid the pain they can cause. In the process, however, we leave behind critical information that can provide guidance to us in our decision making.

Another unfortunate side effect of stuffing our feelings is that we also eliminate the positive (joy, peace, etc.). Dr. Brené Brown (2010) noted that we can't selectively eliminate painful emotion without eliminating positive emotions like joy, peace, happiness, and love. Beginning to address painful emotion can give place for rewarding emotions to emerge.

Addicts and partners enter the recovery process with a lot of emotions. Addicts have been stuffing their feelings and acting out for a long time. On top of their day-to-day emotions, partners also have to deal with the intense pain of betrayal. Looking at and trying to manage those feelings can be particularly difficult in early recovery due to the sheer volume and intensity. As you are able to address them, change and relief can begin.

No Pain, No Gain

One day as I was working with a client, I asked him to try to identify his feelings. He said, "Mark, why do you keep having me focus on my painful emotions? I don't like emotional pain, so why would I want to feel it?" It was a good question that no one had ever asked me before. I paused for a moment to feel my way through the answer, then said, "It's not that I am trying to get you to feel pain. What I'm trying to get you to do is recognize the pain that is there just long enough to get the information it provides you. Then we can focus on coping with and resolving the pain. The more quickly you can identify it and manage it, the less you have to feel it. In the end, I'm trying to help you feel less pain by going through this process." He paused, contemplated and agreed that learning the process of identifying and addressing emotions would be for his benefit in the long run.

In the end, if we can't face the pain, we can't get the gain. We struggle to know how to protect ourselves. We deny the need for deep, connected relationships. We do our best to make decisions, but we're often missing half the data necessary to make those decisions wisely. Additionally, as Richard Rohr states, "If we do not transform our pain, we will most assuredly transmit it." Pain that is not acknowledged, managed and resolved will be perpetuated in our own lives and the lives of those closest to us: partners, children, and so forth.

John Bradshaw (1988) suggested that emotion is energy in motion (e-motion). I have found that when we avoid emotions, the energy from those emotions will eventually push us someplace, usually a place we would not choose otherwise (such as addictive behaviors or trauma responses). As we develop the skills to recognize and manage emotion, we can harness the energy and use it to move to a place that is of our choosing and for our short-term and long-term good.

Thermometer

In order to begin our discussion on how to manage emotion, let's imagine an old-fashioned mercury thermometer. When the temperature goes up, the mercury rises, and when it goes down, the mercury lowers. It is a simple process. Thermometers are useful. They cue us to important things. They let us know when it is hot or cold outside, if we have a fever, when our car is overheating or when that nuclear reactor is going to melt down. Being aware of the temperature allows us to know when we might need to do something. There are skills we have or can develop to know how to manage the temperature changes in many different contexts. These skills require some kind of training or learning. When we are not aware of the temperature, we don't know whether things are on the verge of crisis or going well. Even if we are aware of the temperature, when we don't know what to do if the temperature is high we are often left feeling powerless and scared.

Feelings operate in the same way. They let us know when things are hot and when they are not. They alert us to potential dangers and give us pleasant sensations when things are going well. If we can monitor our emotional temperature and know the steps to respond appropriately when the temperature increases, we can succeed in overcoming the challenges life has to offer. We can continue to learn and grow, developing increased skill and capacity.

When it comes to emotions, most of us would like to live our lives in comfort. On the thermometer, this is represented by low temperatures. When we are in the comfort zone, life is manageable, but growth is minimal. While we can, and need to, experience times like these, life is full of ups and downs, challenges, and trials. If we expect to stay comfortable permanently we will be disappointed and stunted in our growth. As we experience life's stressors, our emotional temperature begins to increase and we cross into the growth zone.

Rises in temperature and opportunities for growth are a natural and normal part of life. Children are continually inundated with the chaos of new information. They adapt to the discomfort of that by developing new skills. As they master skills, they then work on new skills that are not yet developed. Things they cannot do lead to struggle, and struggle can lead to more painful emotions. I have seen my kids get frustrated in many ways as they have tried to master new skills. They feel powerless and inadequate to do it on their own. Sometimes they need my help to learn new skills or remind them of skills they have not yet mastered. When they finally accomplish their goal (walking, tying their shoe, mastering a math problem, etc.), they immediately experience relief and excitement, among other rewarding feelings. As adults we are sometimes less able to manage the painful feelings related to growth and learning. We often want certainty and power more than growth and the joys that can come with it.

The zone of growth on the thermometer represents both the discomfort and opportunities that come with growth. While you are in this zone, you are going to experience some painful or uncomfortable feelings. If you are in tune with your feelings and seek help from others where necessary, you can manage the new experiences and challenges successfully. That leads to relief, comfort, excitement, and *a sense of being enough*. As you master new skills, you are able to handle situations that once would have turned your temperature up. As a result, your zone of comfort has increased, meaning you will be able to experience comfort in more situations than you could prior to growing and learning.

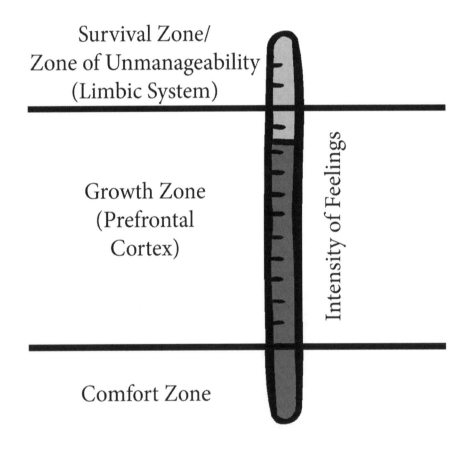

If we ignore or stuff our feelings, we do not even notice the need to learn and grow. We remain vulnerable to the situations we cannot cope with, and gradually that increases the emotional temperature. If we cannot cope effectively with those emotions and do not access help to guide us through that process (friends, family, therapy, Higher Power, books, etc.), we eventually cease to grow and our capacity to manage life decreases.

While we are in the zone of growth, we have full access to a part of our brain called the prefrontal cortex. The prefrontal cortex is where rational thought takes place. It is in charge of helping us know who we are (our personality). It is where we maintain our belief that we are good and capable. The prefrontal cortex helps us to make meaning of our emotions. It is where we make conscious choice, weighing the potential consequences as we evaluate poor, better, and best choices. It also provides the brakes to stop us from doing impulsive things that are dangerous or against our values. It is critical in helping us form relationships and make sense of love, values, responsibility and spirituality. In other words, when our prefrontal cortex is available to us, we know better who we are, can form healthier relationships and can control our impulses and act responsibly. We do what we feel is right and avoid doing what we think is wrong.

Survival Mode: Freeze, Fight, Flight, and Frenzy

As our emotional temperature passes the critical point into unmanageability (too much stress, relational struggles or other threats to our sense of self), another system takes over: the limbic system. The limbic system is dedicated to ensuring survival. Its job is to eliminate any threat to us. Unlike the prefrontal cortex, which isn't fully developed until our twenties, the limbic system is ready early. For example, the amygdala (a very important part of the limbic system) is fully formed eight months into gestation. That means that we are wired and ready for survival before we leave the womb. That makes sense, considering survival is one of our primary goals for the first few years. We have some pre-wired responses: sucking, gripping, crying, etc. All of these help satisfy our basic needs to survive: safety, hunger, thirst, bonding with a caregiver, etc.

The limbic system works wonderfully in moments where there is a true survival threat. In such moments, conscious thought is not necessary or even possible—we *react* to find safety. For example, when a car is about to hit us, we jump out of the way without consciously processing the need to do so. The limbic system organizes our body to react quickly (increasing adrenaline and heightening sensitivity to sights, sounds, etc.). This enables us to react alertly and quickly to potential threats. The typical responses that come from the limbic system are fight, flight and freeze. Some argue that freeze is a flight response because you have "flown" emotionally even though you are still present physically. I also sometimes see another response which I call frenzy. We'll discuss that at the end of this section.

When we are in survival mode, we experience certain emotions: anger, shame, jealousy, and/or survival fear. These are often related to other feelings, but we do not typically register those feelings until we are out of survival mode. We will discuss those underlying emotions in later chapters. Survival fear is the emotion we feel when there is an immediate threat to our life (not to be confused with the fear related to challenges in life that are not life-threatening). These emotions typically motivate us to exhibit survival responses: fight (anger, jealousy, survival fear), flight (shame, survival fear), freeze (shame, survival fear) and frenzy (survival fear).

To better understand survival responses, let's review them individually, starting with childhood examples and then relating them to adult versions of the same behaviors. I learned a lot about these types of responses when I worked with domestic violence. As you consider the temporary effectiveness of these survival responses, remember that they are only functional in environments where survival is the focus. In situations that are not truly survival-oriented, these responses are ineffective at best and very destructive at their worst.

Freeze

When a child's father is raging (physically or verbally), a very common response for children is to freeze. Much like a deer in the woods that senses danger, if s/he can just stay still enough, they might go unnoticed, and therefore remain unharmed.

As adults, freeze behaviors appear when people want to stand up for themselves (assert an opinion, say "no" to sex with a partner, set boundaries, etc.) but are unable to do so in the heat of the moment. It could also include acting like you agree when you do not: going along with things until you can do what you really want to. The primary emotions experienced with the freeze response are shame and survival fear.

Fight

Interestingly, in physically abusive circumstances I have seen normally freeze-oriented children display a fight response towards the abusive parent when a sibling or the other parent is threatened. Because the child has formed attachment bonds with the parent or siblings, s/he recognizes threats to those family members as a threat to themselves and reacts into fight mode. Unfortunately, this is a battle that can rarely be won (attacking the physically bigger parent despite the fact that it will likely lead to being physically abused themselves). Children who are unable to avoid fights or abusive behaviors of others may also react into the fight response.

Adults who display the fight response are a little more obvious to detect than with freeze response. They yell or attack first and ask questions later ("ready, fire, aim" instead of the usual "ready, aim, fire"), demand what they need from others and often repeat abusive behaviors that were inflicted on them as a child. Fight response also takes subtler forms in adults. Passive-aggressiveness is when you look passive or sweet on the outside, but your words are meant to hurt or control others (i.e. sarcasm, double messages, manipulation, etc.). The main emotions connected with the fight response are anger and jealousy.

Flight

Flight response is simple: in the face of a threat, we run. Birds and ducks are good examples. They allow the potential threat to get only so close before the perceived threat is too high, and then they fly (literally).

As children, we run, we hide and we avoid contact with whatever threatens us as much as possible. As adults, this hiding response can be more difficult to notice. We still run, but tactics to avoid social interactions or conflict are more difficult to detect. We also pose. We attempt to portray ourselves as thinking, feeling or doing one thing while we feel something very different. While remaining present physically, we flee emotionally. Posing might include mimicking peers even if we don't think it is right or acting calm or tough on the outside when we are really terrified. The feelings typically experienced with flight responses are survival fear and shame.

Frenzy

The final response is frenzy. I knew a woman whose father would rage if he came home and she wasn't doing something "productive" around the house. No matter what she was doing, when she heard the front doorknob turn, she would jump up and frantically attempt to look busy in some way. It usually worked to help her avoid his rage. Unlike freeze, she was very active and visible. Unlike fight, she did not attack Dad. Unlike flight, she was in Dad's presence.

As a married woman, when her husband experienced distressing emotions or began to *look* upset or agitated in some way, it would trigger her frenzy response. Her frenzy looked different—trying to say the right words, do the right thing, or take all the blame—

but it was still the same behavior for the same purpose: to try to avoid someone's *perceived* or real anger. The impact it had on her husband was not the same as it was with her father. He would feel her anxiety and begin to get more anxious himself. Eventually he would become overheated as well and they would end up having very damaging fights. The emotion typically experienced with frenzy is survival fear.

As was the case with this woman, so it is with most survival skills: they work fairly well when we are in a truly powerless position, giving us as much safety as possible, but they do not generally function well in long-term adult relationships. Much like a deer is very safe with the freeze response in its original, natural habitat (where foliage and nature provide good cover from danger), so is the child safe. But when the context changes, the deer is in a very dangerous position. A "deer in the headlights" is a perfect example of how survival instincts sometimes do not work in new situations. Instead, they often leave us vulnerable to being injured more.

Reflections – Exercise B

1. Which survival responses do you most closely relate to? How do you see them show up in your life?

   _____

   _____

   _____

2. What situations caused you to develop those responses?

   _____

   _____

Survival instincts work in the short term when we are truly in danger of dying. However, my experience with adults is that most of our survival responses occur when we are not truly in imminent danger of death. Rather, we have let our temperature get too high over time or had triggers to shame or trauma in the past. These lead to a triggering of our limbic system and push us into survival mode. Often we can be triggered by small things like a criticism or a child spilling a drink. You can develop skills to help avoid being triggered into "survival mode" when you are not in imminent danger or to help you get out of survival mode when it is not necessary. In the next section I review techniques to help you deal with being triggered. Future sections of this book will deepen your understanding of how to manage your feelings in the present so that you do not have to feel powerless and unintentionally shift into survival mode, causing painful interactions with those who are closest to you.

As you might have noticed, there are only a few emotions that are associated with "survival mode" or "going limbic." Although others label them differently, I call them secondary, survival emotions. They are shame, anger, jealousy and survival fear. They are called secondary because they kick us out of our primary, healthy, prefrontal cortex-guided mode of functioning, into a limbic survival state. These secondary emotions are important to notice because they indicate your temperature is high. They can alert you to the need to do something to take care of yourself and avoid meltdown (like the nuclear reactor we discussed earlier). If you let the emotions continually push you into survival mode, they may destroy the relationships with the people that matter most to you. The loss of connection may lead to an even more intense lack of safety because you have lost the greatest source of safety: a healthy sense of connection with people who care for you deeply and for whom you care deeply.

Reflections – Exercise C

1. What do the survival responses you have developed look like in your current relationships as an adult? What do you do in your current relationships that expresses those responses?

_____

_____

_____

2. How are those responses affecting your relationships?

_____

_____

_____

3. Using a separate piece of paper, draw a picture of what you feel like when you are in survival mode.

Tools for Managing Emotion: An Overview

Certain skills, when developed or enhanced, can help you to stop being triggered into survival mode and manage your emotions more successfully. The first skill is *time-outs*. Time-outs help short-circuit reactivity and avoid survival responses. They allow you to begin to *soothe*, which is the second skill. As you soothe, you can then begin to *identify emotions*, which is skill three, and develop and use *tools to manage the feelings you identify*, skill four. The remaining skills are related to *reconnecting* relationally.

In the next section, I provide an overview of these skills as a road map to the overall process. The following diagram shows the skills in the corresponding zones of the thermometer.

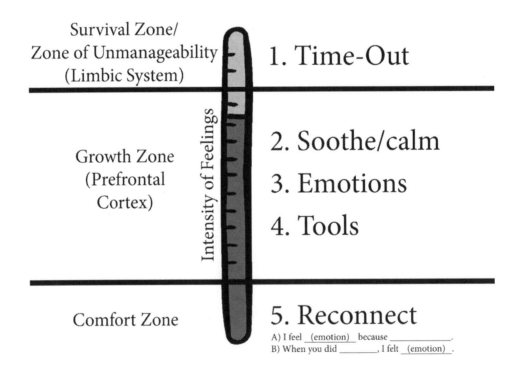

Survival Zone/
Zone of Unmanageability
(Limbic System)

1. Time-Out

Growth Zone
(Prefrontal
Cortex)

Intensity of Feelings

2. Soothe/calm

3. Emotions

4. Tools

Comfort Zone

5. Reconnect
A) I feel __(emotion)__ because _____.
B) When you did _____, I felt __(emotion)__.

The Metaphor: The Overheated Car

I believe the overall process of managing our emotions is like the overheating of a car. When a car overheats, the first thing you need to do is get it off the road and out of traffic. If you keep driving, you will cause significant damage to the vehicle. *Time-outs* help get us to a similar place emotionally: out of the situation and to a safer place.

Once the car is off the road, the engine must be turned off. If you leave the car running, it will actually overheat faster than if you were driving it. A seasoned driver also knows that you should not open the radiator immediately after stopping the car. Pressure and heat are brewing below the lid and if opened will produce an explosion of hot liquid that can seriously injure you. No wise mechanic works on an engine while it is hot. You have to allow it to cool down before you try to investigate what is going on. If time is short, there are things you can do to get it to cool off faster. Applying lukewarm water to the radiator will cool it more quickly. In the end, though, cooling off still takes time.

In therapy language, we use the word rumination—turning something over and over again in your mind—to describe the process of keeping the car running. Once we are already overheated, obsessing about something doesn't get us anywhere but more upset. Instead, we need to turn off the obsessive thinking, give ourselves some time, and use soothing skills to cool off as quickly as we can. *Soothing*, skill 2, will be reviewed in greater detail later in this chapter.

Once the car is cooled, the mechanic can hook it up to a computer to determine what is wrong with the car. *Emotions* are the "readout" that can help you determine what your needs are and alert you to the importance of meeting those needs (skill 3).

My mechanic is a traveling mechanic (instead of having a location he works from, he travels to my house to do the work on my car). On one occasion, I was with him in my garage as he attached a computer to my car to diagnose it. He told me he got a readout of "P4." I asked him what that meant, to which he replied, "I don't know. Let me go check my manual." Less than a minute later he came back with an interpretation of the diagnosis. In early recovery, few, if any, of my clients have the ability to recognize or connect with their feelings. When they begin, it feels foreign (i.e. "What's a P4?"). With a little help, though, people can begin to make connections and better understand the "readouts" related to their feelings.

My mechanic's manual helps him diagnose what is happening with the car. I have my clients use a Feeling Word List to help diagnose what is happening internally (see Appendix). It helps them find words to connect with their feelings. My Feeling Word List contains some of the more common feelings I hear. I have grouped them into three categories:

1. Painful primary emotions, located in the top box.

2. Pleasant primary emotions, located in the middle box.

3. Secondary or survival emotions, located in the bottom box.

The list is organized so it does not have words that are generally interpreted as blaming. I urge you to start with this list and gradually add your own words that you find most helpful.

My mechanic's manual also has a description of what needs to be done to remedy problems. Unfortunately, none of us are given a manual to help us know exactly how to manage emotions. There are many tools, trainings and ideas that can help us figure things out; however, we are all very different "models," so each of us has to take the ideas we learn and create our own personalized manuals. Step four on the thermometer focuses on *developing and using the tools* to respond in healthy ways to emotions as you learn to identify them. Responding with skills that actually meet your needs will restore you to a state of greater health and functionality (just like the car after a mechanic has addressed its issues successfully).

Trauma

Before I move on, it is important to discuss the impact of trauma on our ability to manage our feelings. The word trauma comes from the Greek word meaning "wound." The definition of trauma is, "a psychological or emotional injury caused by a deeply disturbing experience." Let's compare it to physical wounds. My nephew had minor surgery on his toe, and he came to play basketball while it was still healing. None of us were aware of the surgery, and one of our family members stuck his foot out and tapped my nephew's foot in a friendly way, as a greeting. My nephew immediately reacted and doubled over in pain. We react similarly when we have unresolved emotional wounds. We call things that push on these wounds "triggers" or "trauma triggers." In thermometer terms, that means that we can be any place on the thermometer when a trauma occurs and end up overwhelmed.

Often these triggers catch us by surprise. As was the case with my nephew, others may also be surprised and unaware of how they might be triggering you. It is important to acknowledge that our reactions when triggered into the zone of unmanageability can be extremely painful and confusing to both the person experiencing them and their spouse. Whether or not the person meant to hurt you, the pain is still very real. If both addict and partner can develop tools to recognize these trauma triggers and respond in healthy ways, you do not have to remain in (or re-cycle through) these traumatic, painful experiences. Eventually, with time and effort, trauma can be resolved, along with the associated triggers. Let's begin by discussing time-outs and soothing, two tools that are critical in dealing with triggers.

Time-Outs

Step One in the 12-step program of Alcoholics Anonymous (2001) states, "We admitted we were powerless over alcohol—that our lives had become unmanageable." When you are overheated, that is where you are. You may not be powerless over alcohol, but you are powerless over something. It is different for each person and each situation. You might be powerless against your rage or the biting words that come out of your mouth. You might be powerless over your ability to stand up for yourself (freeze or flight). In that moment, your life is unmanageable. Unless you are truly in a life-or-death situation, many of the survival responses that occur when you are overheated are only short-term solutions. They do not serve to help manage feelings in a healthy, long-term way.

In that moment, the relationship is a threat you want to eliminate, so you have to find a way to get away from the threat temporarily without eliminating the person you want to have a relationship with. The only tool I have found that can both eliminate the threat and preserve the relationship is a time-out.

Before you ever begin using time-outs, you should iron out an agreement about how it will work. The first piece of the agreement is what words will be used to call time-out. It may seem silly to have specific words, but couples who try to do it without an agreed upon set of words do not succeed. They end up saying things like, "I'm done," "This is over," "I quit," or "I'm leaving!" All of these statements leave the spouse even more triggered into feelings of abandonment. Another mistake often made is using other phrases that are part of your normal language that are so commonplace that they do not signal time-outs in an effective way, like "I need a break."

Some people just say, "Time-out." Others struggle with that phrase because they feel they are being punished. Couples always seem to come up with words that are good for them, so I encourage you to throw out a few ideas, then choose. I had a family choose to say, "Bubbalicious," because it was really hard to say it in an angry way, which helped prevent further escalation. One couple I worked with struggled with time-outs because they hated that the person calling time-out got the last word. So they decided their time-out word would be Marco, and then the other got to say Polo, which acknowledged the time-out and also let them get the last word. The key is to choose the best language for your relationship.

Reflections – Exercise D

1. What phrases could you use to call a time-out?

_____

_____

The purpose of a time-out is to take a break to soothe, but to make the time-out process effective you also must come back to reconnect. Typically, there is one person in the relationship who wants space and time, the withdrawer, and one who wants immediate resolution, the pursuer. In time-outs, the pursuer commits to give space on the condition that the withdrawer will come back eventually. In other words, the withdrawer is not being given permission to abandon their spouse and avoid resolving the conflict. They commit to return and work through the conflict after they have had time to cool down and soothe.

Attachment theory suggests that it is critical for us to have a sense of a secure place in our lives, a sense that we matter to others, particularly those closest to us. When that sense is threatened, we do crazy things to try to get it restored. So the first premise of a time-out is this message: "You matter to me. I may not like you in the moment, because I'm overheating. But deep down I want to matter to you, and I want you to matter to me. The agreement with a time-out is that I will hold onto myself enough to come back and do the work to reconnect in our relationship, but both of us need some time apart in order for it to work." Time-outs must be based on that agreement or they won't work.

A critical part of the agreement is that a space is created with a commitment to come back. I ask that the person calling the time-out come back in 30 minutes. *Coming back and checking in within thirty minutes, whether or not you are ready to talk, communicates to your partner that you are in the relationship still and committed to the process.* If you are not ready to talk after 30 minutes, you can say, text or email something like, "I'm not ready to talk yet. I will reconnect with you in an hour." By communicating that within thirty minutes, you are letting your spouse know they matter, even though the problem has not yet been resolved.

Sometimes, when it is late, you just need to go to bed without talking the problem through. The saying, "Don't go to bed angry," has some wisdom in it; however, there are many couples who just stay up angry, which leads to lots of fighting. When you need to wait until the next day, let your spouse know when you will come back to reconnect: in the morning, when you get home from work the next day, or after the kids go to bed the next day. Many couples I have worked with have just come up with a general rule for night times: if we need to take a time-out after 9 p.m., we'll talk at a specified, predetermined time the next day.

If you are the one who didn't call the time-out, you may reach out if forty minutes have passed since the time-out was called, in person or by text or email. It cannot be in an accusing way, and it is best when it is simple, something like, "I haven't heard from you and it has been forty minutes. Could you please let me know how much more time you need?" This is a last ditch effort to try to find some assurance that the other person is not abandoning you and the time-out process. It can help you manage the fear of being abandoned enough to allow you to continue to provide the person who called the time-out the space necessary to feel safe and continue their work. In that moment, the person who called the time-out must be respectful (i.e. "I'm sorry. I'm not ready to talk. I need another hour.") If you can't respond respectfully, you are not honoring the time-out. Your choice not to respond appropriately does not give permission for your spouse to stop honoring his/her part of the time-out process. However, abandoning your part of the processes is much more likely to lead to your partner feeling abandoned and being triggered into not honoring the time-out process. This may escalate into old, destructive, and painful patterns.

If the person who originally called the time-out is ready to talk, and the other spouse is not (still needing more time to soothe and sort through their feelings), then the other spouse is now in charge of the time-out. You continue to follow the same rules (check in within 30 minutes, etc.). Finally, in cases where you are unable to soothe and work through your feelings or are scared that the conversation might not go well, you may need to let your spouse know that you are working on it but need to wait to discuss it until you have the help of a therapist. This ensures that the process continues in a safe way and that attempts for reconnection will happen *only* when both of you are ready.

The Appendix includes three tools for time-outs: Effective Time-outs, Time-out Protocol, and Time-out Worksheet. I urge you to review Effective Time-outs and use it as a guide to develop your own Time-out Protocol. As you develop your protocol, learn to use the Time-out Worksheet to help you process through your feelings and needs before coming back together to talk again. Once it is developed, review the Time-out Protocol daily and imagine applying a time-out in your mind (this is called "visualization"). It may sound silly, but I even suggest you go to the places you typically argue, pretend you are getting angry, and practice calling time-outs and going to your different places to soothe. All of this creates muscle memory, both in the physical acting out and in the synapses of the brain, and familiarity with the new way of managing things, which increases the chance of success.

When I was in college and still learning the necessary tools to manage my emotions well, I played a lot of intramural sports. I had a bit of a temper, becoming easily frustrated by the other team's behaviors or the calls the referees were making. As I worked to improve, I decided I would take myself out of the game if I got frustrated. As simple as that solution sounds, it took a lot of failures, new plans, and re-commitments to finally convince myself it was the right choice and actually follow through on that decision. My opportunity to try this commitment to time-out came during a soccer game. I got frustrated and took myself out of the game. As I sat on the sideline and calmed down, the thought came to me: "Why am I upset? Would I rather be in the game or upset?" I quickly calmed down, reoriented on what thing I was upset about, and reentered the game.

I think the same willingness has to exist for every individual and couple who wants to overcome the reactivity of overheating. You must be willing to take yourself out of the game (relationship) temporarily to allow yourself to really be in the game (relationship) in a healthy way. Just like me, you may need to struggle to convince yourself that taking a time-out is the right choice, practice applying it, overcome failure, and finally succeed in following the steps that bring you safety and connection individually and as a couple.

In my experience, time-outs take *at least* a month of practice to work fully. There are often so many negative processes in place that you must allow time to work out the kinks. Below I give a few examples of ways that time-outs commonly fail, as well as ways to correct them.

Ineffective Behavior	More Effective Behavior
Calling time-out on the other person instead of for yourself (e.g. "You need a time-out.")	"I need a time-out." You can call a time-out for yourself if you feel your partner is getting overheated—time-outs are for your safety
Failure of the person who did not call the time-out to allow the time-out to occur (following your spouse around, asking why they need a time-out, etc.)	Going to your own space, following up in 40 minutes if your spouse doesn't come back

Failure to follow the plan you put together for time-outs (leaving the house instead of going to your predetermined space, not returning within 30 minutes, etc.)	Being sure to follow the steps you determined would be most effective for you, including predetermined space and follow up procedure
Failure to create space for yourself when your spouse follows you	Develop a plan to create safety by going to a room with a lock, the car, or someplace you can be separated for a time. Share that with your spouse when they are not triggered so they understand why you are doing it.

I've never known a relationship where both spouses didn't fail in some piece of their commitment to time-outs at some point. Those who succeed are the ones who take responsibility for it and make the necessary corrections. Practicing time-outs will help you figure out what things are getting in the way of your ability to manage your feelings, and that insight will help you improve your part of the time-out process. If you're struggling to succeed, please talk to a therapist to help you and your spouse iron out the process and learn what you can do to make the healthy process permanent. Time-outs work, but you have to really work hard to establish them (often with support from others) to find out how to make them work for you and your relationship specifically.

Reflections – Exercise E

1. What are some of the negative patterns that might prevent you from being successful at separating temporarily for a time-out?

_____

_____

2. What are some new ways or patterns that you could use in place of the negative ones you listed in the last question?

_____

_____

Having begun the time-out successfully, and knowing you need to do your individual work and come back, it is important for each of you to have a plan for how and where you will go to soothe. When you call time-out, slam the door and peal out of the driveway, it is difficult for your spouse to trust that you are in the process of soothing. Often men will try to soothe by playing video games. Their wives will go into a different room and continue to escalate: "I can't believe he's playing video games! Doesn't he care?! How could he just..?!!!" Notice all the exclamation points? While your strategy may be soothing for you, if your spouse doesn't understand what behavior is part of your collection of tools for soothing, then s/he will struggle to trust that you are doing your part. It is very hard to soothe if you do not have a plan prepared beforehand. Sharing your plan with your spouse will also help them to know that you are keeping your commitment to the relationship and the time-out process. Early recovery can be extremely volatile, with intense emotions, and that makes soothing an especially important skill. In my dissertation research (Bird, 2009), a therapist described early recovery in this way: "Every moment [the addict and partner] are just so uncomfortable with their own emotional state and the other person's emotional state that ... the work that you do for a long time is helping them tolerate emotional distress and stop emotionally flooding and learn to self soothe." In early recovery, there are so many triggers that it is difficult for addicts and partners not to constantly react to their own emotions or to their spouse's emotions. That is why learning to feel emotions, learning to tolerate the distress they bring, and learning to moderate reactions through soothing are such important skills in early recovery.

Reflections – Exercise F

1. What locations would be good places for you to go to soothe?

_____

_____

_____

Soothing

At its core, much of soothing is about removing ourselves (physically, cognitively, and emotionally) from the things that are disturbing us so we don't react in a destructive way. I divide soothing into two categories: self-talk and behavioral soothing. Both can be effective, and neither is more important than the other. As you read, you may identify with one type of soothing category more than another, but you'll need both skills to help you through the toughest times.

Soothing does not provide long-term solutions, but it does allow you to get to a grounded and calmer state of mind and body, where good long-term solutions can be determined. Soothing is not a form of denial; it's a way to get centered before moving forward to face problems. I'll begin first with self-talk, then discuss behavioral soothing.

Self-talk

Distress Tolerance

Distress Tolerance is the ability to feel emotional distress and tolerate it for a time (not react to it immediately). It is important to be able to tolerate emotion just long enough to identify it and then work on how to respond to it effectively. If you can't tolerate it, you won't be able to do the work of identifying (labeling) the emotion or the following step of developing tools. In early recovery it can take time to identify emotion, which makes distress tolerance very important at this stage.

Dialectical Behavior Therapy (DBT) addresses how people, when encountering an emotion, struggle not to let that emotion send them over the edge. One goal of DBT is to develop a greater capacity to tolerate and accept emotion as it comes rather than react to it. The term used to describe that process is "radical acceptance." Several other theories also target this type of acceptance/distress tolerance, including Mindfulness-Based Cognitive Therapy (MBCT), Acceptance and Commitment Therapy (ACT) and others. I will not review them in this book, but I mention the theories here so you can explore them as you develop your efforts to practice distress tolerance and soothing.

The self-talk often associated with distress tolerance sounds something like this: "I'm having a feeling now (and it is intense), but it is just a feeling. I will survive this feeling. I accept life as it is right now." Accepting feelings on life's terms and working to soothe are important precursors to doing the work to improve. As you develop distress tolerance, you can put a basic plan in place to help you contain the immediate reactivity of most secondary emotions. In general, that plan should include some form of self-talk (something like, "I can deal with this when I'm calmer") and then have some behavioral steps to soothe (as will be reviewed later in this chapter). While the plan may seem simple, it will not be easy unless you really practice it regularly in your mind (this is called visual imagery) to help it become second nature.

Affirmations

In my experience, toxic shame is one of the most destructive forms of negative self-talk. Its message is this: "I'm a bad person. Because I did something wrong, I am wrong." That's just not fixable. It's permanent. Shame can create hopelessness and fear that others will not accept you. Dealing with shame and the intensity associated with it is so significant that it needs to be addressed throughout the recovery process.

One way to challenge shame and soothe is through affirmations. In the 1990's, Stuart Smalley from "Saturday Night Live" ruined affirmations for me for a long time. His trite "I'm Good Enough, I'm Smart Enough, and Doggone It, People Like Me!" made me feel like affirmations were words you said to yourself that you didn't really believe. Since then, however, I have come to really appreciate effective affirmations.

Affirmations are statements that affirm something that is true, or something you are working to make a reality in your life. These can include pieces of truth that you find along the road to recovery. Sometimes they start as someone else's words, a quote or a saying. Other times, they come as you journal your feelings, then distill them down into concise truths. Regardless, affirmations serve as reminders of what we believe and value. Where possible, attaching affirmations to behaviors makes them easier to apply. I recommend you repeat affirmations ten times, three times a day, to help them become a part of who you are.

I'll share a personal example of how I came across one of my affirmations. I have always highly valued feeling heard and understood. When I don't feel that way, it is hard for me to stay centered. After a conversation with my wife triggered that wounded feeling in me, I sat down and journaled my feelings. As I distilled it down, I came up with this brief affirmation: "I am good. I am known by God. With that knowledge, I can hold myself true in the face of relational challenges."

Notice the truths: "I am good." I've worked hard to recognize that I am a good person, despite my challenges and mistakes. When I feel misunderstood, my sense of being good feels threatened. "I am known by God." I believe in a loving God who truly knows me better than I know myself, and He still loves me! That belief grounds me when other things and relationships are not going well. Finally, I reminded myself that those truths can anchor me in the wind of relational distress, whether that be with my dad, my wife, a friend or a coworker. Being able to "hold on to myself" was a behavior that I needed to have connected to my truth so I could actually do something with my beliefs.

Although I repeated that affirmation 80 times in one day, I still had to look at my sheet to remember the words. Even though it felt true to me, it was hard to remember. Two days later I was emotionally triggered again in a conversation with my wife, and the words, "I am good," came to my mind. Instead of reacting to the trigger, I immediately soothed and stayed connected in the conversation, which was resolved quickly. In just one day, I had significantly reminded myself of my important truths via that affirmation. Results are not always that immediate, but they can be powerful. Some people with different learning styles may benefit from writing it down several (5-25) times each day and visualizing as they write.

Becoming very conscious of the truths you know about yourself and actively affirming those truths keeps you grounded and stable. If you write them down somewhere and keep them with you, they can be accessed more readily in times of higher emotional temperatures. In the following chart, I list examples of affirmations. It is critical you find the ones that fit for you. I suggest that you then write the one or two most important down and review them in your mind ten times, three times a day, for a total of 30 times. If you do this consistently, you will find that these truths will change the way you interact with yourself and others, providing soothing where you previously could not access it.

Examples of Affirmations:

I matter.
I believe in myself and my abilities.
I am strong.
This too shall pass. I will make it through.
I am enough.
I am deserving of love.
I can just be me. Normal is just a setting on a dryer.
I am more than my limitations.
I always have a choice.
I am loved.
I have control over my own life.
I can be patient with myself.
I am beautiful.
I am allowed to have boundaries.
I make mistakes, but I choose to learn from them.
I have the power to write my own story.
I don't have to do everything at one time. I can do things one at a time and one day at a time.
Failure isn't falling down, it's remaining down. I can stand up when I fall.

Reflections – Exercise G

1. Which aspects of self-talk did you connect to?

_____

_____

2. What are some phrases or quotes that might be helpful in your soothing process (what are things you often need to hear when you are struggling)?

_____

_____

3. Pick one affirmation. Use a separate piece of paper to create a meaningful way to represent that affirmation (decorate it, paint it, make a collage, etc.).

Behavioral Self-Soothing

Relaxation

The first place I have people start is with the behaviors that may help them relax. Because in early recovery your emotional system is overloaded and taxed, you need regular opportunities to shut the system down. Relaxation is one way to do that. Some examples of relaxation might include reading, taking a nap, taking a bath/hot shower, watching a TV show, and so forth. I have created a Coping Skills List, found in the Appendix, which includes many ideas for ways to relax. Start with that list and add your own ideas, then figure out how to regularly plan them into your week. When you are consistently filling your life with things that help you relax, you live a more peaceful, less stressful and anxious life. This can help prevent you from overheating as quickly in your day-to-day life. In some cases, these ways of relaxing can also be useful in the moments you are feeling emotionally overwhelmed (see the distraction section below).

Distractions

Distractions can temporarily shift your mind away from rumination, intrusive thoughts, and other disturbing stimuli. While it sometimes feels avoidant, temporarily distracting from a stressor can allow your body and mind to relax and soothe so that when you come back to confront the problem, you feel less unmanageability and can address the issue with greater perspective and capacity. Creating a list of distractions from the Coping Skills List is a great way to begin. Look for things that take 15-30 minutes maximum to do and that also might help hyper-focus your attention (something that really draws your attention is important).

Hyperfocus

Dialectical Behavior Therapy (DBT) highlights the importance of using our senses (sight, sound, etc.) when soothing. The ability to hyperfocus our senses can help drown out the things that are disturbing us in the moment and allow us to cool down. Everyone is different, so be open to trying out different things until you find those that work for you. A significant list of these types of soothing activities is included in the Appendix under "Soothing Skills."

One particular exercise that a colleague shared with me capitalizes on the use of the senses without needing any real preparation. It is called, "2-3-4." You begin by focusing on an object for 15-20 seconds, noticing with your eyes the different aspects of that object. Then choose a second object and do the same thing. Next choose two sounds to focus on. Notice the different aspects of the noises you hear. Then choose two things you can focus on for touch (e.g. the chair you are sitting in, an object you can hold in your hand). In each case, make sure to focus individually on each object or sound for a minimum of 15 seconds. As you complete that portion, you can also add two deep breaths. Once you have completed the round of two, repeat the process. The second time, choose three objects and sounds in each category, followed by three deep breaths. The third time, you choose four objects and sounds, followed by four deep breaths. In many cases, it may not require all the rounds to begin to soothe. If you find yourself feeling better, you can stop at any time in the process.

Mindfulness/Meditation

Mindfulness is experiencing and being aware of your feelings without allowing them to control you. There is no judgment for the emotions you feel, merely observation and acceptance. It does not involve reliving past emotions or predicting future emotions; rather, it focuses on what you are feeling and noticing in that moment.

Probably the most commonly recognized form of mindfulness is meditation, but it can be much less formal as well. Guided mindfulness exercises and meditations are available online or as apps for your phone, many of them at little or no cost. Mindful breathing and listening or other sensory exercises are simple and often help to soothe or ground you. A Body Scan (start with the little toe, moving along all toes, then arch, ankle, and so on) is one example of a mindfulness exercise. Performing an internet search for "body scan mindfulness exercise" produces multiple free video or audio results that can walk you through the specific steps. As you seek to learn about soothing via mindfulness, Jon Kabat-Zinn and Dan Siegel are both leaders in this field and have multiple resources for you to explore.

Journaling (or Venting)

When you are overwhelmed, having a safe place to express feelings can be very soothing. For some, journaling serves that purpose well. Writing or typing things out allows the internal dialogue to be expressed and released (and in some cases sorted through a little as you calm down and continue writing). This journal should be kept private from your spouse, as the words you write when you are overheated are rarely more than survival responses and usually contain words that might escalate your spouse if s/he reads them. This isn't secret keeping. It is a form of containment and self-soothing, but if your spouse were to read it then it would become uncontained and potentially ignite the unhealthy interactions so common in early recovery.

Additionally, having someone to whom you can vent can be extremely helpful. A phone call (email, text, etc.) to your sponsor, peers in your group, or a trusted friend can be a powerful way to feel validated and supported in your pain. It is important that the people you choose to vent to are supportive of your recovery and your relationship. Otherwise they will fuel the fire rather than help soothe it.

Physical Practices

When you are overheated, helping the body release energy in healthy ways can also be self-soothing. It is important to mention first that physical soothing techniques should not compromise your overall physical health; therefore, choose your physical practices carefully, and consult a physician where necessary. Exercise is one important means to help release energy and soothe. Running, hitting a punching bag, roller blading, riding your bike, and countless other types of exercise can bring needed soothing via physical expression, providing relief to the mind and body. Yoga is a combination of exercise and mindfulness practice that can also be very helpful for soothing.

Some physical practices' primary function is to help release tension in the body. Deep muscle relaxation (usually about 15 minutes in length) teaches you how to relax your body by first tensing then releasing your muscles in a systematic way (i.e. beginning with your forehead and working down to your toes). When you tense and release muscles, the body will actually relax more than when you just try to relax the muscles. Massage can also be a useful tool for physical stress reduction and soothing and releasing tension. Depending on how you have acted out, however, massage would need to be something you are particularly cautious with, especially when you have not first soothed in other ways.

Reflections – Exercise H

1. What forms of behavioral soothing did you connect with most?

   _____

   _____

2. What are some ideas from this section that might be helpful to incorporate in your recovery process?

   _____

   _____

3. Do an internet search for mindfulness exercises. Pick one exercise from your results and follow the directions to complete that exercise.

Spiritual Practices

For those who are spiritual and/or religious, your relationship with God/your Higher Power can be an amazingly grounding force in your life. I conducted a study several years ago (Butler, Gardner, & Bird, 1998) about how people use prayer to resolve conflict. There were three types of couples. One type would pray together at the end of an argument to thank God for the resolution they came to on their own. We called this type a "band-aid" couple because God served to provide the seal that would help finalize healing (providing a soothing closure). The second type of couple would recognize they were "on fire" and stop, drop, and pray. For these couples, God would listen, not judge, and bring some neutrality: one wife said, "It is hard to pray and say, 'Please strike my husband with lightning,' when you know that God is on both of your sides."

The first two types of couples were younger. Older couples in the study reported that prayer provided a consistent peace or soothing that allowed conflict never to escalate to the point of "fire" (this would be similar to later recovery). Prayer, reading scripture, reading spiritual books or talks, listening to spiritual or uplifting music, going for a walk while meditating or praying to God, and gratitude lists (reflecting on the good God has given you) are just a few of the many possible soothing spiritual practices. The Coping

Skills List, discussed in more detail in Chapter Four and also included in the Appendix, can also help you to identify spiritual practices that may help you soothe.

Reflections – Exercise I

1. What do you do to feel connected to your Higher Power?

_____

_____

As you develop soothing skills, it is important to recognize that not all of them work well in all situations. For example, if I am triggered at work and get overwhelmed, going for a jog isn't really an option. With practice, you will gradually become an expert on what works best for you in each situation.

As you are able to determine what helps you soothe best, you can create access to those things in your environment: flowers, pictures, a small waterfall, a small Zen garden or sand tray, things to touch (rocks, shells, etc.), smells (scented candles, etc.), tastes (candy, etc.), and sounds (white noise, beach, etc.). In environments where you don't have control, you can keep with you those things that can readily help you soothe. For example, I have addicts create a small collection of pictures, music, and memorabilia that reminds them of what matters most to them and brings other positive emotions. I call it a first aid kit. They can bring this with them and access it fairly easily in almost any environment (some people even have it on their phones via pictures, music, voice recordings, etc.). One particularly useful place for a first aid kit is during business trips, where the environment is completely different from normal life. It can ground people and help them soothe and manage feelings in a very foreign environment.

A first aid kit is not just for addicts. The point of the kit is to help you soothe and feel grounded so that you can figure out which next steps you need to take without extra chaos that comes from being overwhelmed or triggered. There are several different types of things you can include in a first aid kit. Physical things might include: pictures, notes, cards, memorabilia, other items that have personal meaning, and anything else that might help you get grounded and soothed. You can use an envelope or a folder for a flat kit, or a small box or container for one that contains items that aren't flat. You might have a larger kit at home and keep a small envelope in your purse, wallet, glove box or desk. Virtual first aid kits can be made by creating folders of pictures on your phone or computer, or by using tools such as a private board on Pinterest for quotes or photos or ideas that give you hope. You can also use music in your first aid kit, creating playlists on your phone, mp3 player or computer with songs that connect with you in ways that help you soothe. You might create a list of songs to help you soothe when you are angry, one that includes songs you connect with when you are depressed, one for when you feel hopeless, and one that has songs you relate to when you are lonely.

Even when you can't access a first aid kit, you can still work to create a safe place or other resources in your mind. Whatever skills you develop, be sure that the soothing techniques you use do not compromise your overall physical or mental health.

Reflections – Exercise J

1. What changes can you make to your environment that may help you soothe?

_____

_____

2. Pick one type of first aid kit (physical, virtual or audio) and take the time to put it together. Share it with a good friend, your therapist or your group.

The remaining skills on the thermometer are identifying emotions, using tools to manage those feelings, and then coming back to reconnect. I review those processes briefly here to give you a feel for each of them.

Identifying Emotions

As I discussed previously, I believe all of us have the capacity to identify our emotions. Usually it is about giving people words to identify what is going on internally. When you go to the doctor and she asks what is wrong, you don't usually say, "I don't know." We might identify that our throat hurts, our ankle hurts or we have lower back pain. We are trained to have language around what happens inside our physical body. As kids we sing, "Head, shoulders, knees, and toes." Even if we lacked the language to address the specific hurt, the doctor could ask us to point to where it hurts.

We are limited in our ability to do the same thing emotionally. It is rare to meet people who are able to talk about their emotional pain (and even non-painful emotion) as skillfully as they talk about their physical pain. Most of us severely lack emotional intelligence: the ability to identify and manage our emotions. I talk about emotion all the time and there are still many days when I struggle to connect with, and not react to, feelings. What I have found is that when people are given emotional language, it helps them begin the process of becoming more emotionally intelligent.

I have created a Feeling Word List for this purpose, which is in the Appendix. Some experts say there are either only five, eight or nine core emotions. Others provide long lists of emotions. My list represents my best effort to provide enough options without overwhelming you. The words are carefully chosen based on experience; however, I urge you to add words you find that fit for you so the list is personalized.

Occasionally, I have clients who cannot make sense of their feelings enough to identify them, even with the word list. The word that describes this condition is alexithymia. It literally means, "no words for emotions." I have encountered several alexithymic people in my practice. These clients cannot process emotion and connect thought to it using the normal thinking process, so we have to take another path.

When I recognize their struggle, I hand them an emotion sheet again and say something like, "I know nothing connects for you. What I'd like you to do is just look at the list and tell me what words jump out at you. They don't have to make sense." They'll look at the list and say, "Um... powerless... rejected... uncertain." In every instance the feelings they shared were the same as I would have expected for their specific situation. But when I ask if they understand why those might have jumped out, they can never tell me. Over time, even these clients can access emotion better in ways that help them.

My point in sharing this story is to highlight the amazing nature of the human brain to make emotional connections for us (just like the computer to our car). Emotions also connect us to our needs, which restore us to a state of greater health and functioning when met appropriately. I've included a Needs List in the Appendix that can help you better connect with your needs in conjunction with acknowledging your emotions. We are built to heal, and emotions and needs are a natural part of that process. I believe in most cases, clients are actually re-learning skills they once naturally possessed that were trained out of them by family and culture. Learning the skill of emotion identification is important, and the first step in healing is giving yourself the permission to recognize and honor your feelings.

One woman I worked with emphasized the importance of valuing what our amazing systems (our bodies, emotions, etc.) have to offer us. I asked her as we came near the end of therapy to review what had helped her most. She took more than a month to finally share her feedback. She told me, "I remember very clearly sitting in session and telling you about what I was experiencing. I looked at you and had the thought, 'He actually believes me.' I decided then that if you could believe me, I could believe me. That has made all the difference." I have found that when you start to trust yourself and value your impressions, instincts, and feelings, you begin to heal and become all those things you hoped but never believed you could become.

Tools for Managing Emotion

Once you've been able to soothe, connect with, and label your emotions, the next step is to find tools to help respond to and/or resolve those feelings. Just like a mechanic needs expertise to understand and work with the different problems occurring with a vehicle (and even expertise within specific kinds of vehicles), you need to become an expert on how to handle the problems in your life in a way that works for you. Much of long-term recovery focuses on this process of building your own user manual and becoming an expert in managing the emotions that come up.

When emotions emerge, they can take us one of two directions: positive or negative. Research suggests that when we experience painful emotions, we are more likely to think negatively and become reactive. Because of this, it often takes conscious effort to identify and learn to access the healthy meaning that can be taken from even painful emotions. Emotions can alert you when things are not going well and can help you recognize quickly that you need to make some corrections if you are to meet your needs. Here is a list of some of the healthy messages that can be connected to various emotions:

Powerless

I am focused on things outside of my control, and I only have power over myself.

I am powerless over people, places, things and situations, but not over myself.

I'm not taking care of myself.

I'm not God. I can't do it alone. I need others!

Fears (including the feelings that have "fear" beside them on the Feeling Word List)

I am in danger. I need to protect myself.

If I'm scared, I'm not prepared.

If I'm not careful, I could be hurt.

I don't know what to expect or how to care for myself in this situation.

Inadequate/Worthless

I have a need to improve, learn or grow.

I am inadequate in some things but not all things.

Being inadequate in some ways allows me to grow.

I've fallen short. I can learn.

I've made mistakes, but I can recover.

I need to learn something new.

I need/want to sort through my priorities to decide what to put my energy into.

Lonely/Disconnected

I'm not connecting with one (or more) of the following:

- Myself
- Spouse/Partner
- Family
- Friends
- God

I need/want to get connected.

I'm feeling empty and need/want to fill my tank (personally and relationally).

Rejection/Abandonment

I value connection and need it in healthy ways.

I want to work on feeling like I am enough, even when I feel alone temporarily.

I'm not prepared for people to make choices that don't include me.

I don't value me (when you abandon/reject me, I reject/abandon myself, too).

Humility (knowing you are imperfect and cannot do it alone, but still enough and worthy of love)

Boredom

I need to fill my time (tank) with worthwhile things.

I need/want to do something fun.

I need/want to connect with myself or others.

I need/want to get back to planning.

My life is too empty. I need to fill it with more.

Guilt

I have done something wrong (against my own values).

I need/want to correct my mistake.

I have done something that is not in line with my values.

I need/want to take responsibility for what I've done.

Obviously there are many more emotions. I chose to share lessons from some of the emotions that my clients report to be the most difficult to manage and most painful to experience. Hopefully you could connect with some of them as well as their messages. Most people connect with these messages but struggle to hold on to them because of shame and/or past traumas. In some cases, there is a need for further work with a therapist around shame and trauma to be able to fully access the skills I will be discussing.

While more detail will be needed in middle and late recovery, this general idea is enough for now: *feelings are useful data that can be used to help guide us. If we can learn to recognize, identify and manage them successfully by developing tools and processes, we can find a way to stay out of unmanageability and experience peace and joy.*

Reflections – Exercise K

1. What are some emotions you often struggle with? What healthy messages do you think those emotions could be conveying?

_____

_____

_____

_____

Reconnecting

Skills one to four on the thermometer diagram are all individual recovery skills. Once you have learned those skills, you are ready for the relational skill: reconnecting (see Effective Time-outs in the Appendix as a review of this skill). Before beginning to try to reconnect, you should make sure you have written out your feelings in "I-statement" format:

"I feel <u>primary emotion word</u> because <u>specific behavior.</u>"

"When you did <u>specific behavior(s)</u>, I felt <u>primary emotion word.</u>"

As you begin, do not to engage with your spouse at home around any disturbing topic unless both of you have written out your feelings. The chance of reconnecting successfully is so low if that has not occurred. For addicts, because sexual addiction is the result of a connective disorder, unless you have done the work to see into yourself and have written it down, you will struggle to succeed in being able to make yourself seen (intimacy, "in-to-me-see"). The same is true for partners. Your own connective disorders and the intense pain of betrayal often require significant work to know and understand yourself so you can also share in a way that will be safe and connecting. If both addict and partner do not do their own work to identify their feelings, you will also struggle to see into your spouse's world non-reactively. Much of this process occurs during middle and late recovery.

Reflections – Exercise L

1. Think of some of the painful or upsetting things you have experienced this week. Connect with the feelings you experienced and then write those down in the "I-statements" format.

_____

_____

_____

2. Think of some of the happy things you have experienced this week. Connect with the feelings you experienced and then write those down in the "I-statements" format.

_____

_____

_____

3. Did you find happy or painful emotions easier to identify? Which were easier to put into the I-statement format? Why?

_____

_____

_____

Wrap-Up

The purpose of starting with the thermometer is to help you begin to recognize, identify and manage emotion and meet your needs in healthy ways. Most people need these tools, and certainly all would benefit from them, but addicts and partners are in such crisis in early recovery that these tools are essential to successful recovery, both individually and as a couple. In later recovery, these tools will help you to connect in new ways with your spouse so you can establish greater trust and intimacy and experience long-term recovery.

Ideally, the thermometer will serve as a permanent resource (a road map) to consistently refer to as you work to recognize emotions and successfully manage them. While knowing is not the only or final step, keeping a picture of what healthy emotional management looks like will ground you in your efforts to apply the tools. In the next chapter we'll discuss what happens when these emotions are not managed in healthy ways: The Trauma Cycle and the Addiction Cycle.

Chapter 3

TRAUMA AND ADDICTION CYCLES

The Trauma Cycle

As I've discussed, life is about experiencing emotions. Over time we develop skills to help us cope with, manage or resolve our feelings. All of us eventually struggle with managing certain emotions more than others, and those emotions tend to cause the most pain and struggle in our lives.

Reflections – Exercise A

1. What are the three to five emotions that are the most painful for you or the hardest for you to manage? (See Appendix for Feeling Word List.)

_____

_____

In addition to lacking skills to manage emotions, we can also struggle to manage emotions due to two other factors: genes and trauma. Our genetic makeup can provide us with both strengths and weaknesses. Sometimes these attributes can even be both strengths and weaknesses. For example, while ADD can make it hard for me to focus on one thing, it also allows me to integrate a lot of information and manage it well. My ADD causes me to become bored easily and lose focus. This same problem also helps me to be a better teacher in many ways, because I am able to keep things moving and exciting; because if I don't, then I lose focus.

Our environment can either support us in developing skills or prevent us from developing appropriately. In some cases, our environment can even cause significant pain or damage, which we call trauma. Trauma can influence our ability to manage our emotions.

If we have healthy coping skills we are able to recognize the emotions we are feeling, understand the needs those emotions are alerting us to, and know how to meet those needs in healthy ways. This means that we may need to do some work short term (e.g. take the steps to reach out to friends for support); however, in the long term that particular experience with those emotions is resolved.

Trauma Cycle: Emotions and Coping

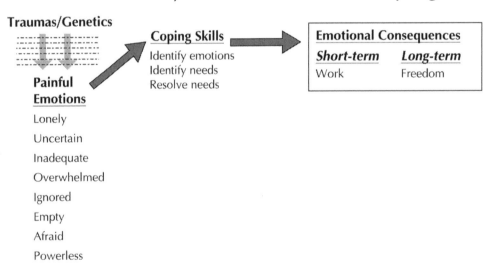

As I discussed in Chapter Two, when we fail to cope with our problems and traumas due to intense emotion, our emotional temperature gets too hot and we become overwhelmed. As traumas have occurred in your life and not been resolved, these wounds leave you more vulnerable to being triggered, which can suddenly and immediately move you to the Zone of Unmanageability. When you get overwhelmed or triggered, you move to your limbic (survival) responses: fight, flight, freeze, and frenzy. When these behaviors occur due to trauma, they are called trauma responses.

Trauma Cycle: Trauma Responses

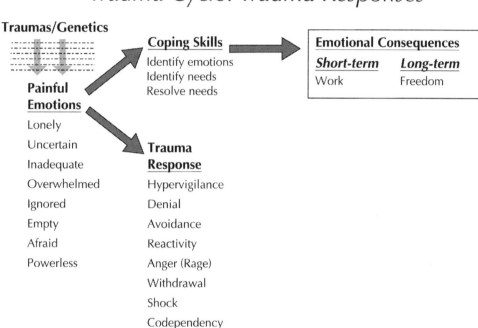

Traumas/Genetics

Painful Emotions

Lonely

Uncertain

Inadequate

Overwhelmed

Ignored

Empty

Afraid

Powerless

Coping Skills

Identify emotions

Identify needs

Resolve needs

Trauma Response

Hypervigilance

Denial

Avoidance

Reactivity

Anger (Rage)

Withdrawal

Shock

Codependency

Depression

Emotional Consequences	
Short-term	***Long-term***
Work	Freedom

In Chapter One we explored how both big T and little t traumas can lead to feeling overwhelmed and triggered. In some cases, the combination of traumas or the intensity of just one trauma can lead to Post Traumatic Stress Disorder (PTSD). As defined by the *DSM–5*, PTSD occurs when a person has been exposed to a traumatic event where the "person experienced, witnessed, or was confronted with an event or events that involved actual or threatened death or serious injury, or a threat to the physical integrity of self or others" that left them feeling "intense fear, helplessness or horror" (APA, 2013).

Additionally, people with PTSD might experience some of the following symptoms:

1. Recurring images, thoughts, or dreams about the event(s) (e.g. the betrayals).

2. Acting or feeling as if the traumatic event were recurring

3. Severe distress due to external or internal cues (triggers) that symbolize or resemble an aspect of the traumatic event (e.g. billboards, locations, songs, etc.)

4. Resultant psychological reactivity to those triggers.

Not surprisingly, people with PTSD avoid conversations, activities and places that might remind them of the trauma, have little interest in activities that normally would be important to them, feel detached from others, and struggle with emotions in general (including being unable to have loving feelings). Finally, they may experience sleep issues, irritability and angry outbursts, difficulty concentrating, hyper-vigilance or can be easily startled. The symptoms have to last more than a month and cause significant problems in social, work, family or other important areas of their lives (APA, 2013) to be diagnosed as PTSD.

In simple language, PTSD occurs when a person continues to experience memories or triggers related to unresolved trauma. When they are triggered, they often react with survival responses that exacerbate the problem long term rather than provide relief. This leads to further problems in their relationships and other aspects of their lives.

Reflections – Exercise B

1. Have you or are you experiencing any of the symptoms listed above? If so, which ones do you most closely relate to?

_____

_____

2. What emotions come up for you when you consider the possibility of having PTSD responses? Why?

_____

_____

Primal Panic

John Bowlby, a British psychologist who developed attachment theory, began a major movement that has redefined the way we now look at love and connection. Unlike those who believe that true success is being totally independent, Bowlby and those who followed after him have amassed an amazing amount of research evidence that suggests that the most successful people have others in their life they know they can count on, depend on and to whom they know they matter. Bowlby called this type of connection "secure attachment" (Bowlby, 1969).

When we feel securely attached to others, we feel better emotionally and physically, and we recover better physically and emotionally. When we feel disconnected from those who matter most, we can develop several insecure attachment styles to try to manage the disconnection and cope in a world that feels very insecure. As we become more insecure in our relationships, or when moments of deep fear about loss of a relationship occur, the limbic system is triggered and we are flooded with what Jaak Panksepp (2010) called "primal panic." In many cases, these insecure attachment styles are very similar to PTSD symptoms. They are responses intended to help you survive in a very insecure, traumatic environment.

Codependence

In the addiction field, the term codependence has been used to describe excessive emotional or psychological reliance on a partner, typically a partner who requires support due to an illness or addiction. I once heard Pia Mellody (1989) describe codependence as, "A state of dis-ease caused by child abuse that renders a person unable to do… five basic things," all of which are related to a healthy, adult sense of self. In the definition of codependence, we find the things we have just reviewed: trauma and a PTSD-like response which attempts to provide stability when someone experiences an insecure attachment to those who matter most.

Basically, codependence occurs when you have experienced enough trauma, including relational trauma, that you lose your sense of self. As part of this trauma response, your thoughts, feelings or behaviors become determined by (or *dependent* upon) the thoughts, feelings or behaviors of others. If feeling like you are good enough is *only* based on whether other people think you are good enough, that is codependent. If the success of something you do (advocate for yourself, create boundaries for yourself, etc.) is determined *only* by how someone else responds to you (instead of your own judgment of your behavior), that is codependent. Obviously, the attitudes and behaviors of those around you will inevitably have some influence on you; however, codependence is when you give up your ability to take back control of yourself and your life because you rely completely on others for your sense of happiness and peace.

My colleague, Laney Knowlton, describes codependency using these three categories from Karpman's (drama) triangle: suffering/victim, rescuing, and persecuting.

Although they look different, all three types of behaviors are trauma responses and attempt to regain control in unhealthy ways: by trying to control the thoughts, feelings, and/or behaviors of someone else other than yourself.

Suffering/Victim. Suffering behaviors place us in the role of victim. These behaviors prevent us from letting go and moving on. Initially, being a victim is a role you are forced into by others; staying a victim, however, is a choice. The victim role may include behaviors such as self-condemnation and obsessive thoughts. This should not be confused with grief. Individuals who are codependent victims are looking for someone to step in and rescue them, whereas individuals who are dealing with grief are in pain but are not attempting to manipulate people through their behaviors. Often codependent victims stay in that role because being rescued is how they try to feel loved.

While it seems that playing victim would make your position weaker, the opposite is actually true. Victims gain a sense of temporary power through trying to control those around them by acting helpless. As with every type of codependent behavior, suffering behaviors do not allow for connection, even if being rescued may feel somewhat like connection. Connection only happens when you are able to show up as yourself, non-reactively (i.e. not a survival response). When you are playing the victim role, you are not gaining long-term power by standing up for yourself. As a victim, you don't allow those who rescue you to have needs or wants of their own, so they are not really part of the relationship as themselves. You might control the situation, or get the surface response you are looking for, but you will not find long-term connection or peace.

Rescuing. Rescuing behaviors block consequences for others. This may appear unselfish; however, it is actually done to prevent pain for the person doing the rescuing. Parents who protect their child from negative consequences due to poor choices (e.g. jail when the child breaks the law), do so because they are reacting to their own fears and pains (e.g. not wanting to see their child suffer because it causes such high levels of personal pain and other negative consequences to the parents). Rescuing might appear to make the situation easier temporarily, but it makes things worse in the long run. Denial is a type of rescuing behavior. In the addiction field, the word enabling is also used to describe rescuing and refers to enabling a partner or family member to continue the addictive behavior. The term "disabling" seems more accurate to me, because it actually prevents that person from learning and developing from their actions, thus disabling them.

It is important to note the difference between rescuing someone and supporting or protecting them in a healthy way. Support, or being there for someone to help them as they go through difficult issues, is a healthy part of connection. Protecting someone in a situation where they do not have the ability to protect themselves is also a healthy part of connection. Rescuing, on the other hand, eliminates or minimizes consequences that might help the person being rescued. It prevents them from experiencing the emotions that will influence future choice and help them learn and grow. Rescuing also prevents the rescuer from learning and growing.

Persecuting. Persecuting behaviors attempt to control someone else's behaviors through exaggerated consequences. This can include threats, shaming, controlling or lecturing. In some cases, persecuting can occur as a reaction to being persecuted. The persecutor hopes that their behavior might be intense enough that the other person will change. As with other types of codependent behaviors, the persecutor attempts to control someone else's behaviors.

With persecuting behaviors, the intent is not to connect. It is to control the other person's thoughts, feelings and behavior in a way that attempts to make your own pain feel better. Sometimes when we go through pain caused by others, we think our pain will not hurt as much if we make the other person hurt. Being able to have your pain heard and understood by the person that hurt you can be a powerful part of recovery and healing. However, persecuting behaviors do not create a sense of connection and actually decrease your chances of being heard.

You cannot show up as yourself in a relationship if your thoughts and actions are constantly being determined by how someone else will feel, think, or react. It is healthy in relationships to process your emotions and express what you think and feel. Being careful to use or avoid specific words and tones can also minimize risks and maximize your chance of connection.

Reflections – Exercise C

1. Which codependent behaviors did you recognize as part of your behaviors?

   _____

   _____

2. Does your codependency show up differently in your different relationships? If so, how does it differ?

   _____

   _____

3. Codependence is a trauma response intended to control others' thoughts, feelings, or behaviors. What is it you are trying to change through your codependent behaviors?

   _____

   _____

4. What are some healthy ways to change those feelings without being codependent?

   _____

   _____

PTSD in Partners of Sex Addicts

The pain that addiction causes in families is real and powerful. Not long after Alcoholics Anonymous began, Al-Anon groups were established to help family members better manage the stress of living with an alcoholic. Similar groups exist for other addictions as well. The term codependency (as described above) emerged as the diagnosis describing the struggles, pain, and reactivity of partners and family members of addicts.

As groups for partners of sexual addicts emerged, a different name was given to them: co-addict. According to leaders in the field of sex addiction at the time, the partner was addicted to the addict and had to recover from that addiction in the same way the addict had to recover from addiction to sex. Many partners of addicts have found that a difficult diagnosis to embrace.

As early as 1999, articles (Milrad, 1999) began to suggest that spouses of sex addicts were experiencing PTSD. Eventually, Barbara Steffens conducted a study that compared partners of sex addicts to others who experience PTSD. Steffens and Means (2009) argued that based on the findings, PTSD is a much more appropriate label for partners of sexual addicts than co-addict.

They make a powerful argument for a shift in our thinking regarding partners of sex addicts. I offer a few examples here (see their book, *Your Sexually Addicted Spouse: How Partners Can Cope and Heal*, for a more in-depth review). They argue that behaviors such as secret keeping and covering for the addict are actually trauma responses intended to avoid activities or conversations that remind them of the trauma, which is typical of PTSD. Co-addicts are seen as obsessing about the partners' behavior. Steffens and Means suggest that this reaction in partners of sexual addicts is really related to having intrusive thoughts, recollections and memories about the trauma related to their partner's addiction. Instead of using anger, blame, and punishment to control someone in a purely co-addict way, partners of sex addicts exhibit these behaviors because they are experiencing intense stress and irritation and are seeking a sense of control due to the instability caused by the trauma of betrayal.

They also suggest that being the partner of a sex addict adds some particularly difficult challenges to the process of managing emotions. Obviously, partners of sex addicts have day-to-day emotional stressors, family problems, other traumas from the past, and other mental health issues like depression, anxiety, ADHD, etc. that they have to manage. In addition, partners of sexual addicts are also forced to struggle with the present-day trauma of discovering the addiction, or in very rare cases having their partners disclose it.

One major factor in the struggle for partners of sexual addicts is the threat of sexual betrayal because it destroys secure attachment. It creates deep insecurities around the partner's sense that they matter and that they can trust their partner to be there for them. Similar responses result from relationships with other types of addicts or abusive relationships, but there is an added relational element when the acting out behaviors are sexual because of the intimate and personal nature of sexual behaviors. Additionally, physical threats such as sexually-transmitted infectious diseases, financial instability, etc. can contribute to the PTSD symptoms. For partners of sexual addicts, their entire world is challenged; the relationship that was supposed to provide the greatest connection and safety for them has become the greatest source of distress and pain in their lives. This primal panic (limbic response) is a major reason that those in relationships with sexual addicts get so triggered into trauma responses.

Perhaps one of the most significant problems of the betrayal trauma is that it can be ongoing since the addict's behavior may still reoccur. The wound remains open until more stability occurs. If relapses are ongoing, the partner (and family) are bombarded with the same fears, confusion, anxiety and pain again, which reopens the wounds.

Reflections – Exercise D

1. Do you connect to feeling primal panic or betrayal trauma? What thoughts and emotions came up for you as you read about this?

_____

_____

_____

_____

2. What issues make dealing with the emotions related to your spouse's behaviors (whether you are reading this as a partner or as an addict) harder for you (e.g. past trauma, depression, anxiety, addictions, ADD, etc.)?

_____

_____

_____

_____

Because of the intensity of betrayal trauma, to heal we need to begin by understanding and addressing the trauma related to sexual addiction. In the previous chapter, I highlighted how trauma and shame triggers can cause a person to go from any location on the thermometer right into survival mode. For partners, the betrayal trauma has the same effect and can result in trauma responses.

Short-Term Consequences

People can be triggered into their survival responses as a way of managing what seems unmanageable. There is a short-term payoff for trauma responses, as is the case for all survival responses: they are effective in the short run. They work well to escape the unmanageability of the moment. I've consolidated these short-term consequences into a list of emotional payoffs:

- Sense of power or control
- Sense of safety
- Numbness
- Sensitivity (including compassion for others)
- Readiness (increased attentiveness to the environment)
- Good Enough/Capable (can function at a very high level)
- Relief (e.g. withdrawal from others relieves stress temporarily)
- Energy (increased dopamine)

Trauma responses provide a temporary set of positive payoffs for partners—temporary relief, energy, safety, and power. Addicts generally experience their partner's trauma responses as painful or attacking and want them to stop "freaking out" (their words for a trauma response), but they don't understand that the partner is triggered by trauma and is searching for some sense of stability in their life, including feelings of being good enough, accepted, and wanted.

Addicts have their own traumas and specific responses to those traumas, such as raging, codependency, acting out, and so forth. Just like partners, addicts will need to learn to recognize those and to connect with how you also want stability and control and to feel loved and connected. This will help you to move forward in recovery and to foster understanding of your own pain and the pain your partner is going through.

Trauma Cycle: Short-term Consequences

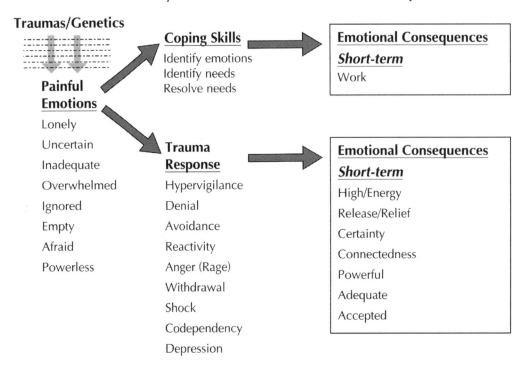

Traumas/Genetics

Painful Emotions

Lonely

Uncertain

Inadequate

Overwhelmed

Ignored

Empty

Afraid

Powerless

Coping Skills

Identify emotions

Identify needs

Resolve needs

Trauma Response

Hypervigilance

Denial

Avoidance

Reactivity

Anger (Rage)

Withdrawal

Shock

Codependency

Depression

Emotional Consequences

Short-term

Work

Emotional Consequences

Short-term

High/Energy

Release/Relief

Certainty

Connectedness

Powerful

Adequate

Accepted

Reflections - Exercise E

1. Referring back to the section on PTSD, what trauma responses do you most closely relate to?

_____

_____

_____

2. What short-term consequences or payoffs do you get from your trauma responses?

_____

_____

3. What trauma responses do you notice in your partner? What short-term consequences or payoffs do you think they might get from their trauma responses?

_____

_____

Long-Term Consequences

Survival-oriented reactions to trauma may bring temporary relief but will lead to greater pain in the long term. It is a package deal: the good will be followed by the bad. Ultimately, the long-term negative consequences are what remain when only trauma responses are used. Below I've listed some of the long-term consequences of trauma responses:

Shock, denial, or disbelief
Anger, irritability
Mood swings
Guilt (which turns into shame/self-blame)
Sadness
Hopelessness
Confusion/Uncertainty
Inadequacy
Anxiety and fear
Withdrawing from others
Feeling disconnected or numb
Fatigue

The end result is that where you temporarily felt powerful, now you feel powerless. For a moment you felt accepted, wanted, or good enough, but you are left with feelings of inadequacy and shame. While you may have felt some relief initially, now you feel anxious or fearful. As illustrated in the following diagram, long-term consequences are what remain after a trauma response. They add to the pile of emotions you had before the whole process started, leaving you feeling even worse. When you feel worse, you are more likely to be triggered again. If you cannot find healthier ways to cope, the trauma response becomes *the only* way to try and cope, and it is almost completely unconscious because it is a limbic reaction rather than a rational decision (prefrontal cortex). Trauma responses lead to patterns of reacting without realizing it and without knowing how to stop it or respond differently. That is why it is so difficult to stop. You likely already have a sense of what you are doing when you are in the trauma cycle, but most clients I work with have not been able to organize what they feel into a conscious model. Hopefully this description will begin to help you become more conscious of the unhealthy cycle you are in.

Trauma Cycle

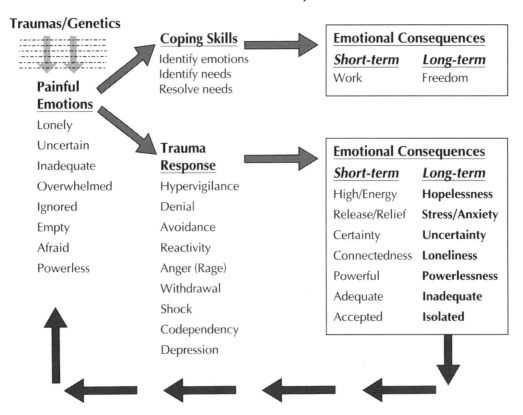

Traumatic events are traumatic because they feel overwhelming and life-threatening, and you do not know how to cope with them. If you felt you could cope with it, trauma wouldn't be traumatic. In order to begin moving forward, it is important to learn very quickly about your trauma response and what you can do to respond in a way that will bring greater long-term relief. In the following chapters we will discuss ways that you can begin to take care of yourself and cope effectively with your trauma in a way that will bring better long-term physical and emotional well-being.

Reflections – Exercise F

1. What are the long-term consequences of your trauma responses?

   _____

   _____

2. Using your answers from question one and the questions from Exercises A through E, draw your trauma cycle on a separate piece of paper.

3. What thoughts or emotions came up for you as you recreated your trauma cycle on paper?

   _____

   _____

4. What are the most important things you learned about yourself from reading about the trauma cycle?

   _____

   _____

5. Using your own music library or online searches, what song or songs most closely fit how you feel when you are in your trauma cycle? Why?

   _____

   _____

The Addiction Cycle

As we try to manage our emotions and are influenced by a combination of genes and environment, we can sometimes begin to feel overwhelmed. It can become a vicious cycle: the more unmanageable we feel, the more we lose confidence in our ability to handle things, and the more unmanageable we feel. Additionally, traumas may trigger us immediately into unmanageability, as discussed previously.

Some people stay in this cycle of unmanageability for years, struggling to control their lives. Living in unmanageability takes a toll. Survival mode becomes *the only* method for managing life. At some point, when these overwhelming feelings come and our efforts to cope do not provide sufficient relief, or even when our pattern of trauma responding seems less effective, we "start to find those things which always comfort, which always feel good, which always are there, and which always do what they promise" (Carnes, 1992, p. 71): at least temporarily. This is where addictive behaviors surface.

Addiction Cycle:
Emotions and Escape Behaviors

Traumas/Genetics

Painful Emotions

Lonely

Bored

Inadequate   **Escapes**

Overwhelmed   Alcohol/Drugs

Stressed   Eating Disorders

Empty   Sexual Addiction

Fear   Rage

Powerless   Gambling/Gaming

                              Codependency

                              Computer Gaming

                              Shopping

                              Lying

Most people first use out of curiosity or trying to fit in with peers and may not become immediately addicted. Dr. Kevin McCauley (2009) suggests that when we use or act out consistently, our brain can eventually adapt our drug of choice (sex, alcohol, eating, etc.) into a survival response. When that happens, our limbic system will adopt the drug of choice instead of the other survival behaviors. So while acting out might initially be a choice, it can rapidly become our main survival response. Thus we become powerless to stop in that moment because we are in limbic mode.

The dilemma is that your body can get confused about whether you are in true survival mode. When emotions build up and a small stressor makes you feel overwhelmed, your system confuses that momentary feeling of unmanageability with a truly life-threatening situation. When that happens, the limbic system kicks you into survival mode. True survival mode, though, is only necessary for immediate, life-threatening situations.

For those who have used consistently enough to convert their drug of choice into a limbic survival response, that feeling of unmanageability almost always leads to using. In the end, that is exactly what Step One of the 12-step program (Alcoholics Anonymous, 2001) describes: "We admitted that we were powerless over our addiction—that our lives had become unmanageable." I sometimes like to reverse the order of Step One to reflect the role of the limbic system in creating powerlessness over the addiction: "We admitted our lives had become unmanageable and we are powerless over our addiction (or behaviors)."

Using temporarily helps addicts to escape the unmanageability that they are experiencing. For this reason, I sometimes refer to using as an "escape behavior." Escape behaviors can include sexual addiction, codependency, drug addiction, rage, gambling, computer gaming, eating disorders, and so forth. All of these behaviors give temporary relief and work powerfully in the short term, much like we discussed with trauma responses previously. See the following diagram, which illustrates the addictive (escape) behaviors and their short-term payoffs.

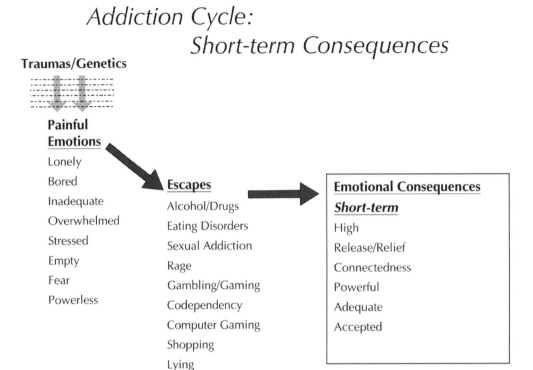

Addiction Cycle:
Short-term Consequences

Traumas/Genetics

Painful Emotions

Lonely
Bored
Inadequate
Overwhelmed
Stressed
Empty
Fear
Powerless

Escapes
Alcohol/Drugs
Eating Disorders
Sexual Addiction
Rage
Gambling/Gaming
Codependency
Computer Gaming
Shopping
Lying

Emotional Consequences
Short-term
High
Release/Relief
Connectedness
Powerful
Adequate
Accepted

Even if you do not identify as an addict, recognizing and dissecting the unhealthy escape behaviors in your life can be helpful. While this section highlights the addictive cycle and focuses on the experience of the addict, I have found that loved ones of addicts benefit from understanding this cycle in two ways: (1) understanding the addict better and (2) understanding how you might "escape" in your own life (we all have unhealthy escapes in some ways, although not always as destructive as addictions can be). If you are a partner of an addict, I challenge you to see how this information connects to your own life and to answer the questions for yourself.

Reflections – Exercise G

1. How do you escape or numb out?

_____

_____

2. What do you get from your escape behaviors?

_____

_____

Short-Term Consequences

Addicts turn to their addiction in an attempt to:
- Handle, remedy, escape, distract, suspend or diminish negative emotions
- Fill the void
- Find nurturing
- Feel pleasure or high
- Self-medicate
- Feel a greater sense of self-worth and acceptance
- Find a sense of power
- Find a sense of connection
- Resolve confusion/pain from childhood traumas or abuse (acting out the abuse in an attempt to feel powerful or make sense of the experience in ways they could not as a child; Bergner, 2002, Goodman, 1992).

Reflections – Exercise H

1. As you review the list above, are there any additional payoffs you would add to the list you created in Exercise G, question two?

_____

_____

Many family members try to convince the addict to just quit using. While eliminating the behavior is a good long-term goal, let me explain why that is so difficult in the beginning. First, you have a person who is in so much pain that they are frequently triggered into a survival response (addictive or escape behaviors). Second, review the list of short-term payoffs! If I told you that you could feel relief, pleasure, high, good enough (or even better), connected, accepted, and powerful, wouldn't you want to feel those feelings? I would. The body integrates this wonderful, powerful, short-term way to feel better into an unconscious survival response: the addiction.

Long-term Consequences

The dilemma here, as you can see, is that addictive/escape behaviors are a package deal. You want the good, but you also have to take the bad with it. And what you are left with in the end are the painful emotions. Here are some of the long-term consequences of addiction, as the short-term positive emotions fade:

- Worthlessness
- Isolation and alienation (including lack of true connection)
- Inadequacy (due to lack of success in truly coping with problems)
- Anxiety
- Powerlessness (not knowing how to manage difficult situations nor the feelings that accompany them)
- Guilt/shame
- Depression

While you initially feel accepted or good enough when you use, in the end you feel guilt, inadequacy and shame. Where once you felt relief, now you feel anxious or fearful. As you see in the following diagram, those long-term consequences are what remain. They add to the pile of emotions you had before the whole process started, leaving you feeling even worse. And when you feel worse, what can make you feel better? The addiction! Quickly your brain alters itself and uses that new addictive process as *the* way to cope when you feel overwhelmed. Because survival responses are unconscious reactions, it is very difficult to stop the behavior. When you are not clear or conscious about what is driving the addictive behavior (survival response to feeling overwhelmed), you have no way of knowing how to stop it.

Interestingly, there is also a response inside our body that occurs as part of the cycle of addiction. Simply put, there is a chemical (neurotransmitter) in the brain called dopamine. It helps you feel pleasure in response to certain behaviors. When you act out addictively, dopamine levels increase to as many as ten times the normal amount, resulting in a high and other good feelings (the short-term effect). After using, the body notes the overabundance of dopamine and ceases creating as much, which then leads to fewer positive feelings than you had when you started (the long-term effect). In other words, what goes up must come down. You cannot use without your body and your emotions eventually feeling worse long term.

Addiction Cycle:
Long-term Consequences

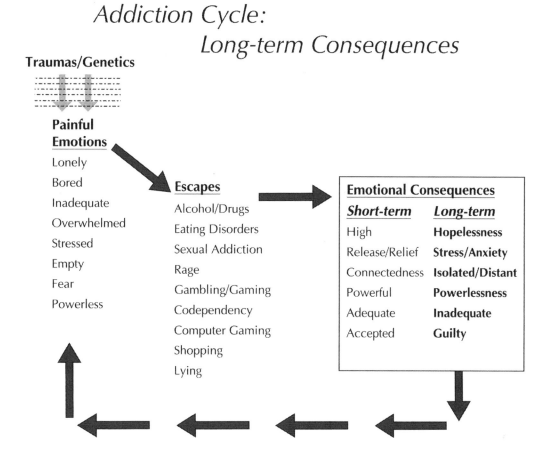

Traumas/Genetics

Painful Emotions

Lonely

Bored

Inadequate

Overwhelmed

Stressed

Empty

Fear

Powerless

Escapes

Alcohol/Drugs

Eating Disorders

Sexual Addiction

Rage

Gambling/Gaming

Codependency

Computer Gaming

Shopping

Lying

Emotional Consequences

Short-term	*Long-term*
High	**Hopelessness**
Release/Relief	**Stress/Anxiety**
Connectedness	**Isolated/Distant**
Powerful	**Powerlessness**
Adequate	**Inadequate**
Accepted	**Guilty**

As I review the addiction cycle in sessions with my clients, they often say things like, "I think I've always known this, but it has never made this much sense." Knowing why addictive responses happen is an important initial step in recovery because it raises the addiction to a more conscious level that you can do something about. Unfortunately, knowing is only half the battle. The other half of the battle is developing positive coping skills.

Just as with the trauma cycle, the way out of the addiction cycle involves developing healthy ways of coping with painful emotions. Healthy emotional coping skills begin with recognition of the emotions you are feeling. As stated previously, emotions are not bad or good: they are simply tools that give us information about what our needs are. The next step to emotional health is to understand the needs those emotions stem from. The last step is to develop the tools that allow those needs to be met in healthy ways.

Healthy coping responses take work. Unlike escape behaviors, appropriate coping skills do not necessarily make the emotions immediately disappear. Once you do the work, however, there is a long-term resolution instead of merely covering the pain temporarily, giving you freedom that is impossible to find when escapes are used.

Addiction Cycle

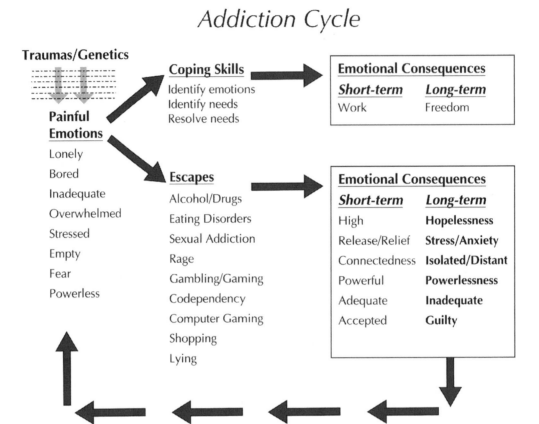

Reflections – Exercise I

Refer back to the addiction cycle, as well as your answers in Exercises G-H, to help you consider these questions.

1. What are the painful emotions that most often start your addiction cycle?

_____

_____

2. What are the short-term emotional consequences of your escapes?

_____

_____

3. What are the long-term emotional consequences of your escapes?

_____

_____

4. On a separate piece of paper, draw your personal addiction cycle, using your answers from questions 1-3. Keep this in a safe place so you can review your cycle regularly to stay consciously aware of your cycle.

5. What thoughts and emotions came up as you drew your cycle?

_____

_____

6. What did you learn about yourself?

_____

_____

Pushing Forward: Learning and
Managing Short-Term Failures

Before we move on to the next chapter, there is one other very meaningful and major impact on people who are consistently being triggered into trauma responses and addictive behaviors. When people react to, escape from, or diminish the experience of negative emotions, it prevents them from becoming familiar with the situation that is causing the emotions and reactions. It also prevents them from experiencing success in managing those situations and emotions. Because they never get resolved and the coping skills are never developed, they continue to experience anxiety and have limited or no confidence in their ability to manage their life, which reinforces this cycle even more.

When I was young, I used to play Super Mario Brothers® on my Nintendo®. Much like life, the goal of Super Mario Brothers is to progress through different levels and experiences, learning new skills that allow you to become successful at even higher levels. Progress in Super Mario Brothers happens in distinct worlds, each consisting of four stages. The last stage in each world is Bowser's castle for that level. To "graduate" to the next world, you must defeat Bowser at the end of the castle.

While the other stages in each world generally have playful music and colorful surroundings, Bowser's castle is always black, gray and red, with ominous music playing in the background. When you first arrive at the castle, your experience is new for each level, so the challenges are unexpected and unfamiliar, with a lot of new context you have never seen before. All these factors always made me anxious and tense, and I never seemed to be able to do as well in Bowser's Castle as in other stages.

The main characters, Mario and Luigi, can have three different sizes: small, big, and fireballs (a skill that allows you to easily manage challenges that are more difficult when you are just small or big). In some ways, those sizes are representative of your emotional skill level, your confidence and your vulnerability. The smaller you are, the more vulnerable, less skilled and less confident you are.

When you arrive at Bowser's castle, you have usually struggled through three other stages that were also initially unfamiliar. The number of lives (do-overs) are limited, and you are usually small. If you start off with good skills and a larger player, you might make good progress, but the situation is so new that you will usually fail to manage the obstacles well and will have to go back to the beginning and try again. For me this would frequently happen even before the halfway point of the castle.

When you start over, you are at your smallest, most vulnerable size. As you repeat the level you will often feel more confident because it is no longer unfamiliar; however, anxiety increases when you make it back to the unfamiliar areas you were not able to master. The heightened anxiety makes it more difficult to perform and easier to make mistakes. In the game, quitting does not seem like a good option, because you have invested a lot of time in the process already.

Much like this video game, in life you have unfamiliar and difficult experiences that may cause you anxiety/fear. Even with good coping skills, you will eventually fall short, fail or make a mistake, and it will set you back. You may not be back at the beginning, but it feels painful to lose any ground. As you approach things that are harder or that you have failed at before, you become more tense and anxious. Life makes you feel so small that you struggle to believe you can succeed. You lose your confidence and every failure seems so painful.

In life, it is often at this point where people begin to escape and avoid. Obviously, there is a lot more risk in life than in a video game, so we tend to avoid the situations that feel risky rather than prepare, work, learn and grow. Gradually, we start to identify most of life's challenges as "too much" for us, and we continue to shrink, as does our own view of ourselves.

In Super Mario Brothers, continuing to try does two things: it allows you to practice what you have already succeeded at, helping you to see that you have the skills to succeed, and it helps you to become more familiar with what was unfamiliar, making it more approachable and less anxiety-provoking. As we discussed in the chapter on the thermometer, working through new and sometimes painful emotions in this "zone of growth" will allow you to learn new skills that will eventually make things that were once uncomfortable feel more manageable and comfortable. In life, quitting or escaping prevents you from gaining confidence, learning and having lower fear/anxiety about hard-to-handle situations.

In Super Mario Brothers, you know that you might shrink temporarily, but there is always an understanding that somewhere soon you will find an opportunity for a boost. In life, you may wonder if you will ever feel big enough again, able to withstand an attack (or two) without feeling like you are a failure, and if a boost will ever come again to make you feel bigger and more confident. At times in this journey you may wonder if you will be able to withstand the pain of real life. The sense of not being enough can be so painful that you might tell yourself you just can't handle it.

In Super Mario Brothers, the assumption is that you will regularly fail and will need to learn by a lot of repetition. In life, we fear failure. We don't think, "Dang! I wasn't prepared for that. I'll do better next time." Instead, we think, "Crap! I can't do it and everybody else can. I hope nobody saw. I'm never going to put myself in that position again." In Super Mario Brothers, you know you have extra lives: another opportunity to try again when you fail. In life you may feel like there are no second chances. However, as you learn to accept failure as a part of life, with new opportunities and available growth, you will recognize that the true measure of success is not whether you fail but how you manage the failures that will inevitably occur.

Even in Super Mario Brothers you cannot do it on your own and need others' help. There were countless times that I would ask my friends how to do things I could not figure out on my own. Sometimes they would know what I was doing and would offer help: "Oh, you can beat that part by doing _____," or, "Did you know you can get some extra lives and coins here?" In life, we tend not to admit we need help, hiding our struggles and assuming we are just broken because we can't immediately figure it out on our own. We struggle to find the courage to admit our imperfection—in a safe way and to the right people—in order to get help and learn the skills to truly succeed long term.

In Super Mario Brothers, if you stick with it you can eventually get to the end of Bowser's castle with fireballs. If you keep trying in life, ask for help and learn from your mistakes, you will also experience success and confidence. With each success, you will become more skilled. You will still need to remember the things you have learned and be careful in how you utilize them, but managing things that were once very difficult will become easier and require less focus and attention. The key is to stay connected and humble. If you drop your guard or stop practicing your coping skills, you can fall backwards. Ralph Waldo Emerson said, "That which we persist in doing becomes easier for us to do—not that the nature of the thing is changed, but that our power to do is increased." You will one day face the challenges that today make you want to shrink with a sense of confidence, power, and support from others if you stick with it, ask for help, and develop the skills and awareness necessary to come off conqueror.

Reflections – Exercise J

1. What are the most important things you learned about yourself from reading about the trauma and addiction cycles?

    _____

    _____

2. Write an example of a time that you confronted difficult things and were able to learn and grow.

    _____

    _____

3. What are some of the challenges you are experiencing now that seem difficult to overcome or cause you a lot of anxiety?

_____

_____

4. Who can you turn to for support with these challenges?

_____

_____

5. On a separate piece of paper, create a self-portrait of your addict or traumatized self. You can use crayons, markers, paint, make a collage out of photos from magazines, create a digital image, etc.

While the Trauma Cycle and Addiction Cycle are different in several ways, there are many similarities. In both cases, triggers occur that leave the person feeling overwhelmed and in survival mode. Survival mode creates a response that is effective in the short term but not in the long term. The long-term goal is to learn to manage triggers and emotions more successfully so that the negative long-term impact is reduced or eliminated.

As stated, it is important for addicts to identify their trauma cycles caused by their own traumatic histories. Many partners of addicts can connect with the struggles of addiction because of their own addictive patterns, past or present. This can bring a degree of empathy for each other's struggles while not giving permission or justification for the actions. These cycles help you see that the root of the unhealthy behaviors is the pattern (emotions and triggers, followed by ineffective escape strategies), not the result of some permanent flaw in you, your spouse, or your relationship. Knowing this can begin to help depersonalize it, decrease reactivity, and reduce shame around the acting out or trauma-response behaviors. Finally, seeing how the Trauma Cycle and Addiction Cycle parallel each other can allow you to better see and understand the emotions of your spouse, without condoning or justifying their behavior. For many, this is the first step in creating empathy for your partner's experience and emotions.

Wrap-up

We have reviewed what addiction is and is not, the Trauma Cycle, the Addiction Cycle, and the steps to managing emotions in a healthy way so that recovery is possible. With this foundation, it is time to focus on the "next right steps" in early recovery. Chapter Four will focus on the remaining important individual aspects of recovery and provide a road map for healthy, long-term individual recovery, including ways to fill your life with positive thoughts, feelings and behaviors as well as ways to intervene in addictive behaviors. I call these tools the Recovery Hill.

Chapter 4

THE RECOVERY HILL
Setting Up an Individual Program

By now you have started to accumulate some knowledge, basic skills and tools to help you in your recovery: the thermometer, time-outs, soothing, the trauma or addiction cycles, etc. Collect these things in a place where you can have easy access: in a folder, binder, on your computer, phone (exercise caution if your computer or phone are one of your acting-out tools), etc. This collection is your "Tool Box." Many of the tools reviewed in this chapter will become essential components of your Tool Box as well.

Over the years of doing my own individual work, studying and practicing as a therapist, I have accumulated a lot of knowledge, skills, wisdom and tools. After so many years, it is difficult to tell the difference between my own thoughts and the thoughts and ideas of others. So I begin this chapter by recognizing all those whose work has impacted me. I'm grateful for the many people who have provided me so much good information and experience with addiction and recovery, including my clients. I have taken all I have been given, added my own understanding and insight, and developed what I call *The Recovery Hill*: one simple picture that represents the different elements of individual recovery that I have found the most beneficial. Throughout this chapter and book, I cite the work of other authors from whose work I have drawn.

While the reasons for their use may differ, the different tools of the Recovery Hill are important and meaningful for both partner and addict. Part of the addict's struggle is for sobriety and healing from the effects of the addiction. Both addict and partner struggle to recover from trauma, manage triggers, increase self-awareness, develop empowerment and establish boundaries and connection. Although the reasons and focus may seem different, I urge you to note the similarities in the healing process for both you and your spouse. Again, I am not dismissing or minimizing the pain that comes to a partner from addictive or trauma-based behaviors. Relating your experience to that of your spouse will increase your understanding of the process and provide the greatest chance of emotional safety and a more complete healing. As I present the tools of the Recovery Hill, I will describe the reasons and ways they are useful for both of you.

While this may seem repetitive, I think it is useful to reiterate that using similar tools creates empathy, connection, and understanding, each of which are powerful elements of long-term couple recovery. When you see your spouse succeed in using a new tool that you have been working on, you understand at a deeper level what it took to make those changes and do things differently. Equally, it is easier to understand when your spouse is struggling to succeed in using the tools because you also will have struggled with finding a way to engage with the tools yourself.

No Silver Bullet

People often wonder why it isn't possible to just "make a choice" to stop these behaviors. As you can see, the reason you can't make just one choice is because it is a group of decisions that combine together, eventually culminating in powerlessness over the behavior. In a similar way, recovery is not just one decision or one tool. Often people think that they find one great tool that will solve all their problems, and they focus all their energy on that. They want one silver bullet to "kill" the behavior (addiction or trauma response) once and for all.

The truth is, there is no silver bullet, although it is exciting to find a new tool that really seems to help. There are many tools that need to be learned line upon line. Some tools have to be learned sooner than others because they are the initial building blocks. The key is to keep looking for the next right step and keep building. The second you think you have found the silver bullet, you are in danger of slipping backwards again.

Struggling to Stop

As you attempt to use the tools in the Recovery Hill, you may find that you are initially unable to create or maintain sobriety. A person who has been sufficiently wounded needs to spend time in the hospital to get healthy enough to go home and do the self-care to finish the process of healing. For addicts in early recovery, part of the initial focus has to be on stopping relapse because of how significantly addiction affects the brain.

In more severe cases, residential treatment is necessary to provide (1) physical safety, such as managing withdrawal, (2) a supportive environment away from most of your normal triggers so you can stop acting out, and (3) the necessary time for your brain to heal and basic tools to be acquired before you go home to continue the recovery process. The different levels of care, from outpatient to residential, are discussed in the "Getting Connected" section of Chapter Five. I mention them here so that if you are unable to stop using, you can refer to that section to see what other resources might be available to provide support and help you through this process more successfully.

Four Sections of the Hill

The tenets and practices of the 12-step program have helped countless people to find sobriety, and you will find multiple references to that program within this book. In the SAA (Sex Addicts Anonymous) Green Book (2012) there is a description of "three concentric circles" (pg. 16) that look like a target.

The inner circle (the bullseye) represents bottom line acting-out behaviors. For partners, bottom-line behaviors are your trauma responses—behaviors that prevent you from being your authentic self, or who you want to be, and behaviors that hurt you, your spouse, or your relationship. For addicts, bottom-line behaviors include both addictive behaviors and trauma responses. The second circle contains behaviors that are not acting out but can leave a person vulnerable to return to the addiction, or bottom-line behaviors, if not addressed. The outer circle represents behaviors that are healthy, positive, and supportive of long-term recovery. You can also visualize each circle as a color: red (inner circle), yellow (second or middle circle), and green (outer circle).

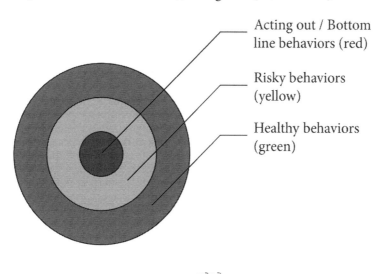

Acting out / Bottom
line behaviors (red)

Risky behaviors
(yellow)

Healthy behaviors
(green)

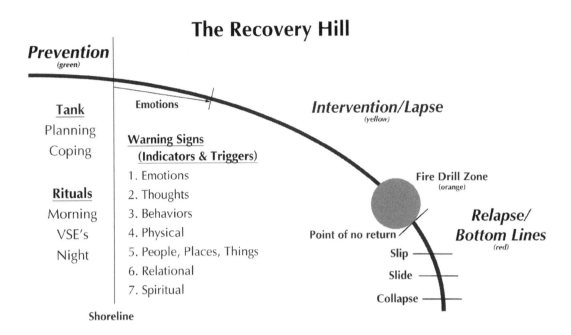

As you look at the Recovery Hill (an idea inspired by Dr. Mark Butler at Brigham Young University), you will see a correlation: relapse (red), fire drill zone (orange), intervention/lapse in self-care (yellow), and prevention (green). I have added the orange fire drill zone; it is a little more intense than the yellow but not yet relapse behavior. I will briefly review each zone and the different skills and tools necessary to manage them, from the bottom right to the top left.

Relapse and Bottom Lines

The term "bottom line" refers to the behaviors in the red zone: relapse behaviors. The bottom line is that if you are doing those behaviors, you are relapsing into destructive behaviors. Bottom lines are more black and white with substance addictions, although new legal drugs K2/Spice and Kratom are creating a gray area where users can try to justify whether it is addictive or not. In process or behavioral addictions like sexual addiction or eating disorders, it is more difficult to define bottom lines, and definitely very individualized. You can't stop eating, but people with eating disorders have to identify healthy versus unhealthy eating behaviors. Sex is a normal part of being human, but you have to understand healthy versus unhealthy sexual behaviors.

Sex addicts have to determine whether or not masturbation, movies with nudity, and other such behaviors fall within the realm of relapse or bottom-line behaviors. Until those boundaries are identified, addicts will justify their behaviors and continue to relapse. In the end, every person's process addiction will have slightly different bottom lines. It is important that you share those with trustworthy people in recovery to help ensure that you have fully considered all aspects of your bottom-line behaviors.

Bottom-line behaviors for sexual addictions might include viewing nudity (and you will need to define that term specifically), viewing pornography, going to a strip club, using prostitutes, setting up a profile on a dating site, flirting with someone other than your spouse, contacting acting-out partners (call, text, IM, email, etc.), physical contact with acting-out partners, lying (overtly or by omission), online sexual activity and so forth.

In early recovery, both of you are in a great deal of confusion, turmoil, and pain. Because of this, trauma responses occur quite frequently. Trauma responses can be very destructive long term, so it is important to identify what those are for you. Part of the initial focus is learning how to identify the trauma responses (bottom-line behaviors that you determine are not safe or productive for you long term) and respond quickly and effectively with other options.

While I reviewed some of the typical trauma responses in Chapter Three, I provide a more extensive list here. Take a minute to review the list, then put a check next to the ones you recognize as part of your trauma responses and bottom-line behaviors.

Emotions

Intense Fear (or high anxiety)
Loneliness
Uncertainty
Grief and Loss (or intense sadness)
Panic
Depression
Despair
Powerlessness (feeling out of control)
Ignored
Worthless
Inadequate
Overwhelmed
Hopelessness
Emotional numbness

Irritability
Worry (or rumination)
Mood swings
Shock or disbelief
Confusion
Exhaustion

Thoughts

Being on high alert and/or very watchful
Increased sensitivity
Obsessive thoughts or images (about the trauma)
Racing thoughts
Nightmares/flashbacks
Reliving the event(s)
Difficulty concentrating
Self-blame
Denial
Pretending the addiction is not a big deal (minimizing)
Avoidance
Thoughts of suicide
Obsession about the future

Behaviors

Detachment
Walking on eggshells
Obsession
Changing yourself to please, accommodate, or pacify (codependency)
Social withdrawal/isolation
Rageful thoughts or behaviors (including name calling)
Denial
Efforts to control the environment (cleaning, dieting, parenting, partner's behavior, etc.)
Diminished interests in regular activities
Acting out via food, alcohol, drugs, spending, affairs, etc.
Avoiding people, places, and things associated with the trauma (including the home)

Physical

Difficulty sleeping (falling or staying asleep)/excessive sleeping
Inability to eat/overeating
Chronic fatigue
Immune/Endocrine system problems
Health problems
Body pain
Difficulty concentrating
Migraines

The goal of establishing bottom lines for addictive behaviors and trauma responses is not to shame or control the partner or addict. Bottom lines help you to increase your awareness, intervene sooner with your destructive behaviors, and develop ways to respond more effectively in the face of potential relapse. My experience is that clients tend to adjust their bottom lines as they move into long-term recovery. Early recovery bottom lines seem to always have a little more leeway, perhaps due to fear of losing the ability to manage things that feel unmanageable in early recovery.

Reflections – Exercise A

1. Which emotions from the list above do you struggle with? Are there any that aren't listed?

    _____

    _____

2. Which thoughts are hardest for you to deal with? Are there any others you would include?

    _____

    _____

    _____

3. Which behaviors do you most closely connect with? Are there any additional behaviors that were not on the list?

    _____

    _____

    _____

4. What physical symptoms do you experience? Are there any that you would add to the list?

    _____

    _____

    _____

Identifying trauma responses can be tricky because they can occur at different intensities. For example, when does a migraine mean you are in your trauma responses or just experiencing a migraine? What's the difference between regular cleaning of the house and trauma, control-based house cleaning? What about when you just don't feel like going out with friends because you are too tired? When you get irritated with your spouse, how is that different from when you would get angry before the betrayal trauma? Because trauma responses can be difficult to identify or distinguish from other behaviors, it is important to try to determine which sets of trauma responses are clearly bottom-line behaviors for you.

Once you have determined your bottom-line behaviors, whether they are addictive behaviors, trauma responses or both, it will give you greater power to notice them and build healthy alternative responses that will provide you both short-term and long-term relief. Over time you may recognize new bottom-line behaviors. Just add them to your list and continue to apply the tools you will learn from the Recovery Hill to help you manage them in healthier ways. Learning the new skills will take time and will not work perfectly, but with patience you will see a positive effect.

Reflections - Exercise B

1. What are your current bottom-line behaviors, including both addictive behaviors (if applicable) and trauma responses, that you have identified as inconsistent with the person you want to be and which have obvious, negative, long-term effects on you and your relationship?

_____

_____

Once you have defined your bottom-line behaviors, the next step is to find ways to prevent yourself from crossing them. There are two ways to help prevent behaviors from occurring in early recovery: internal barriers and external barriers. Internal barriers are the key to long-term recovery. They are formed as you create healthy ways to feel good, better take care of your needs, and build connection with others. Because you feel better, the triggers to act out and/or trauma responses are not as strong. The internal change creates a long-term barrier against the addiction and trauma responses. Internal barriers obviously take time to create.

As you work to create internal changes that act as barriers to relapsing into bottom-line behaviors, it is also important to set up external barriers. External barriers apply primarily to addictive behaviors. For pornography users, this might include filters on the computer and phone or tracking programs to let others know if you are using. For those who act out with strip clubs, massage parlors, or prostitutes, this might include programs which can be installed on the phone that track your location and help provide an external barrier—if you go there, others will know. Others use polygraphs to ensure they are honest and accountable for their bottom-line behaviors.

All of these external barriers are most effective when there is an accountability partner—someone who receives updates from your filter services, can see where you have been with your tracking program, and knows your polygraph results. That person will not be reactive to your failures and can provide support to help you get honest and back into recovery behaviors. You should decide with your therapist or sponsor who should be helping provide accountability. While partners can be aware of your successes and struggles for their own safety, they should not be your accountability partner. These tools can provide accountability by increasing the likelihood of discovery if they act out, which can often motivate addicts to avoid relapse.

What people often see as one of the most powerful external barriers for addictive behaviors is the law. The fear of getting caught or incarcerated can be terrifying; however, over time I have watched clients return to their behaviors again despite their fears and past experiences with the law. Even the external barrier of the potential for legal repercussions cannot provide long-term sobriety. No matter what legal consequences you face, if you do not take care of yourself, the addiction will eventually return as the short-term method for finding relief.

None of these external barriers are foolproof, but they can provide a layer of protection that can provide at least a moment for your prefrontal cortex, the part of the brain that understands long-term consequences and wants sobriety, to have an influence over your decisions and prevent acting-out behaviors. In addition, external barriers can help extend sobriety, which allows the brain to heal. Gradually, the pull of the addictive patterns on the brain and body will diminish as you establish longer periods of sobriety, allowing longer-term recovery skills to be created and managed more successfully (which also leads to self-esteem and connection over time).

For partners, external barriers for the addiction represent greater possibility for sobriety, an increased sense of safety, and opportunities to build trust. Knowing that the addict is willing to take steps to prevent relapse provides a sense that the addict is trying to stop the partner's pain and uncertainty. This often helps partners feel like they matter and improves opportunities to build connection. This safety, connection and trust can help partners feel less triggered into their own bottom-line behaviors.

Reflections – Exercise C

1. What internal barriers would you like to create? How can you start that process?

_____

_____

2. What external barriers might help you work towards recovery and develop trust and safety in your relationship?

_____

_____

Fire Drills

In school, teachers taught me to stop, drop, and roll if I caught on fire. Why? Because the brain's natural response is to run, which is a flight response, but running will ultimately fan the flame and increase the injury. They taught me to stop, drop and roll, had me practice it, and reviewed it with me regularly to make sure it became an automatic response that would override my natural instinct to run if I caught fire.

When you are about to relapse into your addiction or trauma responses, you don't have full access to your prefrontal cortex, and your limbic system (survival instinct) is gearing up to take over. In these moments there is no time to think, so having a trained, automatic process is all you can do at this place on the Recovery Hill. The term "fire drill" refers to steps you must train yourself to do automatically in order to manage the acting out and/or trauma responses that may cause a lot of damage if handled in a reactive way.

Because one of the major goals of early recovery for addicts is to stop acting out, developing fire drills is an essential initial skill in recovery. Active addiction is very chaotic and full of unmanageability, as Step One of the 12-steps suggests (Alcoholics Anonymous, 2001). So when you can move to a place even just a little above active relapse, you will feel you are in a good place. While you are in a *much* better place than you have been, things are still very close to falling back into unmanageability, which is why the 12-step "one day at a time" mentality is such an important principle.

I have heard so many clients say, "I was in a good place and suddenly I relapsed. I just don't understand why." Confusing a "better place" with a "good place," you may assume you are all the way up the Recovery Hill when, in fact, you are still very vulnerable to relapse. Addicts in early recovery, while improving and succeeding, still live close to the point of no return, just in or above the fire drill zone (see the Recovery Hill diagram). When stressors hit, you suddenly find yourself pulled again toward the addiction. Without skills to help you, you will slip quickly past the point of no return—the point where acting out is going to happen and you can no longer choose to stop, even if you have not yet acted out.

Because early recovery for partners is so chaotic and uncertain, it is easy for partners to be triggered into trauma responses all the time. This often applies to addicts' trauma responses as well. One of the major goals of early recovery is to stop the trauma response and replace it with healthy behaviors. Developing fire drills is essential to that process. Like time-outs, fire drills help you to come out of survival mode (trauma response) and into a healthier place. So the goal is to catch yourself before you have gone into a full-blown trauma response, providing the time necessary to soothe and make healthy choices. In my experience, the first few attempts can be difficult and require a lot of preparation and willpower. With time, you will see the positive impact of using fire drills to divert trauma responses into healthy self-care steps.

Many partners and addicts report going from feeling fine one moment to being abruptly triggered into a trauma response. In early recovery, there is so much pain and there are so many triggers that you live on the edge of survival mode. One moment you can be in a peaceful place, then suddenly you are back into trauma responses. Without the necessary skills to help you, it is difficult not to slip continually back into trauma responses. Next we will discuss how to create a fire drill.

Point of No Return

The first step to creating a fire drill is defining the point of no return. I was working with a cocaine addict, and we were creating a fire drill plan for him. I asked him, "Where's the first place you could intervene?" He said he could picture himself in the bathroom, with the lines of cocaine, ready to use. I asked him what he could imagine doing there to stop himself from using. He thought for a while and then said, "Nothing." So I had him take a step back. He pictured himself coming through the door with his drugs. He still couldn't imagine doing anything to intervene there. We took two or three more steps back in the process. Finally, he imagined himself driving to get the drugs from the dealer, and at that point he could imagine doing something to stop himself. Why do I tell you this story? In reality, many times addicts are past the point of no return and headed to relapse well before they are even aware there is a problem. Realistically assessing where the true point of no return is will allow you to plan interventions in a more effective way.

In early recovery, both addicts and partners live on the edge of the point of no return, living with intense fear, insecurity, powerlessness and so forth. Often, triggers come out of nowhere and are unpredictable. It is initially incredibly difficult to stop acting out and/ or to stop a reaction into a trauma response. Because relapse and trauma responses are so unconscious at first, the best laid plans can often fail. The first thing we determine is bottom lines because they can help you acknowledge the behavior and recover quickly.

With time and practice, the frequency and intensity of relapses and trauma responses will decrease. You will notice as you progress that there is more frequently a build-up phase, where poor self-care and increased stressors gradually lead to increased vulnerability to triggers. There will be times where you are triggered by certain things even when you are doing all the self-care you know how to do. In these cases, the goal is still to recover as quickly as possible. While not all acting out and trauma responses can be prevented, you can reduce the frequency and intensity by focusing on understanding how to intervene as you begin to "catch on fire," as well as understanding the build-up that can cause more frequent triggering.

The same concept of fire drills that is used for relapses into addictive behaviors applies to trauma responses. It is often more difficult to see the steps that get you there since they aren't physically definable the way addictive behaviors usually are, and often there is significantly less time from when the process starts to when you have crossed into survival responses. For example, one wife I worked with discovered her husband had re-downloaded an app to his phone that he had used to contact affair partners. She immediately became enraged and she and her husband ended up in a huge fight over it. As she worked through her response with me afterwards, she recognized that she had crossed her own bottom lines by raging. While it was completely understandable, and her husband's behavior was not acceptable, she determined that she wanted to take better care of herself. She did not like the long-term impact of her trauma response, so she worked to develop a fire drill and then better skills for self-care.

Reflections – Exercise D

1. Consider your bottom-line behaviors. Going backwards (because the steps you take are usually easier to see that way), what are the steps that you take to get your high or to try to control a situation when you feel unsafe? (Note—the steps will be different for different behaviors, so you will have to consider this question for each of your bottom-line behaviors.)

_____

_____

_____

2. Thinking about your bottom-line behaviors, where is your point of no return? Where do you still have the ability to stop the process?

_____

_____

_____

To create a good fire drill plan, first identify the most common situations that leave you vulnerable to bottom-line behaviors; that is where you are most apt to catch fire. Come up with a plan based on the feeling you will have in that scenario. To clarify what I mean by feeling, let me refer to the Princess Bride, by William Goldman (1973). In trying to escape from their enemy, the main characters flee into the Fire Swamp. The Fire Swamp is a dangerous place from which no one has ever come out alive. Sometimes addiction can feel that way for both addicts and partners. There are many treacherous things in the swamp, including fire that randomly shoots out of the ground in different places. As the heroes try to maneuver through, they recognize that just before the fire shoots out, there is a popping sound that comes first. They listen intently for that sound, and when it comes they move quickly away from the source of that sound into safety. Knowing what to listen for helped them navigate safely through the Fire Swamp.

I have found that there are things like the popping sound in the Fire Swamp that happen just before acting out or trauma responses. The most frequent things that occur are feelings or body responses. For example, the woman who raged at her husband in the previous section was able to identify the feeling she got in the pit of her stomach when she saw the app: like being punched. She said that was a common physical reaction for her when her husband relapsed into his addictive behaviors. She decided that any time she felt that feeling in the pit of her stomach, she needed to have a fire drill. Identifying these body sensations and other feelings can gradually help you step away from the bottom-line behaviors in critical moments and avoid more serious consequences.

When you are in a safe place, I want you to remember a time where you were triggered or imagine what it feels like when you are about to be triggered into acting out/trauma response. Notice what feelings come up. Notice what happens in your body. Do you notice anything in your chest, stomach, gut, arms, hands, legs, feet, face, jaw or head? Take time to write those things down in Exercise E. If it is difficult to identify, you may need to work with a therapist to become more attuned to those feelings and body responses.

Reflections – Exercise E

1. What feelings do you notice as you imagine/recall being triggered?

_____

_____

2. What body sensations do you notice as you imagine/recall being triggered?

_____

_____

A good fire drill should have a distraction and action associated with it. The best distractions are physical, funny, or both. The distraction is meant to kick the blinders off or get you out of the "tractor beam" (for you science fiction fans) that has you focused solely on the addiction or trauma response. Immediately after distraction, you need an action that will move you away from the situation to safety. If you don't move away from the situation (e.g. out of the room, house, place that is triggering), you'll fall right back into the grips of the tractor beam and continue your descent toward relapse.

To name a few examples of fire drills, I have had clients wear rubber bands that they snap on their wrists, slap their face, scream, "Stop," yodel, talk like Scooby Doo® (and this one was successful for him), run around the room like they were on fire, and throw themselves on the ground or bed and scream. A cocaine-addicted client decided that he would honk his horn as he drove. A sex addict client who frequently relapsed in front of the TV determined that he would not be able to turn the TV off, but he could roll off the couch: both physical and funny for him. Another client who relapsed into pornography made sure he never had his laptop on his lap, and he always had a rolling chair at his desk. His distraction was to push with his legs and propel himself as far to the other side of the room as possible. One partner would sing, "Stop in the Name of Love," with the hand motions from the music video when she was triggered. Another person repeated affirmations she had developed in a British accent in her head. Another partner found it next to impossible to stop herself from verbally exploding all over her husband after calling a time-out, so she decided to physically put her hand over her mouth and run out of the room after saying, "Time-out."

The next step in a good fire drill is an action to get out of the triggering situation. The guy who rolled off the couch decided to do 10 push-ups and then walk out the front door. The yodeler told his wife what his yodeling meant, so when she was home (he worked from home), she would connect with him. The cocaine addict pulled off the road as he honked his horn and got out of the car. He committed not to get back in the car until he called his sponsor or a recovery friend. Obviously, every person will have a different fire drill, but all fire drills need a distraction and an action to ensure success. Getting away from the triggering environment is crucial because it gives people time to deescalate emotionally and improves their ability to choose according to their personal values because the prefrontal cortex will become more active in the process.

Sometimes getting out is an internal process that helps exit the reactive pattern, particularly for trauma responses. For example, one partner found it helpful to imagine her therapist sitting on her shoulder parroting her affirmations into her ear because that grounded her and stopped her from spiraling into her trauma response. The wife who raged as her trauma response decided to repeat the following sentences to herself when she felt the punch in her stomach, after removing herself from the environment: "This will be addressed. It is not OK and I do not have to be OK with it. It never helps for me to talk to him when I'm mad." She practiced doing that before opening her mouth and starting to yell, as that was her point of no return. She trained herself to take a time-out and to contact someone on her support team to vent to if needed, then to contact me and process how to address the relapse.

In each case, as partners start using their fire drills, they see more successful long-term results, even though it is difficult to push through the initial reactivity. This process helps you figure out that you have the ability to decide who you want to be and how you want to respond. That allows you to feel peace without having to sacrifice advocating for your needs.

Reaching In and Reaching Out

Once you have gotten out of the situation and soothed, it is critical to reach in and reach out. Reaching in means getting connected with your feelings and tools for self-care and healthy recovery. Reaching out means letting someone else you trust know that you are struggling, sharing your feelings and struggles, and asking for help when you need it.

Reaching out can be difficult and awkward. In order to make it easier, I have my clients reflect on what they would need from someone after a fire drill. I have them consider to whom they would turn (sponsor, friend, family member, spiritual leader, etc.) and what they might want that person to do for them. I have them write out that plan and share it with that person: "When I'm having a rough time, like after a Fire Drill, I usually need [*a reminder of how to get grounded and centered, to remember my tools for soothing, to get to a meeting, to just vent for a few minutes, etc.*]. When I call, would you help me in that way? If I know what that conversation will look like, I think it will be easier for me to reach out during those times."

Reflections – Exercise F

The goal of Exercise F is to create a fire drill. Once you have completed questions 1-5 below, you will have a plan for the two most common scenarios where you will need a fire drill.

1. Write down the two most common scenarios where you tend to relapse into your addiction/trauma response.

    _____

    _____

2. Write down your initial impressions about what might work for you in a distraction and action for each situation.

    _____

    _____

    _____

    _____

3. Practice your distractions and actions.

4. What are some ways you can reach in, for both scenarios? Do you need a different method of reaching in with the second scenario, or will the resources you listed for the first scenario work equally well in the second? If the second scenario needs different resources, write out your resources for the second scenario.

    _____

    _____

    _____

5. To whom can you reach out? Do you need different people to reaching out to in the second scenario or will the resources you listed for the first scenario work

equally well in the second? If the second scenario needs different resources, write out your resources for the second scenario.

_____

_____

Once you have created your plans, play the entire process out in your mind. Notice what happens within you as you try to imagine going through the fire drill actions (feelings, thoughts, body, etc.). Notice what restricts you as you imagine doing your fire drills. If you can't imagine doing it, it will not work when the time comes to use it in real life. After successfully imagining it, I then urge clients to repeat the visual imagery process at home (imagining the circumstance and the fire drill responses in the context of those triggering feelings). Visualization can sometimes lead to feeling triggered, so it is important to visualize in a safe environment without access to the opportunity to use.

Where possible, I also have clients practice their fire drills. I had the cocaine user practice honking his horn while driving, then pulling over and getting out. The pornography addict practiced rolling his chair, then getting up and leaving the room. The sex addict practiced rolling off the couch, then doing push-ups and leaving the house. The wife practiced singing with her hand out and then walking out of the room. Once it is well-practiced mentally and physically, you have both brain memory and muscle memory to support you in succeeding with your fire drill.

Commitment to Fire Drills

As an addict or partner there is a part of you that may struggle with fire drills because you realize that not using may mean that you will not be able to meet your needs immediately in those tough moments. In the case of trauma responses, especially with angry or controlling responses, it is often difficult not to react because you want to discharge all the painful emotions. I ask you only to commit to the idea that, just for this short period, you are going to experiment with something different for yourself. What are the outcomes you expect? A reasonable outcome or expectation from a Fire Drill is to just get through the "night"—that period of pain and darkness that occurs when you fight off a trauma response or relapse. Once you've made it through the "night," you can sit down and look at the impact that using the fire drill had on you, positive or negative. Because it is just one attempt at managing things differently by using a fire drill, most of my clients are more willing to give it a try and see what happens. Inevitably, they report learning a lot about themselves and a lot about the process. I challenge you to take the same step.

Reflections – Exercise G

1. What outcomes do you expect from trying your fire drill?

   _____

   _____

2. *Come back to this question after you have tried using your fire drill.* What did you learn about yourself and this process from your attempt?

   _____

   _____

Responding After a Relapse

Just because you've been knocked down by a relapse into bottom-line behaviors doesn't mean you have to stay down. For addicts who are struggling to stay off the edge and avoid relapse, and for partners who are faced with a situation where someone else's behaviors have power to devastate you and your life, it is important to have a plan if relapse occurs. This is *not* permission to relapse. It is very scary to consider the consequences of relapse. Most people, including therapists, do not like to talk about what happens after relapse occurs. Family members often won't consider it, and addicts who are trying to stay in recovery want to believe it will not happen. The reality is that if you are not prepared for the possibility, the consequences of a relapse to yourself, your spouse and the relationship can be devastating.

The three types of relapses I identify are slips, slides and collapses. A slip is when you are caught off guard, use temporarily, but then immediately get back into recovery behaviors and start trying to figure out what happened and how to get back on solid ground. A slip may last two minutes or several hours, but you get right back up. A slide is when you don't get right back to recovery behaviors but continue using over several instances or days: "As long as I'm down here and already 'in trouble' with myself and/or my partner, I might as well get a two-for-one, three-for-one, or more." Often slides also occur because it is so difficult to get honest and deal with the pain it causes the partner and addict. The last is a collapse. Collapses are the most dangerous. You lie to yourself and others. You pose and hide. You pick up your 90-day chip at your 12-step meeting, and you know you are not 90 minutes sober. You stop trying. You know your responses are trauma-based or escape behaviors, but you don't care anymore.

If you have a good plan for responding should relapse occur, the hope is that you can keep the relapse to a slip—a temporary setback that you can recover from by being honest and getting back to working your program. You need to have a system in place that interrupts the relapse process and gets you pointed toward healing and recovery. Having bottom lines is the first step because it is immediately clear you have slipped into a relapse behavior.

While relapses into trauma responses are not relapses into addictive behaviors, it is still important to identify them and to stop them as soon as possible. As with addictive behaviors, developing a system that stops you from spiraling farther down and pulls you back towards recovery and peace leads to a temporary setback and not a return to the damaging behaviors. This is why we define bottom lines for trauma responses as well as for addictive behaviors.

Reflections - Exercise H

1. To whom will you report relapses, either trauma responses or addictive behaviors (e.g. accountability person, sponsor, spouse, therapist)?

_____

_____

2. What rules do you need to follow for reporting relapses into addictive behaviors (e.g. report within 24 hours, what details to disclose, etc.)? These rules are intended to help you know how to be honest so you can recover quickly (and not collapse) if you are the addict, and provide the safety to start rebuilding trust in your relationship.

_____

_____

The next thing I have both addicts and partners do is write a letter to themselves to read if they have relapsed into their bottom-line behaviors. It may take a few drafts, but in the end you know yourself better than anyone else, so you can create a letter that will speak most effectively to you when you have crossed your own bottom lines. You are writing this letter to take the burden of shame off your back and get yourself centered in ways that allow you to care for yourself and move forward gently.

One example of a letter an addict wrote is as follows:

> If you are reading this letter, it means you have had a relapse of some kind. Now, your first response when you relapse is usually to go straight to shame and self-loathing and your inclination is to give up and walk away completely from your recovery program. Instead, after reading this letter, I want you to walk away with hope and encouragement. Hope because you don't have to relapse any longer! What's done is done. Unfortunately, you cannot go back and change anything you have already done. Fortunately, you can change your choices for the future!
>
> So, if you haven't already, ask for God's forgiveness, forgive yourself, and strive to move on. You have come a long way… from being a full-blown sex addict who relapses every day, you have made enormous strides to being a more self-aware sex addict who still struggles occasionally with his sexual urges. This is a huge step! This means you can continue to improve over time and one day may put significant time between relapses.

One example from a partner is as follows:

> "Guess what – you're not perfect. That's OK. No one is. I know this sucks. You aren't a failure. You are trying your hardest. You are doing your best. You aren't a horrible wife or mother. Being able to admit to having made a mistake and doing what you can to fix it can be just as powerful a tool as learning to respond in healthy ways. This can be fixed. You aren't alone. You are loved."

In both cases, they then wrote some ways they had developed to recover so they would be able to remember and start working on getting to a better place, including skills to reach in and reach out, as we have discussed previously.

Kelly McGonigal, in her book *The Willpower Instinct* (2011), cites several studies which show that when someone relapses into undesired behaviors (e.g. alcohol, smoking, bottom-line behaviors), the most detrimental way to respond is by shaming yourself. She notes that most people believe that they need to be really hard on themselves when they make a significant mistake (like crossing bottom lines) or they are letting themselves off the hook; however, being gentle with oneself had better outcomes in the studies. In fact, one of the best predictors of relapsing again was how badly people felt about their behavior the previous night. In the end, those who are given permission to be human and make mistakes fare better than those who beat themselves up. This does not justify the behavior; it just allows energy to be put toward recovering rather than beating yourself up.

McGonigal calls it the "what-the-hell" cycle. "I've already messed up and I'm a failure. I might as well just enjoy it." I call it the control-release cycle. The first phase is control. Both partner and addict are white knuckling: (1) partners are trying not to react, to support the addict, not speaking up, etc., and (2) addicts are clinging to sobriety, super-well-behaved, perfectionistic, blaming, or rigid. At some point, the white-knuckling becomes unbearable and then a release occurs. Partners get angry, depressed, suicidal, and even act out addictively sometimes. Addicts release by acting out (sexually, eating, spending, etc.) or respond with their own trauma responses and get angry, depressed or even suicidal. For both addict and partner, releasing seems to mean you have failed, and you believe failing means you are not worthy of love/respect. In an attempt to recover, you pull yourself up "by the bootstraps" and give yourself some floggings, thinking that punishing yourself will somehow make it better. You then go back into the control phase. After continued efforts to control, then release, it begins to feel hopeless and easier to stay down. This can lead to a collapse.

I must clarify here that crossing your bottom lines will bring painful emotions. After crossing your bottom lines, feelings of guilt are appropriate because they signal a need for correction. Feelings of inadequacy signal a need for growth so that you can learn. Similarly, other feelings may exist that require attention. As we've discussed before, painful feelings can be useful in guiding us, but shame will always lead to self-loathing and feelings of worthlessness, hopelessness, etc. While those feelings of shame can be acknowledged, it is important to focus forward rather than backwards, which makes it easier to return to sobriety and recovery after relapsing.

Reflections - Exercise I

1. What are some things that you could include in your letter that would help you to get back up again and keep working if you had a relapse?

_____

_____

2. Take some time to write the first draft of a letter to yourself to include in your toolbox.

Relapse Autopsies and Amends

An autopsy, in short, is the process of going back to understand why the relapse (returning to a behavior you want to avoid, whether that is acting out in an addiction, a trauma response, or merely repeating a pattern you are trying to change) occurred and to develop and/or improve tools to help create and maintain a better long-term recovery. If your relapse hurt your spouse or someone else close to you, the final step of your autopsy should be making amends to them. This usually includes sharing insights and recovery plans related to the autopsy. Autopsies and amends are an essential component of recovering after a relapse and are discussed in more detail later in this chapter.

Prevention (The Tank)

While initially focusing on stopping the addictive behavior or the trauma response is critical, people often focus so much on stopping that they unintentionally eliminate key elements that make stopping possible. Here's the metaphor: imagine an enclosed tank, like a fish tank, that has at the top two sections: one tube where smoke can flow in and a spigot where water can flow in. (See the following diagram, The Tank.) If your goal is to reduce the volume of the smoke in the tank, what can you do? You simply add water, which would push the smoke up and reduce its volume. It would seem a little ridiculous to try to push the smoke up by some other force (pushing it, blowing it, etc.), because no matter how hard you worked, as soon as that effort stopped the smoke would immediately return to fill the tank.

While this might be obvious in physical science, in recovery we often try to "push the smoke out" with some other force, usually willpower. In good faith, we put all our energy into pushing out the addiction or trauma response (smoke). We struggle, huff and puff, exert all our energy, and experience success for a time. But eventually, we become exhausted, feel empty and are focused on what? The behaviors we are trying to avoid! So what is likely to happen when you are exhausted, empty, and thinking about those behaviors? Relapse. If you have nothing left in your tank, you will eventually fall back into your bottom lines. In order to stop this pattern, you need to put some efforts into more than just willpower and other relapse-prevention skills (i.e. fire drills). You have to focus some of your energy on filling your tank.

The Tank

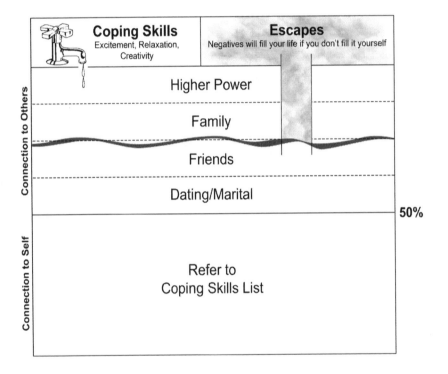

I need to clarify the difference between filling our tank and filling our time. When we fill our time, we ensure that we are busy doing something, anything, that will keep our unhealthy behaviors at bay. But filling our time does not necessarily fill us emotionally. It does not meet the core needs that drive those behaviors, so when our time is suddenly not filled, we are immediately empty. But when our tank is truly full, we can experience difficult times without feeling drained or completely empty. When we are less empty, we are both emotionally better off and have more energy to continue the difficult work of early recovery. Filling the tank also means finding activities that leave us with more energy than when we start them, not less.

The goal is to fill our tank so that we become fulfilled—filled as much as possible. That will take some time. Unlike filling our gas tank, we can't just pour a bunch in and have it last us for weeks at a time. It is true that some big things can carry us for a while. A good vacation, a few days away, or intensely positive experiences (a retreat, a strong spiritual experience, or even just a great day at the amusement park) can do much in terms of helping us feel more emotionally full. But if we are not focused on filling our tank day to day, those experiences will not carry us for long. The pressures from the outside world affect how full our tank is; and as we step back into the day-to-day stress, we need to have a daily focus on replenishing.

The Appendix has lists of ideas, both individual and relational, to fill your tank (Coping Skills List), along with an example of a personalized coping skills list (Coping List Examples). Also, to help make it easier to create a permanent list, electronic copies are available at DrMarkBird.com. Begin by building your own personalized lists, both individual and relational (marriage, family, friends, etc.). If you are married or in a committed relationship, start a marital/dating list. In the end, it is not important which type of relationship you begin with. Choose the one that seems most immediately relevant to you and begin building that relational list.

You will notice in the diagram of The Tank that only 50% of the tank can be filled on your own. Similarly, only 50% can be filled through relationships. It requires connection with yourself and others in a balanced way to create long-term recovery that will fill you enough to provide you with the necessary energy and fulfillment to continue the consistent work of recovery. Be careful not to ask your spouse to fill for you what you need to fill for yourself.

Reflections - Exercise J

1. Go through the list of individual tank fillers in the Appendix or download the list from DrMarkBird.com. Check off activities that you might connect with and use those to create a list of individual tank fillers.

2. Using the list of relational tank fillers, either in the Appendix or from the web site, create a list of relational tank fillers you are interested in using.

Eventually, as we consistently continue the effort, our tank can get full enough to be able to survive very difficult experiences that can rapidly drain the tank. Many clients who are in long-term recovery can experience several very difficult things (job loss, marital distress, death of a family member, etc.) and still manage to stay sober or avoid trauma responses, stay grounded, and stay happy because their tank is full enough to get through tough times without relapsing.

In early recovery, it is not uncommon for both addicts and partners to react code-pendently to each other. It is often difficult not to ignore your own needs as you try to let your spouse have whatever time they need to fill their own tank. Selfishness can also lead to overindulgence by either the addict or the partner, at the expense of the other. The goal in filling the tank is to ensure your tank *and* your spouse's tank are as full as possible, but not at the expense of the other.

Planning

Filling the tank requires fairly consistent, daily effort; however, consistency and structure are not strengths for most people, especially those in relationships where addictive tendencies are part of their pattern.

Take my wife and I, for example. When we first got married, I'd come home from work and this would be our typical conversation:

> Her: What do you want for dinner?
>
> Me: I don't know. What do you want for dinner?
>
> Her: I don't know…

You get the point. We would literally be stuck trying to decide what to eat for nearly 30 minutes. Eventually these discussions would end with us going out to dinner because it was late and we needed something quick. We ended up poorer and more overweight than we liked being, and we decided we needed a better plan.

New research has studied a concept they call decision fatigue (Baumeister, 2011). Essentially, decision fatigue occurs after extended periods of decision making, ultimately causing people not to be as capable of making decisions. In the day-to-day, by 5:00 pm most of us have already made so many decisions that our brain becomes fatigued. In that fatigued state, our brain is unable to make decisions well, even simple decisions like what to have for dinner!

To solve our dinner dilemma, every Sunday we would write down a meal plan. Each day we had something planned. Then as the week progressed we would come home and look at the calendar. The conversation would look like this:

Me: [seeing spaghetti is the meal we have planned] I don't want spaghetti for dinner.

Her: What do you want?

Me: [After trying to come up with some other options] I don't know.

Her: OK. I guess we're having spaghetti.

She would start to get the food out, and I would help her cook the meal. Then we would sit down and eat. In the end, the food tasted good and nourished our bodies. It was a healthier way to live. If I had thought of a better idea, we could have done that instead.

The same process is true for our emotional needs. We have to be willing to plan to meet our emotional needs and follow through on those plans! Shortly after this, my wife and I began planning time for ourselves individually and time for each other. It helped ensure we got some time to rejuvenate and nourish ourselves alone while still making sure that we felt connected and nourished in the relationship. We created a "menu" for the week that included the time and activity we thought might provide good emotional nourishment for our relationship each night. Several examples of planning are given later in this section.

After one particularly long day of work (8 am to 9 pm), I came home and sunk into the couch. At this time, we were on top of our planning and had scheduled to play Dance Dance Revolution (DDR), a video game that includes a dance pad with arrows to step on that guide your steps. It may sound like a silly activity, but I have found that a variety of activities helps life stay novel. In fact, one of the important draws of pornography and sexual acting out is the novelty it brings (multiple images, etc.). I find that as clients can create novel experiences regularly, it helps fill that gap, which has a positive impact on the level of acting out (lowers it).

Coming back to my story... on this night I felt totally exhausted, so I told my wife I didn't want to play DDR. She said, "What do you want to do instead?" I didn't have any other ideas. If I had come up with an alternative idea that seemed to fit better, we would have done that instead. But decision fatigue had set in already.

She was in a good enough place emotionally that she said, "I guess we're playing DDR, then." She got up, plugged in the control pads, and started the game. I reluctantly joined her. I dragged, and gradually began to fall behind in the game. I realized that if I did not start trying, I was going to lose. My competitive juices kicked in, and I started playing intently. The way I remember things is that I came back and won by a hair, although my wife's version of the story may be different. By the time those 15 minutes of DDR were done, we were laughing, smiling at each other and energized. What a great emotional outcome!

I have observed that there is often a "five-minute wall" that has to be worked through in order to fill your tank. This wall represents the energy and time it takes to engage in an activity long enough to quit feeling so drained that you don't want to do anything. I experience the five-minute wall for things I enjoy, as well as things I struggle to do. It takes emotional energy short term to fill the tank long term. For example, shortly after we married, my wife bought tickets to a concert by an artist named Collin Raye to celebrate my birthday. I love his music and had learned to play a lot of it on the guitar. The whole way to the concert I thought about how much money it cost; we were poor students. I worried about whether it would be fun. I felt tired. We got to the outdoor amphitheater and my emotions continued to disturb me. I suppose my "wall" was a little more than five minutes that day. As soon as the concert started, though, my mood immediately changed. It was an amazing concert, and it was such a small arena that it felt like front row seats. In order to begin to experience the joys of recovery, sometimes we have to walk through these five-minute walls.

Everyone needs excitement, relaxation, creativity, and connection in their lives. These four essential parts of healthy living are mimicked by addictive behaviors in the short term. Here are some examples for each:

1. Excitement (drugs like meth, cocaine, etc.)

2. Relaxation (drugs like alcohol, marijuana, opioids, benzodiazepines)

3. Creativity (LSD, PCP, peyote)

4. Connection (most drugs produce a false sense of connection with others)

While drugs usually only seem to fill one or two of these areas, sexual addiction can create a sensation that temporarily fills all four. That is part of what makes sexual addiction such a powerful addiction. When you are not able to meet these needs in healthy ways, you are at greater risk of relapse. Make sure you plan appropriately so that you can ensure some of each of these in your schedule. That will mean that some days you might ride bikes together (excitement), while other days you plan to watch the news, read together, or relax in other ways. Planning with these four categories in mind can help provide a buffer against the pull of the addiction.

I know that there are people who hate putting effort into planning and those who love planning. I like the results of planning, but really dislike the emotional energy it takes to do it. In my experience, many addicts are like me. Others love having a plan and even over-plan, often to the chagrin of their partners. Whichever of those categories you connect to, I suggest keeping it simple. I look at options for ways to connect with my wife, and I email her my thoughts (when we are doing planning well). She also brainstorms ideas for what we might do to connect in the upcoming week. Then we sit down on Sundays and schedule individual and couple times as well as the activity for couple time. On very busy days we don't have much time or energy for either. On other days we have more.

All I'm asking you to do is take five minutes a week to plan in that way: individual time daily and couple time plus the activity. As you plan, consider the activities that will fit best with your schedule. For most clients, that seems more manageable and less overwhelming. Below is one example of how that might look when you are done:

Monday	Tuesday	Wednesday	Thursday
Personal: 5 pm—gym	Personal: 8 pm—Read a Book	Personal: Walk & meditation during lunch	Personal: Personal Big Book study
Relational: 6 pm walk with Wife	Relational: 7 am Morning Men's group	Relational: 8 pm—Watch a movie with wife	Relational: Lunch date with John

There are many other ways to approach planning, and you will need to figure out what fits best for you. For example, I have a colleague, Laney Knowlton, who uses the "Rule of 5" in helping her clients to plan. The rule is this: you need at least five people in your support system, five things to fill your individual tank every week, and five things to fill your relational tank every week. She has found this to be a simple way for her clients to plan so that they ensure enough fulfillment and connection in their lives.

Here is an example of planning using the "Rule of 5" and incorporating all four areas:

Individual
Take a bubble bath
Go on a walk
Watch my TV show
Paint
Take a nap

Relational

Sing the kids to sleep

Date night – laser tag

Girls' night out

Mommy date with son

Weekly check-in with my husband

Finally, I have a few clients who have found that the best way for them to plan is to set a standard weekly routine for individual and relational time. For example, one client set aside Tuesday and Saturday nights as date nights with his wife. While they did not necessarily plan what to do, they always knew they would make time for each other on those nights. Other clients schedule routine gym times, time with friends or time with extended family. The consistency of the routine provides the plan that ensures personal and relational tank fillers each week.

Reflections – Exercise K

1. What are some things you can do to add healthy excitement to your life?

    _____

    _____

2. What are some things you can do to relax?

    _____

    _____

3. What are ways you can express yourself creatively?

    _____

    _____

I suggest that couples touch base every morning or night around their schedule for the upcoming day. If plans have to be changed, rearrange the schedule appropriately. The goal of planning is to provide enough structure to give opportunities to connect, fill your tank and provide a variety of good options that best seem to meet your needs. However, it is important not to let your schedule become your master. Be flexible enough to adapt when your needs or your circumstances change from day to day.

I would like to reiterate one last point before we move on. As we discussed in Chapter One, the opposite of addiction is not sobriety. It is connection: connection with self and connection with others. As we have discussed the tank, I hope you can see how applying these principles can provide you tools and skills to build a stronger connection with yourself in your time alone as well as in your relationship. As you engage in developing ways to fill your tank, you can begin to experience the greatest joy of recovery: a life of connection.

Reflections – Exercise L

1. What steps can you take to start planning more regularly, adding positive things to your life?

_____

_____

Morning Re-mind

The next preventative tool is called a Morning Re-mind. My goal here is not to discuss all the negative ways the brain is impacted due to addictive behaviors and trauma. It is sufficient to note that the brain, including memory, takes time to heal after the traumas and addictive behaviors have stopped. Literally, you could say you are "not in your right mind" early in recovery. Additionally, certain neural pathways, superhighways of nerves, are formed after long periods of repeated behavior. It takes time and practice to Re-mind yourself, forming different, more effective neural pathways. For these reasons, it is critical for people in recovery to consistently take time to Re-mind themselves, reconnecting their minds consistently to the sober way of thinking. Without these consistent reminders, it is easy to become forgetful and fall back quickly into old patterns and old ways of thinking.

If addictive or traumatized thinking is the superhighway, Re-minding is daily work to create a new path. It starts as a barely discernible dirt path through a forest. If you walk it every day, it will gradually grow into a solid dirt path. With time and effort, that pathway can expand to a street, then a two-way road and eventually a superhighway. If you can shut off the exits to the old superhighway (ways of thinking and reacting based on traumas or addictive patterns) while building the beginnings of the recovery super-highway, recovery behaviors will become more natural to you more quickly.

Even those not struggling with addiction or trauma can benefit from this type of Re-minding. Stephen Covey (Covey, Merrill, & Merrill, 1994) talked about the tendency to focus on urgent things, whether they are important or not. Such distractions often take us off course so far that we are unable to accomplish the important things, and ultimately lose sight of them altogether. For whatever reason we are deviating from our path, Re-minding puts our minds back on the new pathway we are trying to form in recovery. Below are some examples of categories that could be part of any Re-mind.

Who I Am

After being in active addiction or significantly affected by trauma, it is easy to lose sight of who you are. As addicts and partners are able to maintain recovery, you begin to get glimpses of your true self. It is important in these moments to write these "glimpses" down and stay connected to them. In the beginning it may just be a few words. Over time it may grow larger as your awareness grows. Here's an example of what someone might include:

> I am a loving, devoted, intelligent and competent person in many ways. I value honesty, authenticity, boundaries and courage. I am still working on making those areas of my life more in line with my values. I am a work in progress.

If you are working on figuring out who you are, there are many ways to begin that process. You can work on a mission statement, you can write your eulogy (giving you a vision of what you would like to have accomplished by the time your life ends) or you can merely write down some goals. One assignment my clients have found particularly useful is called the "hero" assignment. Start by dividing your sheet into two columns. In one column, write down your heroes. After the heroes, write down other people you admire. They can be real or fictional, current or historic. It could be your friend, Spider-Man, Jane Austen or George Washington. Once you have those written down, write the traits you admire in each character in the second column. A small example chart is included here.

Heroes	**Traits**
Superman	Strong, Confident, Capable, Ethical, Powerful
Jason Bourne	Skilled/Competent, Trained, Relentless, Strategic
Neo (Matrix)	Capable, Powerful, Agile (physically and emotionally)
George Washington	Dedicated, Perseverant, Honorable, Valiant
Anne of Green Gables	Quirky, imaginative, strong, funny, passionate, loyal
Joan of Arc	Passionate, leader by example, spiritual, strong
Eve (from the Bible)	Wise, strong, spiritual, kind
Jesus	Real, empathetic, not afraid, strong, human

Once you've finished, you have the beginning of a list of who you are. What we admire in others is part of who we are. For example, I admire Superman's strength, integrity and desire to do good. Whether I have fully incorporated those into my life, am still a work in progress or have not even started, the things I admire are part of who I am and part of who I want to become. I often have clients complete the assignment by dividing the traits they identify into two categories: who I am and who I wish to become. Once that list is created, they can use it to develop a statement or document detailing who they are and who they are working to become. Below are a few examples:

Example 1: I am… creative, nurturing to others, loyal, sometimes humorous, empathetic, compassionate, straightforward, truthful, good at writing, tenderhearted, and kind.

I desire to become… courageous, motivated, open-minded, a good friend, trustworthy, confident, balanced, proud but not egotistical, less sarcastic, a good verbal communicator and have more integrity (behaving and speaking according to my strengths and values).

Example 2: I am strong, real, passionate and empathetic. I am kind, but it is hard for me to let people in. I want to work to build trust in myself and to learn the tools to make connections with others in ways that are safe. Sometimes the passionate parts of me can be really intense, but I like those parts of me as they drive me to work towards things that are important to me. I am not perfect. I am human. I give everything I have to the things that I do. Sometimes that means I am running on empty. I want to work to have more balance in my life, so I will try to be more aware of my needs and take the steps to meet those needs in healthy ways.

Regardless of the format you use, the goal is to keep yourself connected to the good in you and the vision you have of who you wish to become.

Reflections – Exercise M

1. What are some words that describe who you really are (not who your addict or traumatized self is)?

_____

_____

2. Using a separate piece of paper, make a heroes list, including the traits that make those individuals heroes to you.

3. Create a second chart using the traits from your heroes list. Divide them up into "Who I am" and "Who I wish to become." Feel free to add additional traits if they occur to you.

4. Using your heroes list and the chart of traits, create a statement about who you are and who you are working to become.

Affirmations

In the Soothing section in Chapter Two we discussed affirmations in detail. I urge clients to incorporate two to three truths about themselves and their current growth in recovery by including them in their Re-mind. Additionally, the statement about yourself that you created in Exercise M can help you as you figure out what affirmations would be most helpful for you. As a reminder, I urge clients to repeat or write these affirmations ten times, three times a day to help them become permanent.

Reflections – Exercise N

1. What are some things you struggle to believe about yourself?

_____

_____

2. Create an affirmation for at least two of the doubts listed above.

_____

_____

The Trauma and Addiction Cycles

So much is happening in early recovery that it is often difficult for both partner and addict to remember the basics of how to care for themselves when triggered. Additionally, both the trauma and addiction cycles are so unconscious that it is difficult to intervene successfully with them until they become more conscious. In early recovery it is very helpful to remind yourself about your trauma or addiction cycles so that you are more aware of the choices you are making and where they will lead. This gets your prefrontal cortex more involved, which allows you to track consequences and make better long-term choices. Your Re-mind about your cycle might also include your fire drill plans and/or how to recover quickly if you cross your bottom lines. Keep in mind that addicts have trauma cycles as well as addiction cycles that they get stuck in, and partners may have addiction cycles as well as trauma cycles. If you struggle with a codependent cycle, rage cycle or other addiction cycles, those could be included in this section as well. Each cycle you identify gives you more tools to understand yourself and your needs and therefore have those needs met. If you are unclear or confused about your cycle(s), refer back to the work you did in Chapter Three.

Here's an example of a Trauma Cycle in a Re-mind:

I might get triggered into a trauma response today by [be specific here, typically it is certain people, places, or things] today. My normal response when I get triggered is to [control my husband, get angry, withdraw, etc.]. I know those responses can provide me some *temporary* feelings of [power, security, safety, etc.]. In the end though, I end up feeling [exhausted, powerless, inadequate, unacceptable and unloved, distant from those I care about, guilty, etc.]. Then I push others away, including God, and find myself incredibly alone. *It never gives me the things I need in the long term.* When I get triggered, I can use my fire drill, time-out, pull back temporarily, soothe and connect with people I love and trust. I will come back and work through it and create safety for myself.

Here's an example of an Addiction Cycle in a Re-mind:

I might get triggered to act out (get angry, fearful, etc.) today. I may lose track of what I'm feeling for long enough that it will build up and feel unmanageable. I know at those times that escapes can bring *temporary* relief, a high, a sense of power (almost superman-like at times), and a sense of acceptance. If I act out in my addiction, I always end up feeling exactly the opposite in the long term: stressed, powerless, inadequate, unacceptable and unloved, distant from those I care about, and guilty. Then I push others away, including God, and find myself incredibly alone. *It's just not worth it!!!* I've gotten through those times before. I can keep doing so, and I want to!

Why Am I Working So Hard to Recover?

In addition to Re-minding yourself not to go into the Trauma or Addiction Cycle, it can be helpful to remind yourself of the things you are working hard for (the 12-step promises, peace, connection, etc.). This can help you focus on the positive things as well as stopping the cycle of addiction.

Here's an example for the addiction cycle:

Life without acting out brings peace of conscience, love of myself, connection with others, growth and self-acceptance for being able to learn and grow. What wonderful gifts!

Here's an example for the trauma cycle:

Trauma responses give me temporary relief, but I've learned better ways to care for myself and begin to truly heal. I know I can continue to discover the true me and value me. I want a life of connection with others I love. I know I can learn and grow, creating connection and safety in my life with those who are willing to work alongside me.

Reflections – Exercise O

1. Write the section your Re-mind for your cycle(s) (either addiction cycle, trauma cycle, or both).

_____

_____

_____

_____

2. What are your reasons for working towards recovery?

_____

_____

_____

Spiritually Centering Practices

It is easy to forget the spiritual practices that keep you grounded in recovery: meetings, daily rituals (Re-mind, and two other rituals that I will review shortly—nightly rewind and VSE's), gratitude, prayer, meditation, study, etc. The morning Re-mind can help keep you focused on keeping all these practices active in your life.

Here's an example (this one contains a few more ideas than one Re-mind should focus on, but I wanted to model how various ideas might be applied):

I have to do some things every day to remind myself how to stay on course:

1. Review my plan for the day

   2.   VSE: Check in with myself emotionally 3-5 times a day.

   3.   Nightly Ritual.

While each day brings new challenges and problems, I need to do at least the following:

   1.   Study scripture and/or recovery material and take time to meditate/ponder.

   2.   Pray individually morning, noon and night (and have a prayer in my heart).

   3.   Right now—write down at least five things I am grateful for.

   4.   Right now—write down at least five things I love about myself, my wife, and my kids.

Reflections – Exercise P

   1.   What are your current spiritual practices (or the ones you would like to start) that can help you stay more connected and centered in your life?

_____

_____

_____

_____

Current Work

    Doing recovery work can feel like drinking out of a fire hose. There is so much information and it all seems relevant. However, along the way there are elements that are more important at certain times than others. I urge you to determine the most important parts for you right now and focus on just those as a core part of your Re-mind until that work becomes more natural. Then you can choose the next right step and focus on it. Being out of focus and doing a lot of everything can make it difficult to make or see any progress. The most you should probably have in this category at one time is two to three ideas.

    Here is an example of someone's work focused on shame reduction:

I tend to feel a lot of shame, which freezes me and puts me in my cycle of addiction. I need to turn that back into guilt, which teaches me that I've done something wrong (I have values that I contradicted by my behavior), not that I am a bad person. I just need to figure out what I've done and correct it. If I can't figure it out, I need to reach out to God, a sponsor, therapist, friend or my wife and try to sort through it and find solutions with their help. When I do that, the guilt will go away and I will feel better about me.

Reflections – Exercise Q

1. Write down your list of things you need to work on. (This may be overwhelming to write down, but once you do, you can pick two to three to focus on at a time and be able to work your way through the list.)

    _____

    _____

    _____

    _____

2. Pick one to three items from the above list to focus on right now. What work do you need to do on those items?

    _____

    _____

The morning Re-mind is a living document: it is only going to remain useful if you keep altering it and updating it. An affirmation eventually becomes part of who you are. A "current work" eventually stops being the current thing and is replaced by something else. Certain things that are very difficult to do in early recovery eventually become easier, requiring less focus, and will need to be replaced by the next right steps. I recommend a revision every 2-4 weeks to keep it alive enough that it makes a difference. You will notice that if you don't revise it, you will eventually stop doing it (usually sooner rather than later). For more perspective on this concept, consider reading pages 86 and 87 of the AA Big Book (2001).

As you've read some of these ideas, it is likely that you connected with one or more of the concepts or had some ideas of your own. Exercise R will help you combine them into your first Morning Re-mind, and you can start using it immediately. Put your Re-mind where you will see it several times a day, like your bathroom mirror, your desk, your car, the background on your phone, etc. That makes it easier to remember to do your Re-mind daily.

Reflections – Exercise R –
Creating Your First Morning Re-mind
(See Exercises M-Q)

1. Who are you and who are you working to become?

    _____

    _____

2. What affirmation do you most need to use right now?

    _____

    _____

3. What do you lose by acting out, or reacting into your trauma response, and what do you gain when you don't act in those ways?

    _____

    _____

4. What daily activities will you use to keep your focus on recovery?

    _____

    _____

5. What two to three issues (see Exercise Q) are you going to focus on working on right now?

_____

_____

As a reminder, these are the categories that might be included in a Re-mind.

1. Who I am (what I value about me and what I wish to become)

2. Affirmations

3. The Cycle of Trauma and Cycle of Addiction

4. Why stay sober? (List of good things you have or the promises you are working toward.)

5. Spiritual practices (Meditation, readings, scripture, planning, etc.).

6. Current Work

I have included an example of a Morning Re-mind in the Appendix. It reflects aspects that apply to both addicts and partners in early recovery. Hopefully the example provides a sense of how a final Re-mind might look. The example is longer than most Re-minds would be (they should never be longer than one page) because I am trying to model each aspect we reviewed. You do not need to have all categories in your Re-mind, although it is good to revisit the categories occasionally to make sure you are including those that are most important at this time. Remember that over time the Re-mind will be adapted as you progress in your recovery.

VSE's

As I worked with a client about finding time to check in with himself during the day, he commented, "I guess I'm kind of like a leper in that way." To be honest, I didn't really see the connection. First, he noted that lepers are outcasts, and he felt so much shame that he always felt less than and separate from others the way lepers do. He explained to me that there is a book series called *The Chronicles of Thomas Covenant* by Stephen R. Donaldson. The hero is a leper. Apparently, lepers lose feeling in their extremities (hands and feet). Gradually, they get small, unnoticed wounds that become infected, fester and eventually lead to parts of their body falling off. The hero in the book stops every once in a while to look at his hands and feet to make sure there are no wounds that need to be cared for. He calls those checks <u>V</u>isual <u>S</u>urveillance of the <u>E</u>xtremities (VSE's). My client explained that, like the leper, he had lost the ability to feel in his life, and part of ensuring that he stayed connected in a way that he could care for himself was VSE's. As I considered the correlation, I have changed the meaning of the acronym to <u>V</u>isceral <u>S</u>urveillance of your <u>E</u>motions, or gut check.

Partners often report a similar experience, but for different reasons. The intense pain of relational betrayal is difficult to manage. Most partners go numb for a time as a way of avoiding and distracting from the intense pain (the emotional equivalent of going into shock). Unfortunately, this also numbs emotional cues for self-care. Additionally, they feel like they cannot reach out to others about their struggles and feel excluded from society. Because of this, it is also vital that partners engage in practicing VSE's as a means of improving their connection with themselves, their feelings and their ability to care for themselves.

A religious leader named Gordon B. Hinckley, who worked for a railroad company, shared the story of a baggage train intended for New Jersey that ended up in New Orleans, 1500 miles from its destination. Upon investigation, it was discovered that the train had started out in the right direction, but a switchman in St. Louis had moved a switch point three inches. While that changed the direction minimally initially, that carelessness led to a severe discrepancy. He noted the similarity to our lives. We get pulled in many directions and can gradually lose the sense of our desired destination, eventually finding ourselves desperately off course. While the morning Re-mind starts your day off in the right direction, it is easy to hit switch points without even knowing. VSE's provide the opportunity to check our direction and make corrections before it is too late.

I generally suggest that VSE's happen at least three times a day, and it is often easiest to do them at routine times: at meals, when you go to the restroom, during drive time, etc. Some clients have alarms set on their phones, watches, or computers to remind them to do VSE's. It only takes one minute of your time. While each person is different, a VSE can include questions like the following:

- How am I feeling physically?
- What am I feeling emotionally?
- Am I still connected with myself and my purposes today?
- Am I on course? Do I need to make any course corrections?

Reflections – Exercise S

1. What times each day will you perform VSE's (at least three different times)?

_____

_____

_____

_____

Nightly Rewind

Except on very rare days, we don't usually reach our intended destinations perfectly. Nightly Rewinds help to get your bearings at the end of the day. They should take no longer than five minutes to do and include the following questions: (1) What went well during the day? (2) What problems showed up and how did I manage them? and (3) What one to two things can I do differently based on what I've learned from today?

Nightly Rewinds are very much like Step Ten of 12-step programs, which says, "Continued to take personal inventory and when we were wrong promptly admitted it" (Alcoholics Anonymous, 2001). A Rewind allows you to celebrate the positive that happened as well as correct your mistakes from the day and get back on course. A focus on improvement one day at a time brings growth and perspective that will ultimately provide you with greater confidence and security in yourself and in your recovery. A Nightly Rewind's format will change over time. After we've discussed triggers and warning signs in the next section, I will provide an example of a Rewind for someone in early recovery.

The Middle

While it is nice to live in the green zone (preventative), it is rare that any of us spend much time there. Life is full of struggles and challenges, and we have to work daily to stay in the best place possible. Any shift down the Recovery Hill is called a lapse: a temporary decline or deviation from a healthy program of self-care. I had a client who spent three group sessions trying to come up with a name for the line that demarcates the beginning of a lapse (crossover from green to yellow). We decided that line was like the shoreline at the beach; you can stand where there is no water and the shoreline can gradually shift to where the water rises to become ankle deep. Similarly, life can shift on you, and by no fault of your own you can find yourself in a place where you need to make some adjustments to get to a healthier place.

Drifting Toward the Whirlpool of Addiction

Continuing with the beach metaphor, addictive behaviors or trauma responses can be like a whirlpool. When you are standing on dry land and having a good time (prevention), you are safe and can make good, grounded decisions. As you either consciously or unconsciously (i.e. the shoreline shifts) move into the water, you become more susceptible to the waves (the middle of the Recovery Hill) that will pull you toward the whirlpool (the bottom of the Recovery Hill). You will find the water enjoyable, though riskier than land. People are having fun there, and it is easy not to notice the gradual drift away from where you started. If you don't pay attention to what is going on around you, you will find yourself closer and closer to the whirlpool.

At the edge of a whirlpool, the water becomes warmer, which gives you a sense of comfort and/or false security. In a similar way, as you reach the point of no return there is a sense that those behaviors will meet your needs, even though in the long run they will not. Suddenly, the whirlpool rips you out of that comfort and into a crazy tailspin. You quickly become powerless against the whirlpool's grasp, and all you can really do is swim like mad and hope you can somehow make it out (fire drills). If you are only doing fire drills and not using the tools higher up on the Recovery Hill, you will run out of energy and succumb to the seductive pull of the behavior, only returning to recovery when you hit rock bottom.

The rituals and patterns associated with addiction or trauma responses and diminished self-care are so unconscious that you may not even recognize your descent down the Recovery Hill, which generally is a gradual accumulation of seemingly unimportant decisions that leave you vulnerable to relapsing into bottom-line behaviors. It is the lack of awareness and disconnect from yourself that leaves you at risk, so part of long-term recovery is to increase your awareness and watchfulness, which is what Re-minds, VSE's, and Rewinds can help you do.

In the middle (yellow) zone, I like to think of awareness like the cockpit of an airplane. There are many gauges, and trying to understand everything at once is impossible. However, if you focus in on a few of the more important gauges and begin to understand when those gauges start to indicate movement away from healthy recovery, you can become expert in responding effectively to those. In most cases, flying without knowing what gauges to look at or what they mean can be deadly. When things get crazy, you can get vertigo, not knowing up from down. Being disoriented makes it impossible to self-correct unless you understand and trust your instruments.

In recovery, I call these gauges warning signs (see the Recovery Hill diagram above, which I have included again for ease of reference). There are two specific categories of warning signs: indicators and triggers. Indicators are alerts that you may be drifting down the hill; they signal the need for corrections in self-care. Triggers are events or situations that make you want to use; they generally occur further down the Recovery Hill.

If you think of your unhealthy behaviors (acting out or trauma responses) as being at the bottom of a ski slope, indicators would be the trees, rocks, or other physical features that you pass as you ski down the hill. If you are familiar with the mountain, you can tell where you are on it by the physical features you can see. The same is true in recovery. The more familiar you are with your individual Recovery Hill, the better you will be able to tell when you get closer and closer to the bottom and lapse into the behaviors you are trying to avoid. For example, maybe you usually shower every day and you haven't showered in two days. Or perhaps you usually eat very healthy foods, but this week you have eaten fast food three days in a row. These are not relapses; they are alerts that signal a need to look at what you are struggling with so it does not become more overwhelming.

Triggers are directly tied to the desire to relapse and move you toward relapse more quickly. These might be certain words or phrases, or maybe a scene in a commercial or movie. It might be that when you are feeling lonely or disconnected or inadequate or bored, those emotions are so difficult for you that you instantly feel the need to react and do something so you don't feel them.

As you can see on the Recovery Hill diagram, there are seven categories of warning signs. The first thing that you will experience as you drift down the Recovery Hill is some type of painful emotion. For example, if you feel powerless, lonely, etc. it can alert you to the need for self-care. However, because most people in early recovery have lost connection with their feelings and are often experiencing so many different emotions simultaneously (which causes unmanageability), a shift in emotion can go unperceived. The other six categories occur not long after emotions; they can provide additional ways to become alerted to your need for self-care. These other categories include thoughts; behaviors; physical; people, places, and things; relational; and spiritual.

One client recognized that when he broke out in acne, it was a physical warning sign that he was too stressed out, which alerted him to make some adjustments in his self-care. One couple recognized that being short and snippy with each other was a relational warning sign. In neither case was there a desire to cross bottom lines, but the warning signs made them aware that they were slipping into a place where self-reflection and adjustments were needed. Lists of potential warning signs arranged in order by category for both addicts and partners are included in the Appendix to help you with your Nightly Rewind. Hopefully this will help you in creating your own awareness of your indicators and triggers. I suggest that you personalize it; write the list in words you can relate to, and add any ideas that you come up with as you review the list. An electronic copy can be obtained at DrMarkBird.com. Using the electronic copy may make it easier to create the list. Over time, you will discover other warning signs and triggers, so make sure you continue to add to the list as you go.

As you become aware of your warning signs, you will begin to see that this awareness can turn your weaknesses into strengths: every time you feel a desire to go toward your addiction, you know that something is not right in your life. Recognizing warning signs gives you the power to take better care of yourself and your needs. A therapist from one of my studies noted that it is easy for addicts and partners to fall into shame when they notice warnings signs, but that reaction can gradually change:

Instead of saying to themselves, "I'm so awful," they say "Oh, something's not right. What can I do?" It is empowering. That thought can engage their emotions, which then engages a choice to make a different behavior happen: you've just engaged the three most important parts of change (thoughts, feelings, and behavior). So where you didn't have power to change, now you have three different components that are linked together.

In early recovery, I suggest that this initial list of warning signs (both indicators and triggers) be used as your Nightly Rewind. Review it nightly, checking the things you saw occur and noting how you managed them. Celebrate the ways you succeeded. Then review the things that seem most important, and determine one to two small things you can learn to improve your recovery tomorrow.

Example of a Nightly Rewind

1. What went well during the day?

    Today I recognized when I was triggered and stopped myself, and processed before responding to the situation. I did all three of my VSE's.

2. What problems showed up and how did I manage them?

    I got irritated and snapped at my kids when putting them to bed, but I realized what I was doing, apologized to them, and told them I loved them. I was triggered into my shame spiral during a conversation with a coworker and didn't stop to figure out why until afterwards.

3. What one to two things can I do differently based on what I've learned from today?

    I need to do more work around identifying when my shame spiral starts and figuring out ways to possibly halt the situation and figure out how to address it in the moment if possible.

Reflections – Exercise T

1. What are some of your indicators?

    _____

    _____

2. What are some of your triggers?

    _____

    _____

    _____

3. Using the example above as a guideline, write a Nightly Rewind for yourself using the events of either yesterday or today. (You may want to do this electronically if possible, for two reasons: to make it easier to reference and less likely to get lost, and to make it easier to edit as it evolves.)

    _____

    _____

    _____

    _____

Autopsy

I have to admit that autopsy is a pretty morbid word. Outside of cadavers, though, it just means an analysis of something after the fact. It comes from the Greek word meaning seeing with one's own eyes. I had a client suggest that the "auto" means self and "psy" means to know, so autopsy means coming to know yourself better. While that is not the exact origin of the word, I like that definition. Combining all these ideas together, my definition for an autopsy in addiction and trauma recovery is assessing and analyzing your behavior so you can see and know yourself more truly, including how to care better for yourself.

A good autopsy promotes a learning and growth perspective, and is a process that can be useful after an indicator, trigger, or relapse behavior. Early recovery tends to focus around triggers and relapse behaviors. Note the following Autopsies diagram. In early recovery, there are still a lot of holes in your awareness at all levels (indicated in the diagram by the dashes). That's why addiction or trauma response relapses seem to happen "all of a sudden." It doesn't take much early on for the relapse behavior to slip through the holes (indicated by the downward arrow on the far right of the diagram). With each autopsy, you begin to fill in those holes with new awareness, making it easier to intervene and avert more serious problems (indicated by the solid lines). If you can take the lessons learned from a specific event and apply it more generally to your recovery, one autopsy can be used to fill in multiple gaps (instead of just one hole at a time). With increased time in recovery, you will gradually be able to fill in your gaps in awareness around triggers and indicators as well (indicated by the downward arrows that are blocked by solid lines).

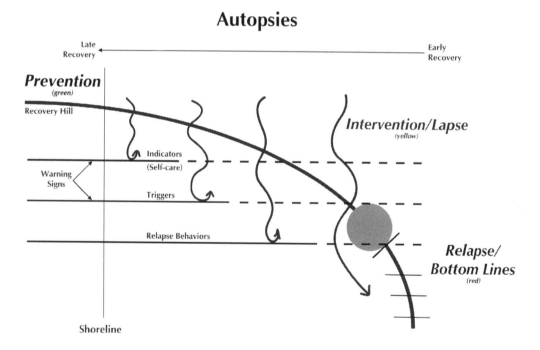

Typically, I suggest that clients begin autopsies by looking at what was happening ten minutes before the event, then move gradually backward in time: several hours earlier, then 12 hours, 24 hours and 48 hours. You can also look at the week in general, trying to identify the factors that might have led up to the indicator, trigger, or relapse you are processing. I find that it is easier to identify more factors when you use the warning signs list that you have already created (from the previous section). It is also beneficial to reach out to safe people to talk about things: sponsor, therapist, group, or spouse. In early recovery, talking about autopsies with a spouse may require support by a third party to help manage the spouse's triggers, so initially I suggest only talking with your spouse after processing with others. Including other people in your autopsy can help provide additional perspectives that can add to your learning. For most of my clients, having support the first time they do an autopsy is critical to understanding how to process it well.

As you complete your autopsy, you should answer two important questions: (1) What did I learn? and (2) What will I do differently? These two questions provide the necessary material to fill the gaps that leave you vulnerable in your recovery. Continued learning about yourself through autopsies will also add new information to your list of warning signs.

I had a client who had been sober for almost a year and felt things were going much better in his life. Then one day he walked into a convenience store and was triggered immediately by someone he could "just tell" was a prostitute. He somehow managed to get out the door and to safety. He came to group that night and was confused about how he had gotten so close to relapse. During the group, we helped him to do an autopsy. He eventually shared with us that during the week his dog had died, he was struggling with job issues, and his wife had entered residential treatment. He was able to recognize the weight he carried (of which he wasn't previously aware), have greater self-compassion, and find ways to better care for himself. His anxiety about the strong trigger decreased (fear and anxiety stem from being unable to protect yourself from something, and his autopsy gave him greater ability to stop that trigger from affecting him that way again), and he was able to maintain sobriety.

In this case, he autopsied a strong trigger. With time, you can go from the autopsy of relapsing into bottom-line behaviors to the autopsy of triggers to the autopsy of indicators (as shown in the Autopsies diagram). As you increase your self-awareness through this process, you will be able to stay further up the hill and manage a lifelong healthy recovery. The Appendix includes an Autopsy Worksheet to help you identify and work through the important elements of a relapse, trigger, or indicator autopsy.

Reflections – Exercise U

1. Name the people who are safe for you to talk to as you autopsy bottom-line behaviors, triggers, or indicators.

_____

_____

_____

_____

Amends

Once your autopsy is complete, if you have hurt your spouse or someone else close to you through the behavior you autopsied, the next step is to work on making amends for your relapse into addictive behaviors or a damaging trauma response. Often after completing an autopsy, clients will, with good intention, move into sharing their autopsy with their spouse without considering how their spouse was affected by their behavior. Completing an autopsy can feel very empowering and freeing. It can take a situation that has felt hopeless and inevitable for years and give you realizations and tools that allow you to step out of those patterns. It makes sense to want to share the hope and peace that comes from that process—to share all the details of what you've learned, how you can improve, and your hope for the future—but in the excitement of wanting to share, it is easy to forget that your spouse is still experiencing pain. All that information from the autopsy will sound more like excuses until their pain has been acknowledged. The Appendix includes an Amends Worksheet that, if followed, significantly increases the chances that the couple recovery from a relapse (or even from triggers or indicators) will be a connecting process.

Reflections – Exercise V

1. What are some struggles you may have with presenting an amends to your spouse or someone you care about? (e.g. "I'm afraid the information I share may be used as ammunition against me in the future," or, "Every conversation we've had about this topic has turned into a fight and I'm scared that bringing it up will make it worse.")

_____

_____

_____

_____

2. Process through these fears and concerns with your individual therapist.

Wrap-Up

There is a lot to accomplish in establishing the tools of the Recovery Hill. I urge you to dedicate the necessary "start-up" work to get each tool preliminarily in place. Once you have the initial documents, it just requires consistently revisiting the tools, using them regularly, and recovering by accessing the tools you have stopped using. As you create your tools, add them to your Tool Box: a folder (physical or on your computer or phone), binder, or document container where you can put all your tools together in one place. You will use and reuse these tools throughout your recovery, so getting them established early is very important.

As a reminder, the tools from this chapter included the following:

- Filling the tank
  - Planning
- Morning Re-mind
- VSE's (check-ins)
- Nightly Rewind
- List of warning signs: indicators and triggers
- Fire drills
- List of bottom-line behaviors

- Recovery-oriented letter to self if you cross your bottom lines
- Autopsy Worksheet
- Amends Worksheet

Recognize that these tools are only part of the process, and they work in conjunction with the other things you will learn later. There is no silver bullet, but creating and combining these tools will provide a great foundation for long-term recovery.

Everyone has holes in their recovery (some big, some small). Your work is to remain consistently watchful, never getting overconfident or believing that it would be impossible for you to be overcome by your addiction. You must realize it is not impossible for you to be pulled back into your trauma triggers or the painful chaos that comes when you are not caring for yourself and are not connected with others. Keep your tools close, remain watchful and humble, and stay connected to your support systems to keep your recovery solid.

Chapter 5

EARLY COUPLE RECOVERY

A Road Map for Creating Safety

So far in this book I have reviewed what connection is, the concept of addiction as a symptom of a connective disorder, the role of emotions in recovery, some tools for managing more intense emotions (time-outs and soothing), the cycles of trauma and addiction, and the different aspects of the Recovery Hill for individual recovery. These concepts and tools can help you to better manage the intense pain and reactivity often associated with early recovery. The final step in this book is to take the individual recovery tools you have developed and create tools and processes for couple recovery.

If you are not in a primary relationship, these skills are still critical for helping you get the support you need from the relationships around you, including planning connection with others, working on your own inventory (Step Four; Alcoholics Anonymous, 2001) and amends process with others, managing triggers with others, and establishing safe accountability people in your life. I would urge you to read this chapter through the lens of establishing healthy relational patterns, even if it is not directly related to a specific primary relationship.

Creating Safety

In the early stage of recovery, because trust has been betrayed, much of the motivation for change for both addict and partner is provided by fear and loss of control or powerlessness. Much of early recovery is about creating safety and stability. Safety in early recovery includes several different aspects: building positive experiences; developing a safe, supportive environment; developing the ability to recognize and soothe intense emotion; full formal disclosure/amends (at least beginning the process); managing triggers (yours and your partner's); creating and maintaining boundaries; and establishing accountability.

Creating Positive Experiences

Due to shame or fear, couples who are struggling to recover from sexual addiction often isolate themselves and focus on controlling the addictive behaviors at the expense of other positive activities. While it is essential to establish crisis management activities that focus on stopping the addictive behaviors, creating (or re-creating) positive individual and relational outlets is also important during early recovery. This idea was previously discussed as part of the Recovery Hill chapter in the section on filling the tank. Generally, though, filling the tank means finding things that bring positive feelings into your lives, individually and as a couple, writing them down, and creating time for them in your lives. This can be difficult in early recovery when trust is low, so you may need to have support in learning how to take appropriate steps to build these positive things into your life individually and as a couple. In my experience, positive individual and relational experiences provide additional stability, increased confidence, positive feelings, and more support for helping the couple move forward in their couple recovery work. As I reviewed in the Recovery Hill, planning as a couple is a particularly important piece of this process as well. If you have not begun to plan or if you have stopped using that tool, review that section in Chapter Four and insert it into your couple recovery.

Getting Connected

Group, Individual, and Couple Therapy

The work required in early recovery to make changes can be difficult and overwhelming at times (Step One of the 12-step program refers to the unmanageability of early recovery; Alcoholics Anonymous, 2001). Because early recovery is such a crisis-oriented time, probably the most important thing to have or put in place is a support system. There is so much shame associated with sex addiction, and both partner and addict can feel isolated and fearful. Coming out of hiding to find support is crucial to long-term success, individually and as a couple. In my dissertation research (Bird, 2009), the overwhelming majority of therapists suggested that each addict and partner participate in group, individual, and couple therapy wherever possible. While each person's recovery is unique, having various forms of therapeutic support for processing and learning provides several benefits.

In early recovery, with so many wounds and struggles, it is often difficult to be honest and vulnerable in front of your spouse, for both addict and partner. A combination of individual and group therapy can be useful in helping addicts and partners sort through their struggles in a less emotionally reactive context, be able to share more honestly, and build a foundation of support to help facilitate recovery. The saying, "You can lead a horse to water but you can't make it drink," applies well here. I have been able to lead many clients toward greater honesty in couple therapy, but in early recovery I cannot get them to drink fully of the opportunities to be honest when their spouse is present. It is just too scary. I can consistently get more honesty from both partners and addicts in an individual or group setting. Gradually and with support, they are able to be more honest about everything with their spouse, including their feelings.

Let me be clear: honesty with your spouse is critical. In early recovery, it is difficult for both addicts and partners to feel grounded and safe enough to share your own realities and feelings. The goal of the skills discussed so far in this book is to help each of you to more quickly understand yourself, as well as to face your fears and be courageous in expressing your feelings and truths appropriately, effectively, and honestly to yourself and your spouse.

Individual therapy with a skilled therapist provides a very private environment to process thoughts, feelings, and pieces of a person's history that are rarely talked about. In individual therapy you can focus on exploring your past and present without judgment from others. Many people have expressed ideas and told secrets in individual therapy that they never imagined they would say out loud, and it gave them the ability to finally face their deepest fears and conquer them.

Group therapy provides an environment where you can explore and share with others who struggle with similar issues. As you listen to others' experiences, often insights will be uncovered that would not be available in an individual or couple therapy setting. Additionally, you can see people who are at different places in their process of recovery, which can help you see your progress. Seeing others in the group who may be further along in some ways and experiencing successes you long to achieve can also bring you hope for the future. Because sex addiction is considered a connective disorder, it is very helpful to have an environment where you can take risks and reach out for connection in ways you normally would not be able to. Almost every one of my clients reports that being in a group setting helps them feel less ashamed, less lonely, and more hopeful.

While individual and group therapy are useful and essential elements for recovery support, couple therapy can provide opportunities to change couple patterns in a way that lowers emotional reactivity. Being able to create mutual understanding and accountability around these healthier patterns is critical in helping individual recovery changes solidify more quickly, which in turn helps your relationship to improve. Unfortunately, most of the literature on sex addiction focuses very little on couple work, and the majority of therapists do very little couple work in the beginning of the recovery process, at the expense of both individual and relationship recovery. I believe that consistent couple therapy (even if it is monthly) is critical because it prevents couples from establishing a firm foundation of individual recovery that is disconnected from each other. This early disconnection can eventually lead to a very shaky and difficult shift when the couple is finally brought together in therapy. Even in early recovery, connection is critical to the process.

I cannot count the number of times I've heard addicts say, "My recovery is good. I've been sober for a year or more. Clearly this is my partner's issue." But sex addiction is a connective disorder, and sobriety is most difficult to maintain when people try to get closer. So if therapy is consistently helping clients create and maintain connection (safety and closeness) from the beginning, it is easier *in the long run* to integrate both partners' individual recoveries and establish connection.

Finally, if the addict is unable to stop the addictive behavior, or if the partner is unable to find ways to manage his or her trauma successfully, they may need a higher level of care. This can include intensive, one- to two-week programs; Intensive Outpatient Programs (IOP); or residential treatment. These more intense and structured environments can provide the necessary stability to move forward quickly and establish a baseline of sobriety. Without the weight of the stressors of your normal lives, you are able to focus on healing and developing emotional strength in ways you are not able to normally. You can gain confidence that additional changes can be made. I compare it to leaving earth to live in space for a physical therapy program: the gravity is less intense, and movement (emotionally) is easier. When clients return to earth from treatment, the gravity of their situation returns (note the double meaning of gravity here) and can make for a very difficult transition. Care should be taken to ensure that the same support systems we have discussed here are in place as quickly as possible as clients transition back into outpatient recovery.

Reflections – Exercise A

1. Which types of therapy are currently part of your recovery program? What do you feel you have gained from those?

_____

_____

2. What additional tools might be helpful to add to your program? What fears do you have about adding them?

_____

_____

You, Me, We

When a couple comes into therapy, I am as clear as possible with them that, as long as they are considering staying together, the couple is the "identified patient." In the words of one of the therapists in my research (Bird, 2009), "Both of you have needs. You've both been through the wringer with this." If I only focus on the addict, the partner is left alone in his or her trauma. If I only focus on the partner, then the addict will continue to flounder and act out. Many articles, books, and therapists still see sex addiction and partner recovery as an "individual" issue. However, if approached only individually, it is easy to lose sight of the important relational processes that are intricately intertwined with individual change processes. In addition, if couple issues are not addressed, painful patterns will continue to re-create pain and trauma. So we have to work on all those areas. I call it a "You, Me, We" approach to treatment.

Individual work creates change that can influence both group and couple work. Group work influences individual and couple work, and couple work can bring about significant changes to individual and group work. Without the influences of each on the other, many individuals and couples get very stuck (and experience longer and more intense pain and struggle).

Addressing all three aspects allows you to develop a commitment to individual recovery in the context of a hopeful relationship. You are working on relationship issues while you are working on individual recovery. But a significant part of early recovery is ensuring that individual recovery work is the primary focus. One therapist in my research (Bird, 2009) said it this way: "[In early recovery] I'm not in the business of saving a marriage. I'm in the business of helping each individual gain a sense of self, self-esteem, boundaries, and abilities or options for a healthier lifestyle, whether they're together or not." So while you are working with hope that the marriage can succeed, the foundation of a healthy marriage is forged in the individual work both partners are willing to do. With that foundation, couple therapy can help merge the individual work successfully and facilitate a much quicker individual and couple recovery process than individual or group therapy alone.

The Therapists: Yours, Mine, and Ours

I began my doctoral dissertation with the belief that couple therapy was the best option for treating sexual addiction and that there was not necessarily a need for group or individual work, except in more severe cases. All the therapists I interviewed, however, suggested that there was a need for all three types of therapy. Additionally, all but one recommended that both addict and partner have the support of their own individual therapist.

After completing my research and practicing for many years, I verify their assertions. Even when a therapist has extensive experience and is well-qualified to manage all the therapy (individual, couple, and group), I do not recommend that the couple be treated in all aspects of treatment by one therapist. There are too many trust issues in sex addiction recovery. It is easy when emotions are high to begin to distrust the process or feel ganged up on, especially when the therapist attempts to hold partner or addict accountable. When trust waivers, and it will at some point, one or both of you will stop feeling safe and may stop therapy. Without a safe place to fall back into (i.e. your own therapist), you will flounder, and either the relationship will end or you and your spouse will have to start the process completely over with a new therapist, which can be excruciatingly painful.

In my experience, there are three scenarios that can work well. First, you can each see an individual therapist and have a separate couple therapist. Second, you can have one therapist act as an individual therapist (to either the spouse or the addict) and as the couple therapist, while the other spouse sees their own individual therapist. Both of these methods have been effective ways to ensure that there is a foundation of trust and support for long-term success. Another approach is for both the addict and the partner to have an individual therapist, and to use cotherapy (both individual therapists in the room facilitating the couple session). I have found this to be the most effective approach, especially for couples where a lot of trauma and distrust have occurred. This method is more difficult to schedule and adds costs at the front end of therapy; however, cotherapy allows partners to move through couple issues and build trust more quickly, ultimately saving time and money while establishing a firm recovery. This method allows each of you to have someone in the room who understands you and advocates for you. It also gives both therapists a much clearer picture of relational and individual patterns. Whichever method you choose to use, it is important that you sign a release for your therapists to be able to communicate and collaborate with each other. When therapists stay connected, they can make sure that there is a consistent message being given with regards to recovery; there are fewer misunderstandings due to comments like, "my therapist says that you need to…," and less confusion about therapist recommendations that might initially appear to be in opposition to each other.

It is especially important with sex addiction to set up guidelines to delineate what to do with secrets and how to work with clients as they struggle to face their fears and get honest. Couple therapy is ineffective when clients are not able to be honest: about their feelings, their needs, and especially about relapses. From the beginning of therapy, I tell my clients that when they can be honest with me but cannot be honest with their partner, I will not see them as a couple until that secret is resolved. Instead, I have the client focus heavily in individual and group therapy on how to get honest with their partner. The only couple work I will do during that time is to resolve crises and establish healthy, safe boundaries. I believe that it is unethical to work on helping the couple to move forward in terms of building connection and intimacy while honesty around critical safety issues is not occurring.

When therapy has clear boundaries, my experience suggests that each individual feels safer being honest. Clients hide less, share more, and are able to go deeper into their core issues when they feel safe.

Other Outside Resources

I can still remember what one of the therapists I interviewed (Bird, 2009) said when I asked her, "Could you just treat sex addiction with marriage counseling?" She paused for a time, then said, "I suppose you could… but it would likely take much longer and the pain will be much greater for most clients, maybe even to the degree they won't make it through the process." Something about how she said it left me knowing that she was right. In addition to the couple therapy discussed in the previous section, I believe that sex addicts and partners are able to recover more quickly and less painfully when they have created a support system and healthy connection in other places in their lives as well.

So what are the outside resources available to people struggling to recover from sex addiction (both addict and partner), in addition to therapy?

1. 12-step meetings such as Sexaholics Anonymous (SA), Sex Addicts Anonymous (SAA), Sex and Love Addicts Anonymous (SLAA), Codependents of Sexual Addiction (COSA), Co-Dependents Anonymous (CoDA), S-Anon Family Groups, Recovering Couples Anonymous (RCA), and even Alcoholics Anonymous (AA)

2. Sponsors

3. Spiritual/religious supports (church, church groups, church leaders, confessor— someone to confess to, etc.)

4. Family

5. Friendships

6. Other medical professionals

7. Any other supports that may be available and appropriate

Establishing additional people (connections) can add several key elements to the recovery process:

1. Come out of hiding and/or isolation (and not feel alone)

2. Reduce shame (being able to talk with others who are "in the trenches" and understand can be invaluable)

3. Manage crises and emotional reactivity (mood swings, volatility in the relationship, etc.)

4. Provide additional perspectives

5. Create connection—opportunities to form meaningful relationships

6. Help fight against well-ingrained negative patterns.

When we talked earlier about Autopsies, we talked about holes in the recovery process that we are trying to fill in order to maintain recovery. Outside resources can provide additional means for filling those holes. Having as many supports as possible provides multiple layers so that if one of them disappears or is unavailable, there are several others nearby to help provide continued support.

There is not one way to do recovery: everyone's approach will be slightly different. Everybody recovers differently, so these resources should be adapted to fit your individual and relational needs as you progress through the recovery process. However, it is critical that you be willing to try at least some of these resources to see if they are a fit for you. Trying to do it completely on your own will lengthen your process of recovery, extend the pain, and potentially have other severe, negative long-term results, including the loss of your relationship.

Reflections – Exercise B

1. What outside resources have you included in your recovery plan? What successes have you had so far in reaching out to outside resources?

    _____

    _____

2. What additional outside resources might be helpful to include? What fears do you have about adding these?

    _____

    _____

Time-outs and Soothing

We reviewed time-outs and soothing in Chapter Two. I urge you to revisit those ideas. One of the most critical elements of couple recovery is the development of this skill in couples. I mention it here so that you are very clear that *time-outs are a major component of early couple recovery.*

Disclosure/Amends

Disclosure is a scary process for most addicts, so much so that research suggests that very few sex addicts disclose the addiction to their partners: almost all sex addicts are initially discovered by their partners (Corley & Schneider, 2002). The history of dishonesty leaves partners feeling fearful and uncertain. The information disclosed under the stress of discovery is rarely a full disclosure. Even if the addict has tried to be honest, details are often left out for various reasons: on purpose (scared to give too much information because they don't want to lose the relationship), the sheer volume of information (it is hard to recall everything in the moment of disclosure), or the addict feels so much fear and pressure that they can only recall certain things in the moment, mostly answering the questions they are directly asked by their partner. Additionally, some partners are so anxious to get past the pain that they want to just forgive and move forward without requiring full honesty (this is part of the denial stage of grief). Without full honesty, however, there is a very high chance of continued relapse.

There are many reasons disclosure is almost never complete when it is done without therapeutic assistance. Most of them boil down to this: addicts have not taken the time to collect their thoughts, sort through their experiences, and present the details in a systematic way. Unless disclosure is done in this way, it is impossible for partners to take all the pieces that have been disclosed and really understand the depth and breadth of the reality of the betrayal. This often takes time and help from a therapist or sponsor to ensure it is as complete as possible.

Based on my research, my experience, the experience of many of my colleagues, and the limited research available elsewhere (Schneider, Corley, & Irons, 1998), disclosure, though very difficult, is a core part of the healing process for both partner and addict. While at the time of the disclosure couples (and addicts particularly) are less convinced it is the right thing to do, over time both addict and partner grow to realize it is a critical step. It lays the foundational bedrock of honesty upon which the couple can begin to grow trust in their relationship. With this foundation, addicts don't have to carry secrets, and partners are less triggered by information they do not remember being disclosed or new information that was never disclosed. This opens space to focus energy on long-term recovery efforts and not on crisis management.

While disclosure is clearly important to a partner's stability and ability to heal, addicts rarely see the benefit to their own recovery. I had an addict in one of my groups announce that he was doing a disclosure with his wife. A newer group member said, "Why in the hell would you do that?!" The client doing the amends said this: "I have spent my whole life hiding, even from myself. It has been a really hard and painful process to look at myself as I've written the amends. Having finished it, though, I have been able to see myself as truthfully as I ever have in my life, and I actually like myself. I want to have a relationship with my wife, but I want her to know the real me and have the choice to stay because she actually likes me. She deserves the truth, too. It is worth the risk to me." His description is the most beautiful description I have heard of the disclosure and amends process.

Disclosure is the presentation of the details of the acting out behaviors. It should be done as soon as possible, but only after the appropriate preparation has been done. The sooner you do a disclosure, the more likely that it will be incomplete and lack empathy. The longer you wait to do the disclosure, the more likely it is that you will get complete disclosure with empathy and ownership from the addict. In some cases, though, it is critical to do a disclosure as early as possible just to get the details (severity, frequency, etc.) of the acting out presented so partners can begin to heal. Obviously, the more serious the acting out and the threat to the partner, the more likely that disclosure will be necessary more immediately.

Amends incorporates how the acting out behaviors have affected your partner: empathy and sorrow for the pain it has caused your partner. Whenever possible, I try to combine the disclosure with the amends because it is a more meaningful, thorough process that has better outcomes overall. Other therapists I have collaborated with strongly suggest keeping the disclosure and amends separate. There is not one right way to manage the disclosure and amends process, and it is very important to consider the needs of each partner in determining how to most effectively carry out a disclosure and amends. In either case, both partner and addict must be adequately prepared.

In most cases, preparing a full disclosure can take several months. If the amends is included, which I have found to be best, the process can take from two to four months or longer. Ultimately, it is the partner and the partner's therapist that determine the timeline that will best meet the partner's needs. The disclosure and amends process is critical. You will not move forward with much success if you do not ensure this process is completed.

I plan to outline how therapists can prepare addicts and partners for the disclosure and amends process in a future book. In the early days of treating sex addiction, addicts would often share their disclosure with their partner outside of therapy or without the partner having any support (no preparation, no therapist to support them, etc.). In many cases, this creates immense trauma for the partner and almost irreversible damage to the relationship. Please make sure that both addict and partner have support and appropriate guidelines for preparing the disclosure and amends so that the process leads to healing. When done correctly, the disclosure and amends process is a powerful tool for couple recovery.

Reflections – Exercise C

1. If you have not already worked through the disclosure process with your therapists, or if you are not currently in that process, what do you need to do to start working towards that goal?

_____

_____

Managing Triggers: Leaning into Your Partner's Pain

Because partners and addicts are usually in very different places with regard to the addiction in early recovery, it is critical that addicts learn to lean into their partner's pain rather than become reactive when partners are triggered. One therapist (Bird, 2009) described the condition of both addict and partner in early recovery:

> …[The] wife is at a place of having to express her anger and being really sad and lonely, and oftentimes the addicts are… in a much better place because they're going, "I'm finally talking about this." There's finally hope, and so they're looking ahead and can't understand why their wife isn't excited that they're in therapy, excited about their recovery. And the wife is sitting there devastated, and really angry and hurt and lonely. And so developmentally, they're just in really different places, because the guy's lived with this and known about this forever, and maybe she's just finding out about it.

Often the addict may want to move through the process quickly while the partner is hesitant. Addicts need to understand and develop empathy for how traumatic and difficult early recovery is for their partners. Recovery is an ongoing process that requires effort and growth over time.

In early recovery, both addicts and partners are often in a lot of fear and pain. Addicts often respond reactively to their partner's pain, taking it personally or getting defensive. Partners also often get reactive when addicts are struggling. In other words, they get triggered when the addict is triggered. This leads to repetitive cycles of intense conversations or battles around the addiction. The only solution to stopping this process is for addicts to learn how to lean into their partner's pain and accept how their addiction has created this turmoil in their partner's life. Partners need to develop a solid sense of how to manage their triggers as well. If both of you are working hard at your own program, you are much more likely to avoid painful, negative cycles. While both of you need to be doing your work, I have rarely seen this destructive cycle around partners' triggers successfully end without addicts being able to lean into the pain non-reactively. This does not suggest that partners have free reign to not manage their triggers by reacting in abusive or controlling ways. Most partners recognize that their triggered or trauma-response behaviors are not in line with who they really want to be. They also become aware that those behaviors are detrimental to themselves and the relationship in the long term.

Much like the amends process, this takes time and effort, and there are very specific things that need to be understood in order for the process to be safer for both partner and addict. I plan to review this process in a future book. As with the disclosure and amends process, learning the process of leaning into their partner's pain is critical—not just an afterthought—in early recovery and beyond. If addicts don't study, practice, and develop the ability to lean into their partners' pain in a way that creates safety for both themselves and their partners, most of the other work of recovery will not take hold in any consistent couple recovery, leading to recycling over and over in trauma responses and gradually destroying any progress toward long-term couple healing.

Boundaries

Because of the intensity of the betrayal trauma, it is crucial in early recovery to begin to delineate boundaries in order to create a sense of safety. Simply put, boundaries are the limits you put in place to provide safety for yourself. They also ensure that there is a "me" (a sense of self), someone separate from those around you. The ability to attune where you end and someone else begins is not as clear to some people, so it is critical in early recovery to develop that awareness. Clearly defining boundaries in relationships actually increases your ability to connect because it ensures that you will be able to protect yourself so that you are safe enough to show up in the relationship. One of my colleagues, Laney Knowlton, provides an excellent overview of what boundaries are and what they are not:

> Trust is an important aspect of boundaries. In reality, trust actually means predictability of behavior: trust = behavior over time. Because we are imperfect as humans, each of us is trustworthy in some ways but not in others. Every experience you have with the people in your life gives you information about the ways they are or are not trustworthy, and that helps you set appropriate boundaries.

Boundaries are often best developed as you form new relationships. Imagine the beginning of a relationship as sitting down at a poker table with someone. You don't know them yet, but you want to start to develop a friendship. Since you don't know how they will respond, you can start by putting $10 down on the table (meaning offering some small part of yourself). They may respond by matching your $10, or they may put down $20, or they may take your $10 and leave the table. If they leave, you're only out $10. If they match your $10 with $10 of their own, or if they put down $20, then you can choose to put down a little bit more. Gradually increasing the amount decreases the chance of you getting hurt. It also allows you to create boundaries as you go, increasing your chance of being able to maintain the relationship long term. If you share something and find out that they told someone else about it, it is much better if that information is a $10-$20 item instead of a $1000 one.

Boundaries are adjustable and can change in relationships. People can change, and we learn new things about ourselves and our friends as we have new experiences. There may be a friend you initially don't trust to keep a secret, but as you get to know them better, you learn you can trust them in that area. The reverse can happen as well.

Discovering ways that you can and cannot trust others allows you to set boundaries that *create safety in your relationships*. Appropriate boundaries allow people to be close in situations where they are trustworthy but help you protect yourself when experience shows they won't be trustworthy. The need for certain boundaries may not become apparent until you have been hurt. You will not know exactly what boundaries are needed in every relationship, even as you become more skilled in creating boundaries.

Boundaries also allow you to ask for what you need and only offer what you are able to offer. *You have the right to have needs and communicate those needs, and this includes being able to say "no."*

When you don't set boundaries for yourself, you give others the control to drain you. Knowing what you are capable of offering to others and giving yourself permission to stick to that allows you to take care of yourself so you can be more present in your relationships and more at peace in your life. Creating boundaries allows relationships to develop and deepen. It allows us the safety to be who we are and creates relationships in which others can feel safe to be who they are. Boundaries allow you to be grateful for your relationship instead of insecure about it.

Appropriate boundaries do not punish others. They do not limit connection. They increase your ability for connection because when you can keep yourself safe, you can allow relationships to continue and strengthen. It's easy to confuse boundaries with selfishness or threats, although healthy boundaries are neither. Boundaries are not about ignoring the needs of others; they are about keeping yourself safe and those around you safe. They allow you to take care of yourself so you can be present in relationships, which actually increases your ability to meet the needs of others in your life in healthy ways.

A threat is an attempt to make another person act a certain way or they will be punished. Boundaries allow natural consequences to happen. If you hurt me (don't keep a confidence I've shared, call me names, or try to punch me in the face), I need to take steps so that I won't be hurt or betrayed again. I might stay a certain distance away from you if you've tried to punch me or limit my interactions with you until you've done whatever work you needed to do so that I have some reassurance that I will not be hurt again. It is not selfish for me not to want to be hurt, and it is not a threat for me to say that I am not going to get close to you in certain ways as long as I feel like the possibility of you hurting me still exists.

As is illustrated in the examples in the previous paragraph, sometimes the need for certain boundaries may not become apparent until you have been hurt. You will not know exactly what boundaries are needed in every relationship, even as you become more skilled in creating boundaries. As stated earlier, creating boundaries allows relationships to develop and deepen. It allows us the safety to be who we are and creates relationships in which others can feel safe to be who they are.

Boundaries are ever-changing and are based on our own experiences and feelings as well as the behaviors of others (trustworthy or not). The first key to boundaries, then, is to learn to trust your own experiences and feelings. Even at a basic level, we have unique experiences that create our likes and dislikes and form who we are. For example, my wife likes more solitary time while I enjoy interacting with people more. Our bodies are set up to naturally favor certain things, and we are all slightly different because we all feel different sets of feelings about different experiences. Who we are adds value to the world even though, and especially because, we are different from others. Knowing what you need and how to ask for it helps to ensure that your needs are met. For example, when I have a hard day, I usually prefer being left alone to process through it. Others may prefer to have someone they can vent to or have someone sit with them. How we feel helps determine who we are. Honoring those feelings will help us honor ourselves.

As you start to identify and honor your feelings, you can begin to establish an identity separate from your spouse. As you develop this identity, it is essential to work to stay grounded and connected with the man or woman you want to be. As you are able to determine who that person is, you can then make decisions in your life based on that vision rather than reactive decisions based in your trauma.

Once you know who you want to be and how you want to care for yourself, you can recognize better what is not safe for you and how to care for yourself appropriately: boundaries. As you determine what is right for you, the next step is to share those boundaries with your partner. For most people who struggle with boundaries, this can be very difficult. Often, people will disregard or challenge your boundaries (consciously or unconsciously) especially if they are not accustomed to you setting boundaries with them. While understanding your own boundaries is a critical first step, it takes time and consistent effort to set boundaries with others. I still recall one wife's comment as she learned to set boundaries: "I'm really good at setting boundaries, I'm just horrible at keeping them!" As one therapist (Bird, 2009) put it,

> It's really hard for people to understand that once you figure [boundaries] out and start making those changes, it's going to feel worse, not better. And it's going to get worse, not better, because people around you will want you to go back to the status quo. And so I think it takes a couple of tries, and sometimes a lot more than a couple, to stay with the course that you have selected for yourself.

It is really important in early recovery that both addict and partner develop a sense of who you want to be and have support and accountability as you struggle to strengthen your sense of self and related boundaries.

Some major boundary issues in early recovery include the following themes:

1. Decision to stay in the marriage for a time to do individual and/or couple work as long as the addict is committed to recovery and sobriety

2. Delineating acting-out behaviors and commitments not to go beyond certain types of behaviors (bottom lines)

3. Partner's negotiable and non-negotiable boundaries

These themes make up the next few sections in this chapter.

Stay or Go?

Because of the trauma of discovery or disclosure, partners are often unsure whether it is safe to stay in the marriage at all. Addicts often struggle to manage their partner's trauma responses and resent the time it takes for partners to heal. This lack of safety often leads to intense swings in emotion and a strong desire to leave the relationship. The dilemma early on is that it is almost impossible to make a decision of such a magnitude when you are in such an intense level of crisis, along with the related emotions. Instead, I urge you to find a way to create some temporary safety for yourself while you work through the first steps of early recovery. I suggest that you take six months to a year to make the decision to stay or go, because it will take time to be certain of the right steps to choose. Leaving the marriage while in crisis will not solve the problems or fix the pain of betrayal; it just creates a temporary distance. Most partners I have worked with have experienced relief when they decided they didn't have to make a decision immediately. It allowed them time and energy to focus on the critical self-care elements of early recovery.

Every partner manages the time in early recovery differently. Some stay in the same house in the same bed. Others decide separate rooms are necessary, but live in the same house. Some separate completely for a time. There is not one right solution. However, whatever the chosen boundary, it is critical that there be a commitment to work through the other steps of creating healthy boundaries (managing the trauma, getting to understand the addiction, your own thoughts and feelings, self-care, etc.).

Let me be clear here: I have seen times where leaving was the right choice. I don't have the right answer for addicts or partners, but I have seen consistently that people who take time to make the choice always heal more completely no matter what their choice is. My goal here is not to influence you one way or the other, just to urge you to take some time to be centered and ready for whatever steps you need to take to create safety and heal in the long run.

During early recovery, if partners commit to take time to make the decision to stay, there are certain commitments that are necessary. One therapist (Bird, 2009) described those steps well:

> …during that time… they agree not to pull the "leaving card:" "I'm not going to stay, I'm leaving, I'm out of here." … I think the purpose is so that abandonment issues don't get stirred up because they [addicts] think lots of times when life gets tough—like around disclosure or relapse… she will either say, "I'm out of here. I'm not going to live like this." Or he'll say, "I'm just such a loser. You're better off without with me. I'm leaving." And I think when you pull those threats of leaving out of the bag it really throws up people's abandonment issues…

To create safety for both addict and partner, it is critical to stay committed to the process until you have had time to determine if you can stay committed to the marriage.

The decision to stay is a commitment to yourself and your own safety and growth. It is important to realize that staying in the marriage temporarily does not mean you will stay permanently. It merely gives you time to work on yourself and make well-informed decisions. During the time that you are staying, one of the major benefits is the work you do for yourself and the growth that occurs. Regardless of whether you stay, you will end up a healthier person because of the work that you do, no matter what happens with the relationship.

The last piece of the decision to stay or go is this: staying doesn't mean giving up on the hopes and dreams of a happy marriage. Initially it might feel like, "My marriage has failed. It's miserable. This isn't what I wanted. How could I choose so horribly?" But with time and processing, most of my clients begin to approach it more like, "I didn't give up my dream of what I hoped to have in my marriage. I merely saw where we were lacking and was able to try and fulfill that dream." Over time, the decision about staying or going is a matter of stepping back and saying, "Now that I'm seeing changes with my spouse, what do I want out of my marriage and can I still have that?" During that time in early recovery, as you put the decision to stay or to go on hold, you can focus your attention on your own recovery, safety, and boundaries.

Bottom Lines

Managing triggers individually requires establishing an awareness of what your bottom-line behaviors are—those behaviors that constitute a relapse for addicts and clearly define a trauma response for spouses. Additionally, the soothing skills described in Chapter Two are a critical component of managing triggers. The individual aspects of establishing bottom lines and learning to managing triggers are covered in detail in Chapter Four as part of the individual Recovery Hill. From a couple perspective, firm bottom lines provide clarity among the chaos of early recovery, accountability to one another, a sense of safety for both partners, and the ability to build trust more quickly.

Boundaries for Relapses

The last component of boundaries that is important to establish in early recovery is boundaries for partners if a relapse should occur. In an effort to stop the addictive behaviors, partners may initially demand that the behaviors never occur again, fearing that other approaches might give the addict permission to continue acting out. Setting black and white boundaries that you may not be willing to follow through with could be more damaging than not setting boundaries at all. Thus, boundaries must be sorted through so that you will be able to follow through if relapses occur.

Before we move forward in this discussion, let me be very clear about one thing: relapsing is never OK. It destroys trust. It creates more trauma. It ultimately does nothing to help the addict. Nobody wins long term when relapses happen. By discussing boundaries here, I am merely acknowledging that addiction is a relapsing disease. By definition, addiction is repetition of a behavior despite attempts to stop. So when people first enter recovery, they may not have enough awareness, enough tools, or enough support to know how to navigate life well enough to stay completely sober.

The overall process of setting boundaries helps partners do some preparation and problem solving beforehand so they can set boundaries that can be successfully followed through with as the addict goes through the process of change. By preparing for the possibility, we are merely trying to ensure that partners can care for themselves should a relapse occur. You need to know that you can and will take care of yourself emotionally.

Non-negotiable Boundaries

Non-negotiable boundaries are definitive cause-and-effect, black-and-white declarations: If you do_____, I will do _____. They are appropriate in certain instances, but must be carefully considered. The danger I have seen with many partners is that they set non-negotiable boundaries and are not able to follow through with them. The goal of boundaries is to create personal power and safety. If you are not prepared to follow through, you set yourself up to lose both power and safety.

Non-negotiable boundaries are necessary. There is ultimately somewhere to draw the line. No relapse is healthy. But which relapses are deal breakers? That is different for every partner. Generally, relapses into pornography are painful, but they don't typically break the marriage for most partners. There are always exceptions, however. I urge you to determine individually if that is a non-negotiable boundary for you, and in a few cases I have seen partners determine that any relapse into pornography was a deal breaker and that they'd leave the marriage. Those cases have been very rare, however, and occurred after a lot of personal work and time in recovery. It has been much more common for partners to set non-negotiable boundaries around sexual acting out that has occurred with another individual in person (affairs, prostitutes, and in some cases strip clubs).

I typically ask partners, "If your partner were to relapse into this behavior, disclose it immediately, take accountability for figuring out why it happened (autopsy), etc., would you leave them?" If the answer is truly yes, then it is appropriate to set a non-negotiable boundary and follow through with it.

Negotiable Boundaries

Negotiable boundaries don't give permission for a relapse, but they put it in the context of the overall effort the addict is making to recover. While sobriety is important, living a recovery-oriented life is what will ensure that long-term sobriety is established. Negotiable boundaries leave room for continued recovery in the relationship if the addict is willing to make the necessary changes. In short, negotiable boundaries look like this:

> If you do A (unsafe/problematic behavior) then I'll do B (safety response),
> until you do C (recovery response). A---B---C

With negotiable boundaries, the partner can feel safer if the addict has had a recovery response after a non-recovery behavior (like relapse). B (the boundary) is not punishing. It is a way to love yourself and the relationship by creating safety with an invitation for reconnection.

For one couple, safety meant spending nights on the couch until a full autopsy was done. The addict at first was resentful, then gradually realized that his program was to do an autopsy (this was part of the program he had established for his own recovery), and she was creating safety until he was active in his recovery program again. She held that boundary strongly, and he spent several weeks on the couch. The longer he was on the couch, the more I became curious why he was not working his own program. When I asked him in therapy why it was taking weeks to do his autopsy, he admitted he was struggling to get through it and had never really done an autopsy successfully. Because she held her boundary, he was able to recognize his limitations in his recovery and address them. He admitted he needed help. We then worked through the autopsy, and he felt proud of his insights and hopeful about his ability to be successful in his ability to do an autopsy in the future. When he finally shared with her, he told her he was sorry it took so long and admitted that he was scared to face something he felt so inadequate to do. They were able to restore connection through the process and she felt safe inviting him back into the bedroom.

Boundaries are a balance between safety and connection. As you set boundaries, you will have to determine how to manage the sense of disconnect (and other related emotions) that come from the necessary distancing required for safety. One wife described that process in this way:

> I distance from you for my safety after a relapse, but I really want to feel safe *and* close to you. So, the way to come back into my life after a relapse is to provide me safety by sharing what you've learned and how things will change (autopsy). If I know that, I can see you growing and feel safer that things will not be repeated. And that work also shows me that you value yourself and me.

Once partners have established their own boundaries, they meet together with the addict in couple therapy to establish a shared vision of these boundaries and accountability. That process is reviewed in the "Accountability Contract" section later in this chapter.

While all boundaries are different, I share some examples compiled from several partners who had spouses who had previously acted out in a variety of different sexual ways. Again, these are merely examples to help you feel your way through the boundaries that are right for you. In many cases, this process might best be completed and supported through the help of a skilled therapist.

Negotiable and Non-negotiable Boundary Examples

> It is not acceptable to me to have you act out. Acting out threatens my safety, so if it were to occur I have established these boundaries to ensure my safety.
>
> If you watch inappropriate content on TV and this leads to masturbation, or if you view pornography or act out sexually (these are things you've identified as bottom-line behaviors), I expect you to follow your commitments in your program, which include the following:
>
> 1. Tell me within 24 hours (or before the next time we have sex, whichever is sooner). I commit to respond with, "Thank you for telling me." If you do not

disclose within 24 hours, I will need some space to create safety for myself by _____ (see examples below for escalation based on severity of the behaviors).

2.   Do an autopsy.

3.   Use your support network within 24 hours (your sponsor, group, ecclesiastical leader, or trusted friend).

Examples of Escalation in Severity of Boundaries

If you are willing to get back to your program, I want to continue to work toward recovery as a couple. While you are working your program, I want you to:

- Sleep on the couch.
- Sleep in another room.
- Sleep on the floor in our room (so there's less risk of acting out).

If you do not disclose within 24 hours, I want you to move into a safe place outside the home (a trusting friend's home, relative's house, hotel, etc.) for _____ days. If you then work your program and can reconnect with me to help me see you are safe (autopsy), I will invite you back into the relationship and/or home.

If you do not follow your program, I will ask you to leave the home until you are back in your program and safe (i.e. you can share your autopsy and help me see that you are in your program).

If you go to a strip club, my safety is threatened more. I will ask you to leave for _____ days. If you then work your program and can reconnect with me to help me see you are safe (autopsy), I will invite you back into the home and relationship.

If you have physical contact at a strip club, massage parlor, etc., I want you to move out for ___. You may not have contact with me or the children for ___. You may have limited contact with the children after ___. If you then work your program and can reconnect with me to help me see you are safe (autopsy), I will invite you back into the home and relationship. However, it will take an extended time for me to feel safe in this situation.

If you have any type of sexual intercourse or oral sex, I want you to move out for ____(longer period).

If you are not willing to work your program after relapse by ____ (set period of time), I will file for divorce.

I repeat again, *these examples are merely models of how boundaries can be created and should be individualized by each partner. They are provided to help you sort through what fits for you and will serve to offer both protection and opportunities for connection as your partner works their program well.*

Reflections – Exercise D

1. What negotiable boundaries do you think are necessary for your relationship?

   _____

   _____

2. What non-negotiable boundaries do you think are necessary for your relationship?

   _____

   _____

3. What specific issues did you identify as needing to form boundaries around but are unsure which category they fall into?

   _____

   _____

4. Work with your therapist to process through your answers to the preceding questions in order to ensure they are right for you, and then put these boundaries into a written document that you can bring with you to a couple session to incorporate into the Accountability Contract.

Accountability Contract for Relapse

Accountability in early recovery is very misunderstood. Often it is seen as being caught or cornered, like the typical confrontation ("calling BS") from partners, groups, therapist, or sponsors. While it is important at rare times for support systems to challenge directly by "calling BS" on an addict or partner, strong confrontations in early recovery sometimes lead to compliance and a sense of powerlessness, which in turn leads to going underground by hiding feelings and behaviors. Challenges of this type should be done rarely, and only when there is enough relational connection (which is typically very low in early recovery) to minimize the shame that such instances trigger.

Initially, accountability can be seen as being controlled, being told what to do, and being "watched like a hawk" to see if you fail. When you feel like you don't have a choice, you tend to live fearfully, begin to pretend and hide, become resentful, and not feel empowered by your recovery. It makes it nearly impossible to work a healthy program.

What accountability really means is acting congruently—consistent with your own healthy vision of recovery—and becoming the man or woman you wish to be. When you, addict or partner, can see the long-term benefits of being the man or woman that you want to be, as well as the ways you can accomplish that, *accountability is empowering*. It provides structure to help create clear ways to manage your own recovery, both individually and in the context of your relationship. It helps couple dynamics improve, focuses more clearly on those areas that need more work, and helps both of you see the positive growth that might otherwise go unnoticed due to the variety of other problems that have not yet been resolved. Accountability also invites those around you to form a healthy support system to hold you to becoming your best self. Basically, accountability helps people hold on to their own recovery.

It is difficult, especially in recovery, to balance justice and mercy. Mercy, which all of us need because we all make mistakes, can quickly turn into enabling if we are not careful. Justice can be turned into punishment. In order to balance these early in recovery, accountability is the key: it recognizes both the need for commitment to healing and long-term recovery (justice) while also addressing your humanness (mercy).

Measures of Success

Because early recovery is so unmanageable, it is difficult to measure success. If you are able to manage some things but not others, it often appears to both of you that everyone is failing. To be able to see success and build trust, I suggest that you both establish clear priorities and determine what is most important to be working on individually and in the relationship. I call these measures of success.

Once established, these measures of success provide a set of markers that can lead to greater trust, increased hope, and healthy accountability as you struggle toward the long-term success of sobriety. Because recovery requires facing the consequences of your behaviors, experiencing your emotions, working to develop coping skills, and taking emotional risks to connect with your spouse and your support network, couples may often feel worse initially instead of better. Measures of success will help both of you see the successes despite the pain you may experience as change is happening.

A major component of holding both partners and addicts accountable in early recovery and establishing measures of success as a couple is the creation of a written Accountability Contract. This contract is a mediated contract, meaning it should be facilitated and supported by a therapist who is knowledgeable in the treatment of sex addiction.

The first step is to establish an agreement about how to manage when bottom lines are crossed. You begin by clarifying your own boundaries for your own individual recovery. This individual work includes bottom-line behaviors for both partner and addict and individual plans for if relapse occurs (autopsy, boundaries for partners, etc.). Once individual boundaries have been clarified, you will share them with each other and work to create a shared vision about what behaviors will be disclosed. The partner will share his/her boundaries, negotiable and non-negotiable, which will provide safety if relapse happens. You will also determine together how each of you will interact when a relapse is disclosed so that there is greater predictability, which makes honesty more likely to occur. It is helpful to delineate when (time between the relapse and disclosure—e.g. within 24 hours) and where disclosure will occur.

While relapse is something that ideally will not occur, this puts a plan in place to better ensure that a slip or slide will not turn into a collapse, where honesty is no longer a part of the recovery process. I include in this section several quotes from therapists included in my research (Bird, 2009). One therapist spoke of how the partner would approach this:

> "I know you might relapse and that doesn't give you permission…but I'd much rather have you relapse and tell me than relapse and hide it from me. So let's set some boundaries around telling me. So I'd like for you to tell me…." And I ask the addict, "When do you feel comfortable that you could tell her about your relapses?" We want it to be an open conversation, and then it's about, "you better tell me that it happened," and not about, "you better never mess up again."

As this plan is created, it gives both partner and addict the necessary preparation to manage a relapse in behavior so that honesty, which is a vital component of trust, can be successfully achieved.

The plan also includes accountability for the partner. This doesn't blame the partner for the addictive behavior, but it does hold them accountable to things they do have control over. These things might include basic self-care (the work of the Recovery Hill), managing trauma responses, addressing addictive behaviors or codependent behaviors, if those exist, and effectively communicating within the marriage. When these things are identified for both of you, some basic ground rules can be set to help provide a healthy pattern for accountability for both you and your spouse—a pattern based on your own vision of becoming and being the man or woman you wish to become.

Part of the Accountability Contract can include ongoing amends. One therapist suggested doing "a 10th step around it with their sponsor and apologize to their partner, not just you know 'I'm so sorry' but 'Wow, I really see the impact this behavior has on you and this is my best understanding of what happened.'" When the partner is upset, another therapist suggested that the addict be supported so that they can "be in a place where he genuinely looks at his wife in the eyes and says—she's furious at him—'Thank you again for reminding me of the consequences of my behavior.'"

The partner needs to own their part of things when they slip into their old behaviors. One therapist shared how a partner was able to do that:

> ...she admitted her side of the interaction that went between them, and even though he went back to his drug of choice, she also went back to her drug of choice. And so she also made amends for that, redid some things they had done early in the couple's work that worked really well for them at critical moments, and then it just reestablished their commitments to each other in their own recoveries and their couple stuff.

If the contract includes amends, it further deepens empathy in the relationship and provides appropriate accountability for both partner and addict.

While appropriate disclosure is important, the contract needs to be clear that the partner is not a babysitter, probation officer, or some other form of a "parent-child" kind of hierarchy in the relationship, and the addict is not a bad child who is being punished.

Additionally, your spouse should never be your accountability person. An accountability person is a person who helps you keep your commitments. This individual helps you sort through feelings, figure out where you may have made mistakes, learn new skills, and be honest with your spouse in a processed and connecting way. They are the one who hold your feet to the fire. This can be your therapist, a sponsor, a well-trained religious leader (those who are not well-trained may cause more pain than support), a 12-step group, or a therapy group. Ideally, both of you (addict and partner) would be sharing your work with several of these resources as a form of accountability and support.

Although your spouse cannot be your accountability person (for either addict or partner), the goal of the Accountability Contract is to outline how both of you can connect in healthier ways during the recovery process. Establishing healthy boundaries will help create predictable and healthy ways to do the following:

- Interact more safely around difficult topics, including disclosure.
- Protect yourself when your spouse crosses a bottom line.
- Be supportive when the other person is struggling.
- Work together to support each other in achieving your goals in recovery, both individually and relationally.

If the Accountability Contract is done well, it can help you to create a context that allows you to move forward in both your individual and couple recovery process. The contract is meant to ensure that, as long as both of you are doing what you have committed to do, the addict does not go into a shame spiral or continue to act out if a relapse occurs, and the partner does not go into a shame spiral or get trapped in a trauma response. A good couple disclosure plan helps you to respond in ways that identify and honor your needs and your authentic self, rather than responding reactively. Each of you can measure your own success clearly, even in the face of your spouse's blame if necessary. This helps manage shame while focusing on those things you need to learn and improve.

Additionally, the contract will set up a plan that permits you to check in with each other if you are feeling insecure or scared. Although being an accountability partner is not appropriate for spouses, a therapist shared that one of the things a spouse said was, "I want to know when you're triggered. I want to know when you're struggling, and I want to know what you're doing to take care of it.'" One therapist said that the addict "needn't come home at the end of the day every day and say, 'Here's the 20 things that I felt tempted by today, hon.' Because that's a problem." Instead, the contract can put a structure in place that outlines how each of you can check in in a way that builds connection and safety while minimizing reactivity.

It is also important for either spouse to be able to check in when they feel uncertain about the recovery process or disconnected from each other. One therapist said:

> It's important that periodically through the recovery if she has—not that she's allowed to badger him—but even if she has questions two, three, five years down the road, just a general question. "So I'm kind of feeling

insecure, honey. I'm just wondering, how are you doing?" He can certainly say, "I'm doing fine. Sometimes I struggle. But I haven't acted out. I'm going to my meetings. I'm doing fine." I think they can keep that communication open between them.

Another therapist set up a rating scale,

> …where 0 to 100—and we had discussed in therapy what 0 meant, what 100 meant—and if she at any time was feeling anxious or sensed that a relapse occurred, she had permission to inquire, "Where are you at?" And they had this very simplified language that was not attacking. They could just in a very non-defensive way say, "I'm at a 57." And… she could then gauge the direction of progress as well. And so couples that are… successfully dealing with this have developed a way to talk about this that works for them.

In the end, a healthy Accountability Contract will establish ways to talk effectively about both the process that leads up to relapse, either into addictive behaviors or trauma responses, as well as relapses, should they occur. This helps to establish a very clear process for both of you to feel more prepared, safe, and grounded despite the challenges that may come up in early recovery.

After you work together to write down the agreement, you should establish a regular check-in point to be held accountable to the contract. Initially I suggest this happen with your therapist(s), although that can change as more long-term recovery has been established. I also suggest that each of you review the contract as part of the re-mind process for your individual program. Your plan should be revisited in therapy at least every few months, because over time you will need to address changes in the contract. For example, there may be new goals that each of you are trying to accomplish individually. In these cases, you may need to negotiate how to provide support in a connecting but boundaried way. In this way, the Accountability Contract is a "living" or changing document. Until much later in recovery, and when agreed upon with your therapist(s), all changes to the accountability contract should be made with the support of a therapist to ensure they are healthy and balanced.

Reflections – Exercise E – Accountability Contract

1. Find the version of the accountability contract that applies to you (either addict or partner) in the Appendix and complete it. Once you are done, review it with your therapist and group for feedback, then set up a time and present it to your spouse in a couple session.

Wrap-up

In this chapter I have reviewed how to bring together early individual recovery tools in a way that can create a more stable, connected, trust-building process for couple recovery. Through an accountability contract, both partners are able to see the recovery process more clearly, recover from mistakes and struggles quickly, and stay connected. As you work in tandem, both couple recovery and individual recovery will move forward much more quickly and effectively.

Chapter 6

WORKING YOUR PROGRAM

Congratulations on finishing this book and the various aspects of early recovery, individually and relationally! If you have read, answered the questions, and applied the concepts in this book, by now you have a solid program of early recovery, which includes the following:

1. Greater connection (God, family, friends, groups, 12-step meetings, etc.)

2. Filling your tank

3. Planning, including opportunities for connection

4. Daily Rituals
   a. Morning Re-mind
   b. VSE's
   c. Nightly Rewind

5. Recognition of warning signs (Triggers and Indicators)

6. Fire Drills

7. Relapse Recovery Plan
   a. Letter to yourself
   b. Accountability person/people

Having a program ensures that you are able to care for yourself, form connections with others, focus on what you have power over, and feel greater peace even when things around you are not going as well as you might wish (struggles in your relationships, job, etc.). These tools will also be used throughout middle and late recovery and will act as building blocks to other things you will learn.

After the Crash

I began this book with the journey of two people on a tandem bicycle, suddenly faced with a painful reality and a decision regarding how they might recover from a very devastating crash. Each of your crashes might be very different, as will your recoveries.

For those of you who didn't start the journey in a primary relationship, the measures of success that matter most to you might include individual recovery and the creation, maintenance, and improvement of your connection with others. In some cases, that may include forming a primary relationship, but that more often happens later in recovery. Remember that long-term recovery requires individual steps *in tandem* with steps to improve connection. Hopefully the tools you have learned so far have made it easier to maneuver through difficult terrain and brought you joy as you have begun to travel with others.

If you are in a primary relationship, you have most likely begun to connect your individual recovery work with your partner's recovery work. In small ways, that builds connection, empathy, and trust. For those of you where both partners are working actively on their individual recoveries, the chances of having a long-term individual recovery that also includes a long-term relationship recovery is higher. Through very painful, difficult, committed steps, many of you have begun to experience small joys as you are able to ride *in tandem*.

After the crash, there is not always the fairy tale ending that people hope for. Just because you do the work of recovery does not mean that there will not be significant losses, individually and relationally. Some couples separate, some divorce, and some stay together but struggle to hold on to individual and relationship recovery because of an inability or unwillingness to change patterns.

In some cases, ending the relationship is a success, especially in cases where one partner continues to be dishonest, unwilling to change, or abusive. Moving away from that relationship can be extremely lonely, and you may wonder what you did wrong to deserve all the pain and abandonment you are experiencing. I have watched many clients go through the sense of being in "no-man's land," and have also seen the other side of that as they have held to their recovery. The most important part of that time for my clients has been the connection they have built with others. I know that, despite the pain of ending the relationship, you will slowly begin to experience the joy of individual recovery and connection with others who are willing to do the work, including friends, family, etc. Even though it was not what you wanted or expected, you will begin to understand the joy of working a recovery *in tandem* with those who are willing to do the work.

In an upcoming book, I plan to look at individual and relational aspects of middle and late recovery. I will introduce several new tools for individual recovery and growth, as well as tools for creating healthier connection. These tools will build upon what you have learned in this book.

Individual Tools

1. Understanding shame and anger, including how they can destroy connection when not managed well.

2. Managing primary emotions more successfully.

3. Amends and impact letters: this is listed under "individual tools" because a successful amends and/or impact letter leads to greater personal insight and growth.

Relational Tools

1. Learning to build greater connection in all your relationships.
    a. Understanding connection as a process that occurs gradually over time.
    b. Managing social situations in ways that build greater connection.

2. Catching and Pitching: tools for safe communication within caring relationships.

3. Developing two types of empathy.
    a. Empathy related to the trauma of the addiction.
        i.   Disclosure and/or Amends letter (addict).
        ii. Impact letter (partner).
        iii. Responding in a safe way when triggers occur.
    b. Empathy related to pain experienced in the past and present, including pain from the relationship and family-of-origin.

4. Healthy sexuality.

Again, congratulations for the work you have done. I urge you to take the next step and begin to work on the elements of middle and late recovery. Those who continue forward report that many of the promises of healthy recovery are able to be realized more quickly as they take the next right steps.

REFERENCES

Alcoholics Anonymous. (2001). *Big Book* (4th ed.). New York, NY: AA World Services, Inc.

Adams, K. M., & Robinson, D. W. (2001). Shame reduction, affect regulation, and sexual boundary development: Essential building blocks of sexual addiction treatment. *Sexual Addiction & Compulsivity, 8(1)*, 23-44.

Alexander, B. (2010). *The View from Rat Park*. Retrieved from http://www.bruce-kalexander.com/articles-speeches/rat-park/148-addiction-the-view-from-rat-park

American Psychiatric Association. (2013). *Diagnostic and statistical manual of mental disorders* (5th ed.). Washington, DC: Author.

ASAM. (2011). *Definition of Addiction*. Retrieved from http://www.asam.org/quality-practice/definition-of-addiction

Baumeister, R., & Tierney, J. (2011). *Willpower: Rediscovering the Greatest Human Strength*. New York, NY: Penguin Press.

Bergner, R. M. (2002). Sexual compulsion as attempted recovery from degradation: Theory and therapy. *Journal of Sex & Marital Therapy, 28(5)*, 373-387.

Bird, M. H. (2009). *Sexual Addiction and MFT: Therapists' Perspectives on Facilitating Individual and Relationship Healing* (Doctoral dissertation). Virginia Polytechnic Institute and State University, Blacksburg, VA.

Bowlby, J. (1969). *Attachment. Attachment and loss: Vol. 1. Loss*. New York: Basic Books.

Bradshaw, J. (1988). *Healing the Shame that Binds You.* Deerfield Beach, FL: Health Communications.

Brown, B. (2010). *The Gifts of Imperfection.* Center City, MN: Hazelden.

Butler, M. H., Gardner, B. C., & Bird, M. H. (1998). Not Just a Time-Out: Change Dynamics of Prayer for Religious Couples in Conflict Situations. *Family Process, 37,* 451–478.

Carnes, P. (1992). *Out of the shadows: Understanding sexual addiction.* Minneapolis, MN: CompCare Publishers.

Carnes, P. (1991). *Don't call it love: Recovery from sexual addiction.* New York, NY: Bantam Books.

Cooper, M., & Lebo, R. (2001). Assessment and treatment of sexual compulsivity: A multi-modal perspective. *Journal of Social Work Practice in the Addictions, 1(2),* 61-74.

Corley, M. D., & Schneider, J. P. (2002). Disclosing secrets: Guidelines for therapists working with sex addicts and co-addicts. Sexual Addiction & Compulsivity, 9(1), 43-67.

Covey, S., Merrill, A. R., & Merrill, R. R. (1994). *First Things First: To Live, to Love, to Learn, to Leave a Legacy.* New York: Simon and Schuster, 1994.

Earle, R., & Crow, G. (1989). *Lonely all the time: Recognizing, understanding, and overcoming sex addiction of addicts and co-dependents.* New York, NY: Pocket Books.

Flores, P. (2004). *Addiction as an Attachment Disorder.* Lanham, MD: Jason Aronson, Inc.

Goldman, W. (1973). *The Princess Bride.* New York, NY: Houghton Mifflin Harcourt Publishing company.

Goodman, A. (1992). Sexual addiction: Designation and treatment. *Journal of Sex & Marital Therapy, 18,* 303-314.

Hari, J. (2015). *Chasing the Scream: The First and Last Days of the War on Drugs.* Bloomsbury, USA.

Jackson, P., Osborne, B., & Walsh, F. (Producers), & Jackson, P. (Director). (2002). *The Lord of the Rings: The Two Towers* [Motion Picture]. USA: New Line Cinema.

Leiblum, S. (1997). Sex and the net: Clinical implications. *Journal of Sex Education and Therapy, 22 (1),* 21-27.

Linehan, M. (2015). *DBT Skills Training Manual* (2nd Edition). New York, NY: Guilford Press.

Magai, C. (1999). Affect imagery and attachment: Working models of interpersonal affect and the socialization of emotion. In J. Cassidy, & P. Shavers (Eds.), *Handbook of Attachment: Theory and Research* (pp. 278-802). New York, NY: Guilford.

McCauley, K. (2009). *Pleasure Unwoven.* [Motion Picture]. United States: Institute for Addiction Study.

McGonigal, K. (2011). *The Willpower Instinct: How self-control works, why it matters, and what you can do to get more of it.* New York: Avery.

Mellody, P., Miller, A., & Miller, J. (1989). *Facing Codependence: What it is, Where it comes from, How it sabotages our lives.* New York, NY: Harper & Row.

Milrad, R. (1999). Co-addictive recovery: Early recovery issues for spouses of sex addicts. *Sexual Addiction & Compulsivity, 6(2),* 125-136.

Panksepp, J. (2010). Affective neuroscience of the emotional BrainMind: evolutionary perspectives and implications for understanding depression. *Dialogues in Clinical Neuroscience, 12*(4), 533–545.

Reed, S. J. (2000). Shame and hope in sexual addiction. *Journal of Ministry in Addiction & Recovery, 7(1),* 9-17.

Schneider, J. P., Corley, M. D., & Irons, R. R. (1998). Surviving disclosure of infidelity: Results of an international survey of 164 recovering sex addicts and partners. *Sexual Addiction & Compulsivity, 5(3),* 189-217.

Sex Addicts Anonymous. (2012). *Sex Addicts Anonymous* (3rd Edition). Houston, TX: International Service Organization, Inc.

Sprenkle, D. H. (1987). Treating a sex addict through marital sex therapy. *Family Relations: Journal of Applied Family & Child Studies, 36(1),* 11-14.

Steffens, B., & Means, M. (2009). *Your Sexually Addicted Spouse: How Partners Can Cope and Heal.* New Jersey: New Horizon Press

Washton, A., & Boundy, D. (1989). Willpower's Not Enough. New York, NY: HarperCollins.

Wilson, B. (1958). *The Next Frontier: Emotional Sobriety.* New York, NY: AA Grapevine, Inc.

Wolfe, J. L. (2000). Assessment and treatment of compulsive sex/love behavior. *Journal of Rational-Emotive & Cognitive Behavior Therapy, 18(4),* 235-246.

APPENDIX

Accountability Contract (for Addicts)

My program of recovery is (e.g. honesty, ongoing disclosure, autopsy):

_____

Specific steps I am taking to move through recovery (e.g. individual therapy twice a month, couple therapy twice a month, attend group weekly):

_____

_____

_____

Relapse into my addictive behaviors is defined as:

_____

_____

Relapse into my trauma response is defined as:

_____

_____

How relapses into addictive behavior will be disclosed (e.g. within 24 hours or before sex, whichever happens first; sitting in the bedroom after the kids are in bed; details to be included):

_____

_____

_____

How I will respond to relapses into my behaviors both addictive and trauma-based (e.g. do an autopsy, report to therapist and group):

_____

_____

_____

Steps I will take for self-care following a relapse (to ensure that my needs are met and to bring me back up towards the top of Recovery Hill):

_____

_____

_____

How I will stay safe if my partner relapses (e.g. attempt to lean in twice, then leave the conversation until my partner has done and presented an autopsy):

_____

_____

_____

Steps I will take for self-care following a relapse by my partner to ensure that my needs are met and to minimize the effect of the relapse on me:

_____

_____

_____

Who is safe for me to contact for support?

_____

_____

Accountability Contract (for Partners)

My program of recovery is (e.g. honesty, boundaries, autopsy):

_____

Specific steps I am taking to move through recovery (e.g. individual therapy twice a month, couple therapy twice a month, attend group weekly):

_____

_____

_____

(If applicable) Relapse into addictive behaviors for me is defined as:

_____

_____

Relapse into trauma responses for me is defined as:

_____

_____

How I will respond to relapses into my behaviors, trauma-based and addictive if applicable (e.g. do an autopsy, report to therapist and group):

_____

_____

_____

Steps I will take for self-care following a relapse into my behaviors to ensure that my needs are met and to minimize the effect of the relapse on me:

_____

_____

_____

How I will respond to disclosure of a relapse (e.g. "Thank you for telling me," followed by 24-hour time-out):

_____

_____

_____

How I will stay safe if my partner relapses (e.g. no sex for ___ days, sleep in separate rooms until my partner completes and presents an autopsy):

_____

_____

_____

Steps I will take for self-care following a relapse by my partner (to ensure that my needs are met and to bring me back up towards the top of Recovery Hill):

_____

_____

_____

Who is safe for me to contact for support?

_____

_____

Addiction Cycle

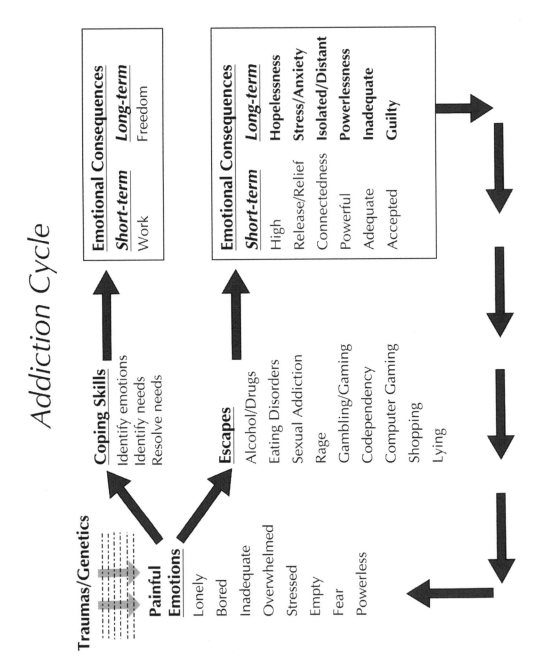

Traumas/Genetics

Painful Emotions
Lonely
Bored
Inadequate
Overwhelmed
Stressed
Empty
Fear
Powerless

Coping Skills
Identify emotions
Identify needs
Resolve needs

Escapes
Alcohol/Drugs
Eating Disorders
Sexual Addiction
Rage
Gambling/Gaming
Codependency
Computer Gaming
Shopping
Lying

Emotional Consequences

Short-term	Long-term
Work	Freedom

Emotional Consequences

Short-term	Long-term
High	Hopelessness
Release/Relief	Stress/Anxiety
Connectedness	Isolated/Distant
Powerful	Powerlessness
Adequate	Inadequate
Accepted	Guilty

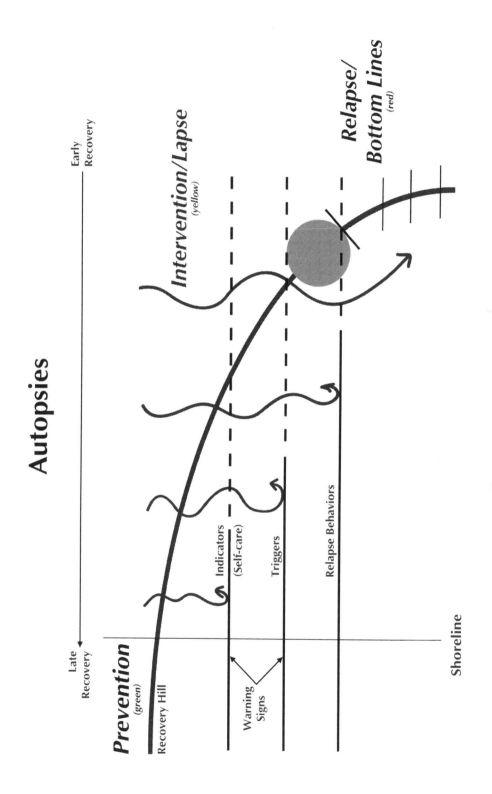

Autopsies

Prevention
(green)

Recovery Hill

Late Recovery

Early Recovery

Intervention/Lapse
(yellow)

Relapse/
Bottom Lines
(red)

Indicators (Self-care)

Triggers

Relapse Behaviors

Warning Signs

Shoreline

Autopsy Worksheet

This behavior crossed one of my bottom lines:

_____

I was feeling these emotions prior to crossing those lines (refer to Feeling Word List):

_____

The needs underlying those emotions (refer to Needs List):

_____

Other times I have struggled with those emotions:

_____

_____

Considering my individual Recovery Hill, these triggers happened before I crossed my bottom line:

_____

Considering my individual Recovery Hill, these indicators were present before I crossed my bottom line:

_____

Steps I had set up to meet those needs in a healthy way:

_____

_____

Reasons those steps did not work in this case:

_____

_____

Changes I will make to those steps so those reasons won't affect my ability to avoid crossing my bottom line in the future:

_____

_____

Ways crossing my bottom line in this case hurt me:

_____

_____

Ways crossing my bottom line in this case hurt others:

_____

Steps I need to take to make amends:

_____

_____

Amends Worksheet

I crossed one of my bottom lines or boundaries by:

_____

I know that my actions have hurt you. I would imagine you feel:

_____

I would imagine this probably affected you in these ways:

_____

_____

These are the steps I would like to take to make amends to you:

_____

_____

To help rebuild trust, I want to share part of my autopsy with you.
I realize that my behaviors happened because I felt _____ and needed

_____.

These were the steps I had set up to meet those needs in a healthy way:

_____

_____

Reasons those steps did not work in this case:

_____

_____

Changes I will make to those steps so those reasons won't affect my ability to avoid crossing my bottom line in the future:

_____

_____

_____

Connective Disorder Screening Questionnaire

Note—Sexual behaviors may include physical interactions, cyber interactions, viewing pornography, masturbating, or any behaviors that cause sexual arousal.

Y   N   Do you often find yourself preoccupied with sexual or romantic thoughts?

Y   N   Do you feel shame more often than you think is healthy or normal about your sexual or romantic behaviors?

Y   N   Have your sexual or romantic behaviors ever created problems for you or others in your life?

Y   N   Have you ever tried to stop certain sexual behaviors or romantic thoughts and been unable to do so?

Y   N   Have you ever sought help or wanted to seek help controlling your sexual behaviors or romantic thoughts?

Y   N   Have your sexual behaviors hurt you or those you love?

Y   N   Are any of your sexual behaviors against the law?

Y   N   Do you feel you need to hide your sexual behaviors or romantic thoughts from others you feel you should be comfortable discussing them with?

Y   N   Do you feel degraded by your sexual behaviors or romantic thoughts?

Y   N   Do you feel depressed after sexual or romantic encounters?

Y   N   Have important events in your life been missed due to sexual or romantic behaviors?

Y   N   Is sex or romance the most important thing in your life?

Y   N   Have you ever broken promises to yourself or others regarding your sexual or romantic behaviors?

Y   N   Have you ever paid or been paid for sex?

Y   N   Do you lose track of time when engaged in sexual behaviors or romantic thoughts?

Y N Do you use sexual behaviors or romantic thoughts as an escape?

Y N Do you ever engage in sexual behaviors that pose a risk to your health (e.g. unsafe sex, anonymous sex, use of prostitutes, sadism and masochism (S&M) behaviors that risk your life)?

Y N Do you seem to alternate between periods of increased sexuality or fantasy and periods of abstinence?

Y N Have your sexual behaviors or romantic thoughts negatively affected your life emotionally, physically, mentally, socially, or financially?

Y N Have you found that you need to increase your sexual behaviors or romantic thoughts to achieve the same satisfaction?

Y N Does the thought of living without your sexual behaviors or romantic thoughts seem impossible?

Y N Do you avoid sexual or romantic interactions at all cost and/or view sex as disgusting?

Y N Do you use substances (alcohol, illegal drugs, prescription drugs, etc.) to numb out, isolate from other or escape from emotions or difficulties?

Y N Do you feel you can only be yourself if you are high or drunk?

Y N Do you only feel connected to and accepted by others if you are high or drunk?

Y N Do you use food as an escape?

Y N Do you feel you have to hide your behaviors involving food from others?

Y N Do you feel that acceptance and connection are based off of physical appearance?

If you circled "yes" on three or more of these, you might be struggling with a connective disorder. The more "yes" answers you have, the more likely your problem is affecting you and/or your relationships in significant ways. Each "yes" is a red flag that should be discussed with your therapist or group to better understand why you have struggled in that particular area.

Coping Skills List

Picnic
Camping
Sky diving
Orienteering
Rappelling
Boat ride
- Sailboat
- Canoeing
- Rafting
- Motorboat

Skiing (water or snow)
Go to the lake
Go to the beach
Bonfire
Fishing
Scuba dive
Hiking
Horseback riding
Sit by pool
Swimming
Sunbathe/Sun tan
Driving
- Off-road
- Road trips
- Drive and sing
- Mud bogging

Sit outside
Star gaze
Watching the sunrise
Hammock
Nap
Long hot shower
Hot tub
Bubble bath
Pray

Meditate
Hug myself
Plant flowers
Mountains
Make-over
Get nails done
Puzzles
Sudoku
Crossword puzzles
Woodworking
Sewing
Group dates
- (See relational list for ideas)

Cook
- Grilling
- BBQ
- Smoking food
- With kids
- Cookie/decorating

Coin collecting
Guns
Drafting/architecture
Cross stitch
Photography
Flower arranging
Build web site (web design)
Astronomy
Astrology
Family history
Learn a foreign language
Antiquing
Collect stamps
Calligraphy

Crafts
Video editing
Draw
Ballet
Pottery
Paint
Acting
Build/design something
Redecorate
Remodel
Reorganize things
Home projects
- House painting
- Rearrange furniture

Wash car
Yard work/gardening
Cleaning house
Chopping firewood
Water flowers
Rake leaves
Skip
Make a collage
Finger paint
Water colors
Write
- a book
- poems
- journaling
- letters

Fly a kite
Hopscotch
Sidewalk chalk
Climb trees
Coloring
Bubbles

Jump on bed
Trampoline
Sprinklers
Slide
Throw football
Hide and seek
Playground
Eraser chase
Square chase
MASH
Sardines
Kick the can
Skip rocks
Swings
Jump rope
Watch children play
Obstacle course
Races
Feed ducks
"Kidnap" a friend or partner
Air hockey
Babysit
Daydream
Listen to/Watch it rain
Board games
Card games
- Solitaire
Chess
Horseshoes
Bird watch
Butterfly kisses
Have a group of people over
- book club
- board games

- themed parties
- video games
- (see relational list for more)
Paintball
Caving
Capture the flag
Water park/water slide
Arcade games
Six flags
Midway games
Circus
Monster trucks
Aquarium
Arboretum
Motor home store
House hunting
Car shows
Festivals
Safari park
Scarborough Faire
Science place
Symphony
Concert
Plays
Service/Charity work
- Homeless Shelters
- Hospitals/Hospices
- Churches
- Library/Museum
- Nursing Home/Care Centers
- Animal Shelters
- Kids Athletics
- Schools
- Orphanages

- Arts Programs
- Local Government
- Parks and Recreation
Zoo
Rodeo/bull rides
Art gallery
Museum
Shopping
Play Santa Claus at office
Look for bargains
Clip Coupons
Gratitude list
Positive affirmations
Self-improvement tapes
    Cataloging
Call friends and family
Bookstore
Racquetball
Swimming
Jog/Run
Ice skating
Read
- magazines
- meditations/devotions
- scriptures
- study
- recovery material
- study other religions
Tell stories
Tell Jokes
Basketball
Volleyball
Soccer
Golf
Driving range
Tennis

Miniature golf
10k race
Bike race
Skeet shooting
Pistol shooting
Rock climbing
Ping pong
Weight lifting
Sit-ups/push ups
Walk
Roller skating
Rollerblading
Skateboarding
Rip stick
Frisbee
Frisbee golf
Ultimate Frisbee
Wrestle
Biking
Yoga
Softball
Punching bag
Box
Kickboxing

Flag football
Taekwondo/Karate
Video games
Play pinball
Cuddle
Music
- Listen
- Play
- Karaoke/sing
- Compose a song
- Choir
Make music videos
12-step groups
Walk dog
Pets
Ask questions
Observe
Plan
Cry
Go downtown
Watch TV
Computer/Internet
Movies
- Theater

- Drive-in
- Rent
- Home movies
Dinner with friends
Go out to eat
Ice cream
Neighborhood parties
Supermarket
Send yourself a letter
Travel (US or abroad)
Church
Breakfast in bed
Bowling
Tubing
Sledding
Snow angels
Snowball fight
Hockey game
Baseball game
Football game
Motocross
Go to races
Ride motorcycle/moped
Go-karts

Effective Time-outs

1. While you don't always feel loving at the time you call a time-out (especially when you are angry), the premise of time-outs is this: "**I love you**, and because I love you I do not want to say or do things that would harm you. Therefore, I am going to stop myself any time that I feel like I am getting close to that point."

2. **You call a time-out for yourself, not for your spouse**.

3. **Call a time-out *early on*.** Knowing your warning signs can help you stop sooner.

4. **Explicitly call the time-out** using the word(s) you have agreed to use.

5. Time-outs can initially feel like abandonment. If after **30 minutes** you are not ready to talk, communicate to your partner that you need more time and that you will return at a **specific time to reconnect** after doing more work.

6. Find a **separate, safe space** to **soothe/calm down**.

7. After you have soothed, connect with and **write down your feelings** in this format:
   a. "I feel <u>primary emotion word</u> because <u>specific behavior</u>."
   b. "When you did <u>specific behavior(s)</u>, I felt <u>primary emotion word</u>."

8. After soothing and writing down your feelings, make sure you feel **grounded in your understanding of yourself** and how you can cope with your own feelings before reconnecting with your partner. It is unwise to go back looking for more soothing/understanding from your spouse than you can give yourself.

9. Once you are grounded, **COME BACK!!** Both partners must have the list of feeling statements from step 7. One partner is the speaker (pitching) and the other listener (catching). You then switch roles after the first speaker finishes.

10. **While you are in the listener role, DON'T DEFEND YOURSELF!** The goal in listening is to see into the other person's world and understand better how they see the world and the emotions that arise for them due to that view. Remember that you will get a chance to be heard when the roles switch.

Feeling Word List

Primary Emotions

Lonely	Scared/Fear
Powerless	Rejection (fear)
Helpless/Hopeless	Abandonment (fear)
Stuck/Trapped	Unappreciated (fear)
Bored	Unloved (fear)
Stressed/Tense	Inadequate (fear)
Shocked/Surprised	Insecure(fear)
Blah	Worth-less (fear)
Guilty	Ignored (fear)
Regret	Anxious/Worried (fear)
Torn	Uncertain (fear)
Sad	Discouraged (fear)
Grief/Loss	Confused
Distant/Disconnected	Restless
Overwhelmed	Tired

Happy/Joy	Rested
Hopeful	Energetic
Grateful	Calm/Peaceful
Love(d)	Relaxed
Connected	Serene
Playful	Surprised

Secondary Emotions*

Shame (embarrassed)	Jealousy
Anger (frustrated, irritated, annoyed, hate, upset, resentful)	

*Secondary emotions are important to recognize and validate within ourselves; however, they typically motivate us to hide or attack rather than take care of ourselves and be assertive with others. Thus, we move from secondary to primary to find the tools to care for ourselves and connect with others.

Morning Re-mind Example

Who I Am

I am a child of God. He knows better than I do and loves me deeply. I am a loving, devoted, intelligent, and competent person in many ways. I value honesty, emotional intelligence, and boundaries, and I am still working on making those areas of my life more in line with my values. I am a work in progress.

Affirmations

Challenges bring opportunities. I am strong, but not on my own. I can have the strength to ask for help. I can find love and support. I can make healthy choices when I am connected to others I trust.

Cycle

I will be tempted to escape today. I may lose track of what I'm feeling for long enough that it will build up and feel unmanageable. I know at those times that escapes can bring temporary relief, a high, a sense of power (almost superman-like at times) and a sense of acceptance. In the end though, I end up feeling exactly the opposite: stressed, powerless, inadequate, unacceptable, unloved, distant from those I care about, and guilty. Then I push others away, including God, and find myself incredibly alone. I am working on changing that reaction and learning to reach in and reach out.

What I Want in Recovery

Life without escapes brings peace of conscience, love of myself, connection with others, growth, and self-acceptance for being able to learn and grow. I have tasted some of these things recently and want to keep experiencing them.

Spiritual Practices

While each day brings new challenges and schedule problems, I need to do at least the following:

1. Study scripture and/or recovery material.

2. Take time to meditate/ponder.

3. Pray individually morning, noon and night (and have a prayer in my heart).

4. Right now—write down at least five things I am grateful for.

5. Right now—write down at least five things I love about myself, my wife, and my kids.

I have to do some things every day to remind myself how to stay on course:

1. Review my plan for the day.

2. VSE: Check in with myself emotionally two to three times a day.

3. Nightly Rewind.

Current Work

Reminders:

I tend to feel a lot of shame, which freezes me and puts me in my cycle of addiction. I need to turn that back into guilt, which teaches me that I've done something wrong (I have values that I contradicted by my behavior), not that I am a bad person. I just need to figure out what I've done and correct it. If I can't figure it out, I need to reach out to God, a sponsor, therapist, friend, or my wife and try to sort through it and find solutions with their help. When I do that, the guilt will go away and I will feel good about me.

Needs List

Physiological/Physical needs
Breath
Water/Food
Sleep
Hygiene
Health (including exercise)

Safety/Security needs
Physical security (from violence,
    aggression, crime, etc.)
Financial
Space/Privacy
Structure, predictability, stability, order
Justice and Mercy (balance)
Relational competence

Esteem needs
Identity
Cultural security (identity in community)
Self-respect (worth)
Respect for others
Contribution
Competence (adequacy)
Achievement/productivity
Expression
Power/Freedom/Control/Agency/Choice

Growth needs
Learn (explore, discover, create, curiosity)
Stewardship (responsibility)

Love/Acceptance/Intimacy needs
Friendship/Social
Support/Nurture
Guidance/Mentoring
Belonging (Family, Community, Higher
    Power)
Sexual intimacy

Versions of acceptance
—heard
—acknowledged
—recognized
—noticed
—understood
—admired
—appreciated
—approved of
—important
—needed
—valued
—worthy
—respected

Spiritual needs
Connectedness (see love/acceptance)
Mindfulness
—connection w/ and awareness of self
Purpose/meaning (including
    stewardship)

Hope
Comfort

Rejuvenation
Play
Relaxation/Soothing
Adventure/Excitement
Novelty/Variety
Connection
Excitement
Comfort

Personal Coping List Example

Bubble bath
Hot shower
The beach
Hot tub
Listen to rain outside
Make music videos
Garden
Makeovers
Make a collage
Puzzles
Rake leaves
Wash car
Observe
Family history
Waterskiing
Meditate
Pray
Study religions
Movie theater
Nap
Give self a hug
Home videos
Watch children play
Skip class
Cry
Get a massage
Acting
Play with pets
Give
- • Cookies/Food
- • Service
-   - Soup kitchen
-   - Visit Elderly
-   - Yard work

Outdoors
Bird watch
Duck pond
Go to the lake
Skip rocks
Feed ducks
BBQ
Picnic
Festivals
Carnivals
Circus
Fishing
Caving
Camping
Horseback riding
Bonfire
Hammock
Sit in the sun
Sit outdoors
Sunset/sunrise
Star-gaze
Horseshoes
Bochas

Snow Activities
Sledding
Snow angels
Snowball fight
Tubing
Skiing
Snowboarding

Hobbies
Collect Things
- • Stamps

- • Coins
- • Cards
Crafts
Pottery
Photography
Cross stitch
Sew
Build/design
Paint
Draw

Places to Go
Bookstore
Learn a language
Concert
Visit animal store
Go to the zoo
Sporting event
Rodeo
Ballet
Go downtown
Plays
Art gallery
Aquarium Museum
Shopping
- • Wal-Mart
- • Supermarket
- • Target
- • Mall
Drive
- • and sing
- • Off-roading
- • Mud bogging
- • Motorcycle/moped
- • a Scenic route

- Mountains
Pool

Decorating
Remodel
Redecorate
Reorganize
Move furniture

Cook
Cookies
Hot chocolate
Milkshake
Ice cream

Kid Things
Watch clouds
Finger paint
Water colors
Hopscotch
Sidewalk chalk
Daydream
Draw
Trampoline
- Wet/Sprinkler
Jump in leaves
Coloring
Bubbles
Jump on bed
Run a race
Swim
Play pinball
Skip
Wash car
Nintendo/Atari
Playground
- swings

- slide
- monkey bars
- merry-go-round
- hanging bars
- obstacle course
Fly a kite
Run in sprinklers

Eat
Fruit
Veggies
- With dip
Crackers
Cheese
- Cottage
- Cream
Nuts
Toast
Sandwich

Exercise
Walk
Run
Hike
Skateboard
Rollerblade
Roller skate
Ice Skate
Bike
Swim
Frisbee Golf
Golf
Miniature Golf
Ping pong
Weight lifting
Push-ups/Sit-ups
Bowling

Aerobics
Climb a tree
Jump rope
Batting cages
Martial Arts
Yoga
Kickboxing
Punching bag

Read
Fiction
Jokes
Reader's digest
Scriptures
Other religious lit.
Therapy-related
Self-help
Meditations
Journals
Kid's literature

Write
Jokes
Stories
Journal
Letters
Letter to yourself
Notes
Poetry

Music
Sing
Karaoke
Compose
Play
- Piano
  - Classical

- Religious
- Kids
- Popular
- Duets
• Guitar
• Trumpet
• New instrument

Listen
• Classical
• Old rock
• Country
• Religious
• Random radio
• Kid stuff
• Oldies
• Memory music
- Kid
- Teen
- College

<u>LIMITED</u>
TV
Computer
Search web
Play solitaire
Watch a movie
Video games

Relational Coping List Example

Hike
Skateboard
Rollerblade
Roller skate
Ice Skate
Bowling
Batting cages
Golfing/driving range
Service
- Target
- Soup kitchen
- Visit elderly
- Yard work
- Cookies/food

Movie theater
- Drive-in

Hot tub
Playground
- Obstacle course

Fly a kite
Play pinball
Bochas
Slumber party
Air hockey
Go to the lake
Skip rocks
Feed Ducks
BBQ
Board/Card games
Festivals
Fruit picking
Amusement parks
Garage/Yard Sale shopping
Letterboxing
Auction

Take a walk
Car washing party
Out for ice cream/dessert
Dessert contest (making
    or eating)
Chocolate making/dipping
Candy making
Fortune cookie making
Out for dinner
Basketball
Billiards
Make a video with child-
    hood photos and
    home movie clips
Dutch oven cooking
Crepe/pancake breakfast
Horseshoes
Drive
- to small towns
- around your town
- Downtown in a nearby
    city
- Motorcycle/moped
- a scenic route

Bookstore
Concert
Sporting event
Ballet
Drama/play/musical event
Art gallery
Drawing class/instruction
Dance Instructions (ballet,
    country, tap, swing,
    square dance, high-
    land, etc)

Aquarium
Museum
Ceramic/pottery store
Build-a-Bear
Dance (country)
Story writing contest
State parks
Canoeing at a local lake
Nickel-cade
Swap meet or flea-market
Rodeo
Theater
Ice show
Demolition derby
Lecture
Rewrite the newspaper
History tour
Go visiting (surprise)
Give blood
Historic church trip
Temple
Hot chocolate and talk
    (highlights of month)
Take a class together
Animal Habitat
Bubble blowing contest
Creative Story (write/say
    one or two lines of a
    story, the next person
    continues with another
    line or two)
Crock pot party
Dehydrate fruit
Donate blood
Fashion show (modern/

oldies/clothes from scriptures/other cultures)

Bonfire (hot dog/ marshmallow roast)

Factory tour

Family history (genealogy)

Fireside

Boating

First aid class

Fondue party

Chili cook-off

Food storage

Football

Balloon volleyball

Street or field hockey

Bowling

Formal dinner

Games

Gardening (plant a tree!)

Charades

Badminton tournament

History class

Hold a free musical concert (instruments/choirs/etc.)

Puzzle party

Hot air balloon ride (make sure your date/group is okay with this!)

Water park

Instrument class (everyone tries using different instruments)

Scavenger hunt

Leather working class

Subway trip

Make a video

Miniature golf (can even make your own course)

Bikes (Tandem/individual)

White water rafting

Revisit old memories from growing up

Sundae party

Musical show

Opera

Painting

Petting zoo

Pillow fight

Pizza party

Poetry readings

Popcorn fight

Potluck meal

Pottery class

Sculpting class

Progressive dinner

Racquetball

Jogging

Rock climbing

Roller blading/skating

Sand castle building

Museum

Self-defense instruction

Paper folding

Chalk drawing

Miniature marshmallow fight (big ones can hurt, I know!)

Homemade pizza

Sign Language class

Skiing (water or snow)

Volleyball

Tennis

Softball

Watch sunrise or sunset (tell stories/share testimonies)

Snow ball fight

Yoga (or other type of relaxation/exercise)

Walk-a-thon

Story telling

$5 to spend on the best item at the mall

Tie-Dye shirts

Relay ping pong (run around the table)

Name that tune

Paint your own pottery

Fishing

Take turns playing advice columnist and help seeker (who can come up with the best problems and the best answers

Capture the flag

Mark off boundaries throughout the town, and play hide and go seek with cars. You and your date go hide, and then call the other couple with a clue

Lego building contest

Family Feud

Public Garden
Hollywood Squares
Paper boat races
Swimming
Litter clean up party
Taffy pulling
River Float
Snow sculpting
Theme parties (medieval, Hawaiian, etc.)
Train ride
Nature walk
Marathon run
Treasure hunt
Skits
Tubing down a river
Ultimate Frisbee
Sledding
Sleigh ride
Visit the elderly (read to them too!)
Patriotic class/history of your country
Wood working
Pool/Darts
Roller Skate (Rink)
House "Hunting"
Indoor Rock Climbing
Archer/Firing Range/Rifles
Dress Rehearsal Tickets
Restaurant.com (Dinner Deals)
Share spiritual experiences
Test Drive Cars
Photography (everyone has a camera, takes pictures, develop in one hour/upload to a computer, and look at pictures together)
Chocolate/Candy Factory Tour/Visit
20 Questions (open-ended about each other) or everybody brings a question everybody answers
Act Pretentious at an art show
Window shop on the square
Classes (Art, Dance, etc.)
Baseball game
Middle/High School Plays
Home videos
Book of remembrances
Bubble bath
Hot shower
Massage
Watch clouds
Finger paint
Water colors
Hopscotch
Sidewalk chalk
Trampoline
• Wet/Sprinkler
Jump in leaves
Coloring
Wash car
Run in sprinklers
Make music videos
Garden
Makeovers
Family history
Make a collage
Puzzles
Learn a language
Dance
Mutual Hobbies
• Class
Cook
• Fondue
• Green eggs & ham
• Taffy
Learn a relative's story
Missionary letters
Sunset/sunrise – watch or activities such as:
• Push-ups/sit-ups
• Aerobics
• Yoga
• Jump Rope
• Bochas/Bocci Ball
Pajama party

Read
Fiction
• Kid's literature
• Sci-Fi
• Church
Reader's digest
Scriptures
Jokes
Ensign
Self-help (Colors)
Journals
Study religions
History (person or period)

Write
- Stories
- Journal
- Letters
- Notes
- Poetry
- Personal Histories (one talks, the other types & asks questions)

Music
Sing
Karaoke
Play
- Piano
- Duets
- Guitar
- New instrument

Short Times at home
Video Game (DDR, Dr. Mario, Atari, etc.)
Trade massages
Hot tub
Talk about the day
Watch a show (only 1)
Read a short story
Read a magazine article
Listen to an inspirational talk
Karaoke
Piano or guitar duets

Seasonal
Haunted House
Santa at the mall
Gingerbread house contest & apple cider
Christmas music
Caroling

Dates at home
Make birthday cards for the upcoming year
Story writing contest
Play a game (make a list)
Picnic in living room
Video games
Piano/guitar and sing
Pick a historical person/period and read about it together
Rewrite the newspaper
Take an online class together
Get to know a relative's life story
Write missionary letters
Look at photo albums from since we've known each other
Country dancing video
Stargazing (use a book to help)
Rent a movie
Read a book together
Invite extended family over
Cook (taffy, fondue, green eggs & ham)
Homemade Ice Cream
Make a gingerbread house

Group/Social Dates
Ancestor potluck dinner
Banana Splits, Fondue, appetizers, snacks or desserts
Pizza decorating contest
Passover feast
Supermarket sweep
Play games
Race ("Olympics" – skip, 3-legged, wheelbarrow, egg, etc.)
Play basketball at park
Scavenger hunt at mall
Bowling
Country dancing
Frisbee golf
Horseback riding
Picnic
Nickel-cade
Rodeo
Theater
Demolition derby
Miniature golf
Go to the temple
Laser Tag
Pump-it-up/extreme sports
Planetarium
Out for dinner
Flip a coin to turn until you arrive at a restaurant

LIMITED
Computer
Search web

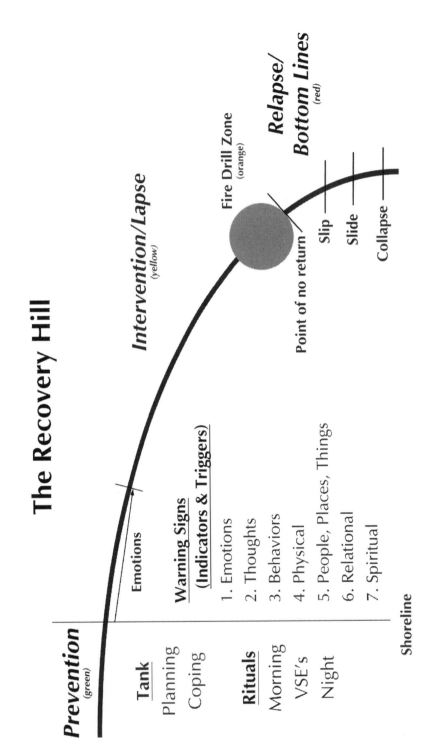

Soothing Skills

Soothing techniques should not compromise your overall physical or mental health.

Sight/Vision

Keep a beautiful picture/scene on your wall or desk to focus on.
Walk in a pretty part of town.
Look at the nature around you.
Buy a flower and put it where you can see it.
Sit in a garden.
Watch the snowflakes decorate the trees during a snowfall.
Light a candle and watch the flame.
Look at a book with beautiful scenery or beautiful art.
Watch a travel movie or video.
Watch a funny movie, TV show or comedian.
Read a book.
Look at pictures of loved ones.
Look at pictures of a past vacation or places that you would like to visit.
Watch the clouds.
Make one space in a room pretty.
Set a pretty place at the table, using your best things, for a meal.
Go sit in the lobby of a beautiful old hotel.
Watch the stars.
Fix your nails so they look pretty (even "real men" can do this).
Look at beautiful pictures in a book (picture/photography books).
Be mindful of each sight that passes in front of you, not lingering on anything.
Lower the lights (not so bright).
Clean house or organize a messy area (restoring a sense of order can be calming).
Create art (paint, draw, color), even if you are not good.
Watch people.
Polish your furniture.

Hearing/Sound

Listen to beautiful or soothing music.
Play nature sounds (ocean waves, whale songs, rain forests).
Listen to a baby gurgling or a small animal.

Sit by a waterfall.

Listen to someone chopping wood.

When you are listening, be mindful, letting the sounds come and go.

Listen to relaxing music.

Sing to yourself.

Say positive statements to yourself or self-encouragement.

Play a musical instrument.

Listen to beautiful or soothing music, or to invigorating and exciting music (many people recommend that country music be avoided, since the lyrics tend to be depressing). Classical music can be very good, since there are no lyrics to trigger specific thoughts.

Pay attention to the sounds of nature (waves, birds, rainfall, leaves rustling) or listen to tapes of nature sounds (I use a whale song tape, and a rain forest tape).

Sing your favorite songs.

Hum a soothing tune.

Learn to play an instrument.

Call 800 or other numbers to hear a human voice.

Be mindful of any sounds that come your way, letting them go in one ear and out the other.

Meditate.

Call a friend or family member. The sound of another voice can often be calming.

Go someplace quiet, like a library or a bookstore.

Get quiet and read a really good book that totally engrosses you. Keep such a book handy for times when you need to calm yourself.

Smell

Bake/cook and take in all the smells.

Notice all the different smells around you.

Walk in nature (garden/woods) and breathe in the smells.

Light a scented candle or incense.

Shop for flowers.

Smell lavender or vanilla.

Deeply breathe in fresh air.

Use your favorite perfume or lotions.

Spray fragrance in the air.

Put lemon oil on your furniture.

Put potpourri in a bowl in your room.

Smell flowers/roses.

Plant an herb garden—Smell the thyme, rosemary, etc.

Bathe in scented bath oil, etc.

Boil cinnamon or other spices to fill the house with scent.

Taste*

Have a special treat, and eat it slowly, savoring each bite.

Drink a soothing drink like herbal tea or hot chocolate. Let the taste run over your tongue and slowly down your throat.

Go to a potluck, and eat a little bit of each dish, mindfully tasting each new thing.

Eat a comforting meal.

Slowly suck on peppermint, hard candy, or other candy.

Have a favorite soothing drink such as herbal tea or hot chocolate (no alcohol).

Treat yourself to a dessert.

Sample flavors in an ice cream store.

Chew your favorite gum.

Have a little bit of a special food you don't usually spend the money on, such as fresh-squeezed orange juice.

Eat one thing mindfully.

Eat an orange (touch, smell, and taste).

Bake cookies, cake or bread. The more elaborate the process the better.

Eat foods which are very spicy or rich.

*Using taste to soothe may trigger issues with an eating disorder, or may cause health issues for those with medical problems (diabetes, etc.).

Touch

Take a bubble/warm/cool bath.

Pet your dog, cat or other animal.

Put on a silk shirt or blouse (feel the fabric on your skin).

Sink into a comfortable bed or chair.

Float or swim in a pool (feel the water on your body).

Get a massage.

Relax in the warmth of the sun.

Stretch.

Change into comfortable clothes.

Draw, color or paint.

Put clean sheets on the bed.

Soak your feet.

Put creamy lotion on your whole body.

Put a cold compress on your forehead.

Wrap your face in a very warm, damp facecloth.

Wear fur-lined gloves, fur coats or artificial furs.

Brush your hair for a long time.

Hug someone.

Experience whatever you are touching; notice touch that is soothing.

Do yoga.

Take a nap.

Go for a walk.

Go for a run.

Walk your dog.

Play with your children.

Work in the garden.

Wrap yourself in a very comfortable blanket.

Breathe. Concentrate on slowing and calming your breath.

Write in your journal.

Hold ice cubes in your hands.

Some other examples of soothing:

Name 5 things you can see in the room with you.

Name 4 things you can feel ("chair on my back" or "feet on floor").

Name 3 things you can hear right now ("fingers tapping on keyboard" or "TV").

Name 2 things you can smell right now (or, 2 things you like the smell of).

Name 1 good thing about yourself.

- 5 things you see in front of you.
- 4 colors.
- 3 body sensations.
- 2 sounds.
- 1 smell.

<u>Breathing Exercises</u>

Sit or stand in a relaxed position.

Slowly inhale through your nose, counting to five in your head.

Let the air out from your mouth, counting to eight in your head as it leaves your lungs. Repeat several times. That's it!

Tips:

As you breathe, let your abdomen expand outward, rather than raising your shoulders. This is a more relaxed and natural way to breathe, and helps your lungs fill themselves more fully with fresh air, releasing more "old" air.

You can do this just a few times to release tension, or for several minutes as a form of meditation.

If you like, you can make your throat a little tighter as you exhale so the air comes out like a whisper. This type of breathing is used in some forms of yoga and can add additional tension relief.

Other things that can be very powerful but take more time and practice include: Progressive Muscle Relaxation (PMR), Body Scan, Self-Hypnosis, Guided Imagery, Autogenetics, diaphragmatic breathing, and other mindfulness practices. You can search for these on the internet and quickly find out how to apply these practices for yourself.

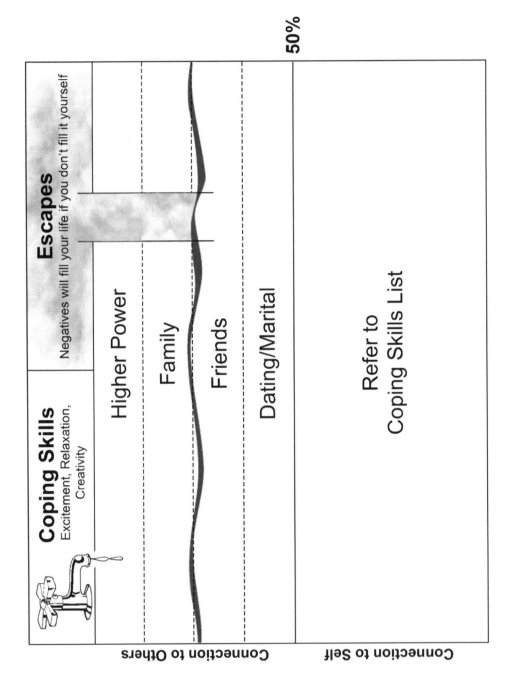

The Tank

Coping Skills
Excitement, Relaxation, Creativity

Escapes
Negatives will fill your life if you don't fill it yourself

Higher Power

Family

Friends

Dating/Marital

Refer to Coping Skills List

50%

Connection to Others

Connection to Self

The Thermometer - Tools for Managing Emotion

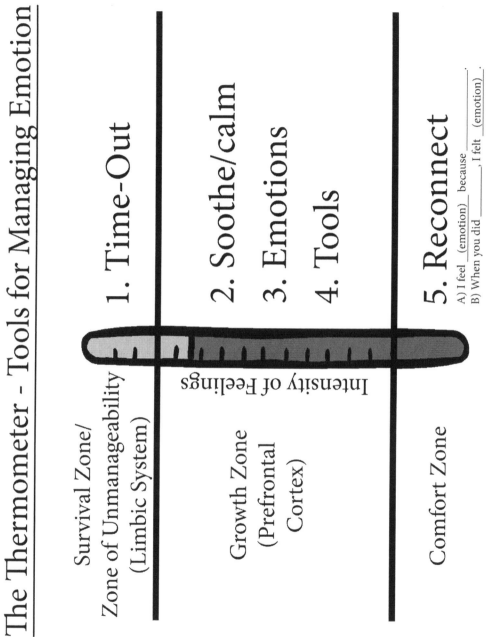

1. Time-Out

2. Soothe/calm

3. Emotions

4. Tools

5. Reconnect

A) I feel (emotion) because _____ .
B) When you did _____, I felt (emotion) .

Intensity of Feelings

Survival Zone/
Zone of Unmanageability
(Limbic System)

Growth Zone
(Prefrontal
Cortex)

Comfort Zone

Time-out Protocol

The word or phrase that will be used to call a time-out:

_____

Soothing methods the wife might use:

_____

_____

Soothing methods the husband might use:

_____

_____

Specific steps each will take to process before sharing with your partner and after calling a time-out (e.g. each will complete the time-out worksheet):

_____

_____

_____

Any additional specifics regarding time-outs (e.g. if a time-out is called after 9 p.m., we will reconnect the following day at _____):

_____

_____

_____

Steps to be taken if time-out protocol is not followed (e.g. it will be addressed in the next couple's session, both partners will autopsy why the protocol didn't work):

_____

_____

_____

Time-out Worksheet

How did I soothe:

_____

_____

Using the Feeling Word List, these are the emotions I am feeling:

_____

_____

Translate your emotions into one of these two formats:
"I felt _____ when you _____." Or "When you did _____, I felt _____."
Make sure you keep the emotions as what you felt instead of what you think someone
did to you (e.g. you felt abandonment, not that someone abandoned you).

_____

_____

_____

_____

The need behind each emotion is:

_____

_____

_____

Other times in your life you have struggled with these emotions (this helps to separate
the energy around this situation from energy that is related to other instances in which
you've felt similar emotions and helps you to more completely understand the pain
you're feeling):

_____

_____

Using your answers to each of the above questions, use a separate piece of paper to write up your processing to present to your spouse. Make sure you focus on your emotions and how things felt for you, and avoid telling them they "did" something to you or what they need to do to fix it. Identify times when you assumed things they thought or the meanings behind their words or actions and use phrases such as, "The message I got when you did this was…," or, "I make up in my head that you thought…." Avoid putting "spikes"—harsh statements or attacks—in your processing (if you feel you need to do that, more processing is needed before you present it to your spouse).

How you will respond if your spouse's response is not connective:

_____

_____

Trauma Cycle

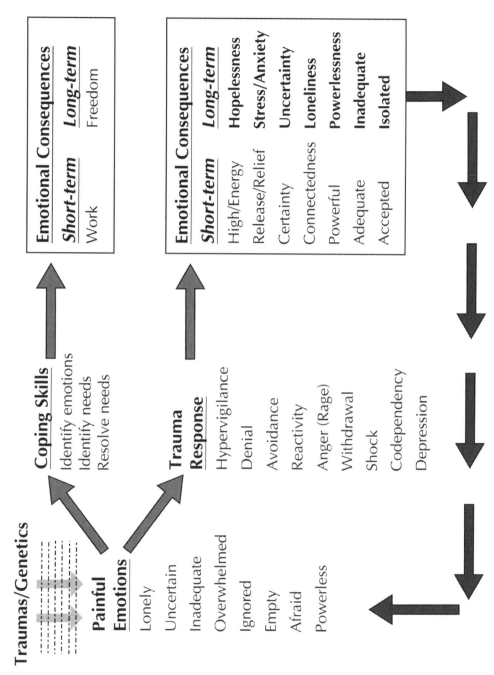

Traumas/Genetics

Painful Emotions
Lonely
Uncertain
Inadequate
Overwhelmed
Ignored
Empty
Afraid
Powerless

Coping Skills
Identify emotions
Identify needs
Resolve needs

Trauma Response
Hypervigilance
Denial
Avoidance
Reactivity
Anger (Rage)
Withdrawal
Shock
Codependency
Depression

Emotional Consequences
Short-term	*Long-term*
Work	Freedom

Emotional Consequences
Short-term	*Long-term*
High/Energy	**Hopelessness**
Release/Relief	**Stress/Anxiety**
Certainty	**Uncertainty**
Connectedness	**Loneliness**
Powerful	**Powerlessness**
Adequate	**Inadequate**
Accepted	**Isolated**

Warning Signs for Addicts

1. Emotions
Loneliness/disconnected
Powerlessness
Fear/Anxiety
—Inadequacy/worth-less
—Rejection/abandonment
Guilt
Boredom
Anger
Shame
Numb

2. Thoughts
Euphoric recall
Wanting to fix others
Using computer w/o safeguards
Moving too fast (dating, career)
I'm a bad person/I'm unlovable
Get over it
Dreams
Racing thoughts
Fantasy
Suicidal ideation
Objectifying
Nobody cares what I do
Missing drug friends
I've got to be perfect
I am stupid/bad/unworthy
Poor me (perpetual victim)
Nobody gets how I feel
I'll never get through this
I'll never be enough
Criticizing others (thought/behavior)

3. Behaviors
Cruising (for drugs, sex, triggers)
Not doing therapy/homework
Isolating/not being present
Keeping secrets
Disorganization (car, home, job)
Not planning/following plan
Over-commitment
Overspending
Movies/TV (content/extent)
Not pursuing hobbies/interests
Unnecessary shopping
Not sharing thoughts/feelings
Unhealthy risk-taking
Dealing with surprises
Driving aggressively
Internet surfing
Not expressing gratitude
Defensiveness
Driving too fast
Objectifying others
Lying
Stealing
Depression/anxiety
Fixing others
Not planning/over-planning
Sarcasm
Procrastination
Swearing, yelling, etc.
Tobacco
Overeating

4. People, Places, & Things
Uncomfortable at social events
Seeking out positive places
Messy home
Drug friends (bad choice of friends)
Billboards
Personal ads/phone lines
Chat line
Using computer w/o safeguards
Driving in sex or drug areas
Dealers/bars/night or strip clubs
Contact with ex-partners
Internet (time, reasons, etc.)
Hanging out at the mall

5. Physical
Not exercising/too much exercise
Unhealthy eating habits
Staying up/getting up late
Sleep (too much/too little)
Poor personal hygiene
—Not brushing teeth
Too much personal grooming
Headaches/muscle pain
Major weight loss/gain
Illness (chronic or temporary)
Injuries (or wounds, bruises, etc.)
Breaking out (acne)
Tension (shoulders, jaw, etc.)

6. Relational
Taking other's inventory
Harboring resentments
Not connecting with others (friends,
    group-members, sponsor, etc.)
Not keeping commitments

Treating people poorly
Gossiping
Not socializing
Not trying to make new friends
Being closed off with others
Snapping at others
Being critical/judgmental
People pleasing
Break-ups
Isolation/withdrawing
Losing focus in conversations
Unwillingness to talk about me
Always talking about myself

7. Spiritual*
Prayer
Meditation
Spiritual Meditation Reading
12-step meetings
Gratitude
Morning Ritual
Evening Ritual
Calling a friend in recovery
Church
Scripture/Spiritual readings
Poetry
Yoga
Nature
Religious addiction/obsession
Community participation/service
Connectedness
Loss of interest

*The warning signs here are not doing
    these positive spiritual practices

To turn this into a Rewind, start by reviewing all the items on the list to see what showed up during the day. Celebrate your successes, recognizing your progress. Then look at the one to two things that need to be improved upon today. Do an autopsy on those to learn more about yourself and come up with a game plan to intervene better with those few things.

Warning Signs for Partners

1. Emotions

Loneliness/disconnection
Powerlessness
Fear/Anxiety
- Inadequacy/worth-less
- Insecure
- Rejection/abandonment
- Helpless/hopeless
- Stuck/trapped
- Uncertain

Grief
Overwhelmed
Anger
Unappreciated/unloved
Resentment
Ignored
Tired
Discouraged
Shocked

I've got to be perfect
I am ugly
Poor me (perpetual victim)
Nobody gets how I feel
I'll never get through this
I'll never be enough
It will never get any better
Will it ever get better
Will it ever be good enough (for both
   of us)
Why have I wasted so many years
Our whole marriage has been a lie
Was anything real
How do I trust again
Is trust even possible
Is intimacy ever possible again
How do I trust what I feel
How will I know when I can trust him
Criticizing others (thought/behavior)

2. Thoughts

Memories of past experiences
Wanting to fix others
Checking computer history/email
Stagnant recovery progress
I'm not good enough for him
I'm unlovable
If only I were . . .
Dreams
Racing thoughts
Suicidal ideation
I'm completely alone
There is no one I can talk to

3. Behaviors

Checking computer/phone
Blaming/shaming
Not doing therapy/homework
Isolating/not being present
Keeping secrets
Disorganization (car, home, job)
Not planning/following plan
Over-commitment
Overspending
Movies/TV (extent)
Not pursuing hobbies/interests
Unnecessary shopping

Not sharing thoughts/feelings
Unhealthy risk-taking
Dealing with surprises
Driving aggressively
Expressing gratitude
Defensiveness
Lying
Depression/anxiety
Fixing others
Not planning/over-planning
Sarcasm
Procrastination
Swearing, yelling, etc.
Tobacco
Overeating

4. People, Places, & Things
Uncomfortable at social events
Not seeking out positive places
Messy home
Negative friends
Forming inappropriate relationships
Internet (time, reasons, etc.)
Avoiding the home

5. Physical
Not exercising/too much exercise
Unhealthy eating habits
Staying up/getting up late
Sleep (too much/too little)
Poor personal hygiene
—Not brushing teeth
Too much personal grooming
Headaches/muscle pain
Major weight loss/gain

Illness (chronic or temporary)
Injuries (or wounds, bruises, etc.)
Breaking out (acne)
Tension (shoulders, jaw, etc.)

6. Relational
Taking other's inventory
Harboring resentments
Not connecting with others (friends,
    group-members, sponsor, etc.)
Not keeping commitments
Treating people poorly
Gossiping
Not socializing
Not trying to make new friends
Being closed off with others
Snapping at others
Being critical/judgmental
People pleasing
Break-ups
Isolation/withdrawing
Losing focus in conversations
Unwillingness to talk about me
Always talking about myself

7. Spiritual*
Prayer
Meditation
Spiritual Meditation Reading
12-step meetings
Gratitude
Morning Ritual
Evening Ritual
Calling a friend in recovery
Church

Scripture/Spiritual readings
Poetry
Yoga
Nature
Religious addiction/obsession
Community participation/service

Connectedness
Loss of interest

*The warning signs here are not doing
    these positive spiritual practices

To turn this into a Rewind, start by reviewing all the items on the list to see what showed up during the day. Celebrate your successes, recognizing your progress. Then look at the one to two things that need to be improved upon today. Do an autopsy on those to learn more about yourself and come up with a game plan to intervene better with those few things.

Mark H. Bird, Ph.D., is a speaker, author, researcher, supervisor, and practicing Marriage and Family Therapist with more than 15 years of experience. In 2009 Mark established Healing & Recovery, a clinic for the treatment of chemical and process addictions. The clinic offers groups for both sex addicts and their partners, including female sex, love, and relationship addicts and their partners. Mark is passionate about connection and believes it plays a critical role in helping people heal and thrive. He believes the best type of recovery includes healing and building strong relationships.

Mark is also a husband and father, and his favorite activities include singing as well as playing the guitar, piano, and trumpet. He loves cracking jokes, playing basketball and volleyball, roller blading, and playing board games with friends. Mark and his wife, Stevie, and their six children live in the Dallas–Fort Worth Texas area.

Dr. Bird would be delighted to hear from you. Visit him at DrMarkBird.com

Made in the USA
Columbia, SC
23 February 2022

56671277R00148